Home Waters

Home Waters
A Year of Recompenses on the Provo River

GEORGE B. HANDLEY

THE UNIVERSITY OF UTAH PRESS
Salt Lake City

The Defiance House Man colophon is a registered trademark
of the University of Utah Press. It is based upon a four-foot-tall,
Ancient Puebloan pictograph (late PIII) near Glen Canyon, Utah.

Excerpt from "We are many" from Extravagaria by Pablo Neruda, translated
by Alastair Reid. Translation copyright © 1974 by Alastair Reid. Reprinted
by permission of Farrar, Straus and Giroux, LLC.

14 13 12 11 10   1 2 3 4 5

LIBRARY OF CONGRESS CATALOGING-IN-PUBLICATION DATA
Handley, George B., 1964-
  Home waters : a year of recompenses on the Provo River / George B. Handley.
    p.   cm.
  Includes bibliographical references.
  ISBN 978-1-60781-023-0 (pbk. : alk. paper)
  1. Handley, George B., 1964—Travel—Provo River Watershed.
  2. Provo River Watershed (Utah)—Description and travel.
  3. Provo River Watershed (Utah)—History.
  4. Mormons—Utah—Provo River Watershed—History. I. Title.
  F832.P76H36 2010979.2'24—dc22

Cover painting by Frank Magleby, *Upper Provo*. Used by permission of the artist.

Printed and bound by Sheridan Books, Inc., Ann Arbor, Michigan.

For Eliza, Paige, Camilla, and Sam
"We *live* here!"

Contents

I would like to know if others

go through the same things that I do,

have as many selves as I have,

. . . .

and when I've exhausted this problem,

I'm going to study so hard

that when I explain myself,

I'll be talking geography.

—*Pablo Neruda,* "We are many"

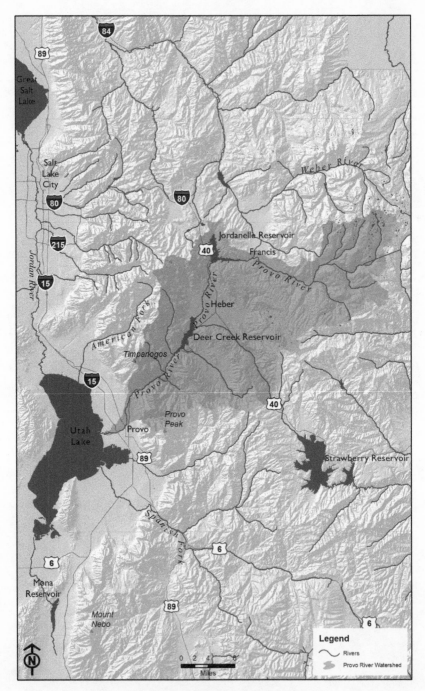

THE PROVO RIVER WATERSHED

Prologue

The wilderness and the solitary place shall be glad for them;
and the desert shall rejoice, and blossom as the rose.
— Isaiah 35:1

ISAIAH, OF COURSE, IS NOT AN UNKNOWN IN THESE PARTS. BUT FOR WHOM does the desert rejoice, "even with joy and singing?" For whom shall the "parched ground...become a pool, and the thirsty lands springs of water?" These are the hopes of any desert people striving to be worthy of providential grace, hoping to merit a land that provides sustenance, home, and belonging in the face of nature's unpredictability. It is not too sweeping to say that this has been the hope of all humanity. To find abundance, rest, and protection from the whims of biology, to live in a forbearing and forthcoming world— this is the first and oldest dream since Eden. We who live in a fallen world and who humbly fear for our survival hope for what Isaiah calls the Lord's "recompenses."

Recompense is payback. It means to weigh together, to bring back into balance. So recompenses are just deserts, and our pronunciation notwithstanding, those are "deserts," not "desserts." Recompense is to get the desert or garden that we deserve. Little wonder then that for a persecuted and destitute Mormon community that arrived in Utah in the middle of the nineteenth century, these verses were seen as a promise of an end to their suffering. Many came to believe the promise was fulfilled by the irrigation and settlement of the semi-arid climate of the Great Basin. Their just desert was one that blossomed and bloomed with orchards, crops, and a thriving human economy.

But the tense of prophecy is always future. The paradox of the written word of tradition is that even when it might be fulfilled, it still appears to await final resolution. I am not like the Mormon pioneers of the nineteenth century whose feet were firmly planted on the soil of their sustenance. I am a twenty-first century Utah Mormon, a citizen of a globalized world, breathing the brown cloud of Chinese as well as local coal factories, eating food from as far away as Chile and New Zealand, and casting my long American consumer shadow across lands unknown to me.

And soil is hard to see these days. All across the Wasatch Front, the Utah mountain range that has fed fresh water and fish to the human populations on the edge of the desert for millennia, houses spring up and farms and fields disappear. The Aquarian Age of water gatherers has given way to the mechanized Hydraulic Age of water engineers; a land of webbed and braided arteries of mountain streams—hardly a desert in need of blossoming—is now a carefully engineered and mapped zone of straight or symmetrically curved lines: canals, dikes, and pipelines—some of them drilled right through mountain ranges—the occasional swollen reservoir, household piping, and candy cane–shaped sink taps.[1]

In his promise of a blossoming desert Isaiah speaks not only to humankind but to all of creation. "Let the earth hear," he says, "and all that is therein; the world, and all things that come forth of it. For the indignation of the Lord is upon all nations." He promises "the year of recompenses," but this year of recompenses doesn't bring springs flowing onto desert soil but instead turns rivers to "burning pitch." This time, he promises that only the screeching owls, cormorants, vultures, and the wild beasts of the desert will have a mate and shall "possess [the land] forever, from generation to generation shall they dwell therein."[2] This recompense is payback of an unpleasant kind—no promise of human survival but divine vengeance for human hubris; it is the desolation of humankind and the final, unfettered regeneration of the wild. That's not so comforting all of a sudden, unless you are a cormorant. I guess you could say that the recompense Isaiah promises is another word for ecological law. Living in or out of balance, we will get what we deserve.

Which begs the question: Is our homeland a garden or a desert? Does its blossoming beauty depend on human engineering or on the unfettering of the wild? I like to think that this is a false dichotomy. We have had enough of those cheerleaders of all things human who will always see whatever our technology and economic prowess can do to nature as a categorical virtue. Likewise, it won't do to see ourselves as the categorical disease that ruins all we touch. If the desert demands submission to limitations, it also requires human ingenuity and innovation. Hannah Arendt was right to say that "man cannot be free if he does not know he is subject to necessity, because his freedom is won in his never wholly successful attempts to liberate himself from necessity." We are exceptional in the creation, to be sure, but our exceptionality will only remain innocent if we choose to respect the desert's integrity. In our heady embrace of the recompenses of an engineered world, we rejected the recompenses of its wilderness, failing to see that the desert blossoms with its own brilliant colors. It was always already a blossoming garden.

There are recompenses, of course, for working with nature—the pleasures of gardens, orchards, and yards—but the desert's engineered blossoming has reached the aesthetic equivalent of cosmetic surgery. We make snow, prop plastic deer on our front yards, decorate highway exits with colored rocks and manicured bushes, hang landscape calendars on our walls, design waterfalls and streams by our shopping malls, fertilize and water our Kentucky bluegrass, and buy every kind of enhanced and processed food you can name. Perhaps our only hope now is to fulfill Isaiah's prophecy by a persistent working back toward a restoration of the desert's own native beauty. Ecological restoration is neither technophilia nor antihuman escapism. It is repentance, plain and simple.

Of course, our most important and difficult acts of repentance pertain to those areas of life where our deepest affections lie. Love of the land is needed to make things right, but it is no facile panacea for environmental degradation. As Wallace Stegner famously warned us, "we may love a place and still be dangerous to it." Stegner, one of the West's most important writers and an adopted son for many Mormons because of his brief upbringing in Utah and his appreciation for Mormon pioneer history, remains a vital voice of warning about the need to live in balance with the semi-arid climate of the Rocky Mountain West: "We have no business, any longer, in being impatient with history. We need to know our history in much greater depth, even back into the geology.... History," he explains, "was part of the baggage we threw overboard when we launched ourselves into the New World.... Plunging into the future through a landscape that had no history, we did both the country and ourselves some harm along with some good....'The land was ours before we were the land's' says Robert Frost's poem. Only in the act of submission is the sense of place realized and a sustainable relationship between people and earth established." He suggests that an increasingly mobile, commercial, and acquisitive American life keeps too many of us distracted from the particulars of where we live and the deep human and natural history of our environment.[3] No longer assuming responsibility for collective memory or shared knowledge, we pursue our individual and family pleasures at the expense of civic strength and collective ethics.

But the problem is more complicated than this. Stegner admired people with a sense of history and a sense of place, and he knew this came from being "stickers," people who remained to cultivate deep belonging in their landscapes. Strangely, Mormons, an example of stickers if there ever was one, do not have the record of exceptional stewardship his belief in the value of rooted communities would have predicted. Perhaps this is because, as Jared Farmer writes, a sense of place is often paradoxically at odds with the preservation of history and of the land itself: "Collective memory involves forgetting as much as remembering." More history would no doubt help to overcome forgetfulness, but as long as our relationship to the land remains deeply invested in territorial claims to identity, the complexity of history will never truly open to our view. Consequently, individual *and* group needs will supersede those of the land.

For Mormons, Utah is Zion, a sacred homeland and refuge from the world. This is a vital place to start. But environmental problems are never going to be solved by one political party or one religious community. Utah is not unlike most places in America today, resisting dialogue across the lines that divide us—lines of politics, religion, ethnicity, and "lifestyle." And because no one would mistake the notion of homeland as the kind of inclusive, cross-cultural, and cooperative community that is needed, I want to consider a new definition of a sense of place. I have chosen to borrow from the fly-fishing term for one's favorite riverbend and defined that common ground as *home waters* as a way to convey a more fluid, ecological, and plural inheritance. My hope is to tap the potential of Mormonism to inspire better stewardship in the interest of all communities in the West. We face the steep challenge of cultivating a collective environmental ethos and a sense of place that are animated by the precious particulars of a variety of ethnic and religious experiences. We can only hope that we are nearing the end of open hostilities in the West over environmental issues, but tepid and distant tolerance of one another will not do, either.

Mormonism, at least the kind I have inherited as a descendent of early pioneers, can function as an ethnicity like any other. And that means that I confess to the weakness of occasionally bristling at criticisms of my culture and people, even when they might be deserved. In writing this book, however, I have wanted to offer something more than structural criticism of a religion and culture that I know intimately and believe in and also something more than a defensive apologist tract. I have wanted instead to use the literary imagination as a vehicle for exploring the uniqueness of a Mormon relationship to land, as I see it, in the paradoxical hope that my exploration of those particulars will expand rather than narrow communion with my more-than-Mormon and more-than-human neighborhood.

This book began as a nature journal over the course of one year as an experiment in building a relationship to the Provo River watershed, but one year extended into several as I revisited the same places at different times and in different conditions. Describing one place on one day, like an impressionist, opened the channels of memory. But I discovered that the shape of experience is more like the repetitive motions of a cubist painting. I found the years blurring and the places mingling as memories surfaced, memories of ancestral legacies on and around the river I had been learning, and personal memories.

Moreover, while making my voyages into my environment, I was reading about the environmental history of Utah and the ecology of rivers, and the Native American, European, and early Mormon history of Utah Valley. So as the years accumulated, whenever I sat down to write about the watershed, I found myself increasingly unable to separate place from story, outdoor recreation from ecological and spiritual restoration, the present from the past, and, even against my will, the historical from the personal.

At first this was distressing, but it became apparent to me that to write in this fashion was a way of resisting the disintegration of landscape, community, and memory that characterize modern life. This is the way of things with watersheds. They gather tributaries from upstream and connect all that is above, beneath, and beside and give life through unseen processes of exchange. They shape and are shaped by our common history. Their mystery and beauty as well as the tragedy of their degradation are key to understanding who we are.

Aldo Leopold once argued that in order to learn to respect ecological integrity, we need to learn to think like a mountain. This essay is an exercise in thinking like a river. The prose is not restricted by the rules of literary genres. It seeks to embody the form of a river, with all of its whimsical bends and turns, its competing current speeds and sudden encounters with boulders, its peripatetic flow and interdependencies, and its relentless carrying forward of the detritus of all that lies upstream in the dark past. The writing arcs loosely over time—the course of a metaphorical year—because a river's course is a journey through space as well as through time. And it follows loosely the flow from the headwaters to Utah Lake. But because water's journey is also a cycle, it challenges the illusion of chronological time and of the singularity of one life story. Instead of the stand-alone human memoir, I sought something more true to the porous boundaries of my biological being. I prefer to think of how each stone in a river begins utterly *sui generis* but the grinding and refining power of relentless currents smoothes them all, not to the same shape, of course, but to the same pebbly touch. It is the Romantics' dream that a deeper penetration into the ecological imagination leads to anonymity. As Walt Whitman once said, "If you want me...look for me under your boot-soles."

Anonymity is not the same thing as self-annihilation, of course, because it is a discovery of our human nothingness in the face of beauty, a discovery that is paradoxically our unique human privilege. Whatever environmentalism seeks to be, it must not denigrate the uniqueness of human experience. This is because environmental degradation is itself our own suicidal impulse. And this self-destructiveness is not only an indifference to beauty but an intolerance for the bald fact that we are subject to death and dying. We need to rehabilitate what it means to be human. We cannot risk self-hatred.

As I have come to understand from the irrevocable loss my family suffered when my oldest brother took his life, it is all too tempting to acquiesce to self-destruction. Love of beauty motivated by nothing more than a fear of death is hedonism, but acceptance of death without deep attachment to beauty is pure nihilism. I have drawn strength from Mormonism's unusual articulation of the intimate and proximate relationship between spirit and body, heaven and earth.

My understanding of Mormonism and Mormon experience offered here are, of course, entirely idiosyncratic (even if, in the interest of complete disclosure, they are filtered through the lens of what could be called devout personal belief and practice). But it is precisely the idiosyncrasies of experience in which I have placed my greatest hope. There is little value to community if it can't be inclusive, but it also fails when we demand renunciation of the intimacies of experience and belief in the interest of a generic collective good. Landscapes are never generic. And neither are people. Only a sense of place feelingly attuned to the particulars of home yet wisely aware of the global and cross-cultural is worthy of sustaining. Suffice it to say that the idiosyncrasies that follow are offered in the greater interest of our collective and sustainable well-being in a sometimes unforgiving, chastening, but still staggeringly beautiful place. They are my songs of praise and my lamentations—Isaiah's recompenses, then—for a watershed I undyingly love.

Summer

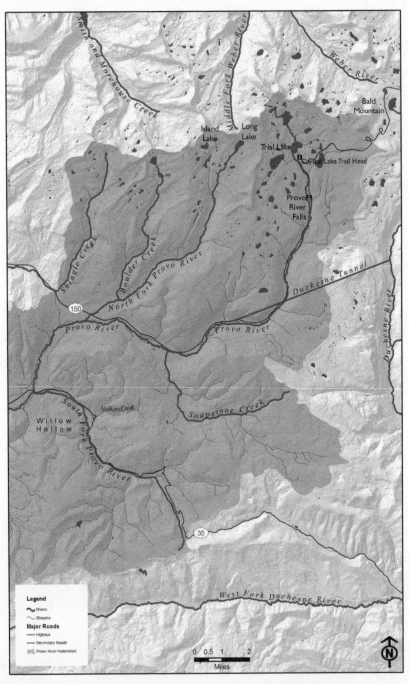

THE HEADWATERS OF THE PROVO RIVER

One

THE DRIVE UP THE MIRROR LAKE HIGHWAY TO THE HEADWATERS OF THE Provo River offers views of soft valleys of aspen and pine until about mile 20, when suddenly you feel the hardness of the high wilderness. On an early day in July like this one, you begin to catch sight of the still snow-patched peaks of the high country, and as the Provo River grows thin, it spills over tan rocks, slated at angles or dropped as erratics in the middle of some deep slow labor of time. This is water in its fast cycle, rushing from the pores of rocks seeking the sea or finding its way back again to groundwater or to atmospheric vapor, the attenuated veil of fresh water that sustains life in this corner of the planet.

The color of the water turns to a light copper hue as the thin light of high altitude penetrates through it to the stones beneath. At the Provo River Falls, a spectacular display of white rushing syllables echoes against the layers of stone that create steep and impatient stairs leading to the higher realms of lakes and springs. I find it hard to believe at these reaches that water is still moved by an accumulated higher source above. If it weren't for the grace of gravity and the infinite variety of the earth's surface, there would be nowhere for this heavy matter to go.

At Washington Lake, one of the main feeders of the river at close to ten thousand feet, I find a trail that ascends along well-worn white rock, with pockets of snow and mud surrounded by firs and spruce and the occasional aspen. In July, summer is in full swing in the valley where I live, but here there is still a hint of spring. The wind blows strong, blending the song of the trees with the intoxicating sound of mountain water. Nothing is still. Rising more closely to the ear are gurgles of excess runoff spilling indecently at every turn, often trapped in deep, glassy ponds where the dead bodies of trees lie buried.

I memorize the form of some white and yellow wildflowers in order to mark them later in my wildflower book at home. I feel ashamed not to know what perhaps should be the common language of my world. This is really why I have come. To find that shared and rooted vocabulary missing in my suburban and placeless way of life. To do this, I have only the occasional hours I can steal for private recreation away from my job as a professor and a busy home life with my wife and four children.

At first my hikes started simply as a means of exercise, something to keep my health and spirits up through the long months of responsibilities—teaching college students, parenting, nurturing my marriage, and giving time to my church—but it has become something more, a deeper yearning for absolute connection or maybe absolution itself for what Annie Dillard once called that "unwonted, taught pride" that makes us indifferent to place. Either way, it seems I can't stand any longer not knowing where it is I find myself. *Reconnaissance*—the French word for recognition—implies that what I seek I may have always known. As T. S. Eliot put it,

> We shall not cease from exploration
> And the end of all our exploring
> Will be to arrive where we started
> And know the place for the first time.

So I have decided to start at the headwaters, to explore the watershed down to the lake near my home, and to write everything and anything that comes to mind, to see what kind of relationship I can make with my place.

I find myself staring at one flower in particular, a flower with thin petals so long that in full bloom they droop into a small ball, like so many heads covering themselves with tiny yellow arms. Maybe it is only because I am no naturalist, or because I forgot my wildflower book, but I like the idea that this extravagance deserves a good metaphor more than it needs a proper noun. Collapsed Planets, Shameful Marys, or maybe Star Hearts. (Later at home I find the entries for Glacier Lily, White Avens, and the small, pale violet Rock Cress, all possible candidates for what I saw.) I am pleased to learn that even a proper noun doesn't have to be unpoetic, but because each flower stands alone and tremulous in the naked air, impervious and indifferent to what anyone might call it, I know that my quest for a language of home must begin with the imagination, not with the borrowed words of books. The payoff of naming is that I have made the experience mine even though the risk is the isolation of idiosyncrasy. Something about the books feels like cheating, as if home could be found and photocopied instead of made, so I have taken this risk of idiosyncrasy in the hope that my metaphors will facilitate my homemaking.

I rise over a slope. Running on the trail at the speed of a butterfly, the likes of which are sometimes found fluttering alongside me, gives an intoxicating sense of freedom. I admit that there is no inherent virtue in this, however, since I am running with a CamelBak backpack, running shorts, and a wicking shirt, just to stay young and probably to avoid depression. Not one to punish others with the appearance of my pale flesh, there is nevertheless pleasure in the hint of a bite in the air on my goose-pimpled skin.

I head northwest and find myself on a large flat range of exposed rock. Needlelike pine trees, many dead, pierce the blue sky with their alternating dark green and gray strokes. I don't know if this is evidence of acid rain, the pine beetles that are enjoying a feeding frenzy in the age of global warming, or just nature's law of death, but the scenery, though beautiful, is marked by staggering numbers of the dead. Here and there trees lie in various stages of decay, including faint lines of rust-colored soil where a trunk once lay. Wherever I see a peak—Notch or Watson, or others that are not named on my map—they appear rough, patched with white, and almost bald (Bald Mountain, appropriately named for its smooth, treeless face, lies to the southeast).

I continue to cross snow patches and small catches of water leaking through spaces between stones and tree roots, all heading south to the Provo River. I arrive at Long Lake, about half a mile long to be precise. The water level reaches a few feet below the man-made dam—a heightened retaining wall, really—the likes of which were constructed along many of these lakes in the 1920s to prevent water loss during spring runoff and to facilitate late summer irrigation. No signs of fish feeding, although a gentle wind whisks oxygen into the water.

Rising over another climb to the northwest, the trail suddenly drops a hundred feet or so through a pine grove of soft soil before turning sharply to the northeast where a steep ravine appears. I hear water and air together vibrating everywhere with no single identifiable source. I glance down, as if in expectation that I will find the sounds coming from the ground. The trail rises sharply, some three hundred feet, led by the promise of another lake that appears to be spilling over the ridge across from me.

I run beneath an array of cakelike layers of lichen-covered stones where dark stains of spring seepage trickle almost silently, like leaking milk. At the top of the next ridge, Island Lake finally appears. Its contents spill over the ridge and down a steep slope of pines below, disappearing into Duck Lake and eventually to the North Fork of the Provo. The lake offers an even larger body of glassy amber, with a stunning island of stone and pine emerging from its center.

There are hundreds of such lakes here in the Uinta Mountains in northeastern Utah, and dozens feed the Provo River, which runs some seventy miles to the southeast before reaching Utah Lake on the edge of the Great Basin. What was once a dangerous and peripatetic passage of mountain water building up and cutting through various canyons now flows steadily throughout the year, owing to two dams along the river's course. Who is to say which particles of high mountain spring water and runoff will then slowly ease their way to the north, catch the movement of the Jordan River, and spill into the Dead Sea of the New World, the Great Salt Lake?

The allusion to biblical landscapes is not my idea. Early Mormon settlers saw the parallel: a Jordan River connecting two large lakes, one saline, one freshwater, although it was American cartographers interested in national exceptionalism who exploited the idea. After years of wandering in the wilderness, these Mormon exiles sacralized the desert landscape of their homelessness; sacralized, too, their fall from the gardens and endless rainy days of the British Isles and Scandinavia. This was to be their land of milk and honey away from the threats of Babylon.

Everywhere in the state names bear witness to Mormon zeal to be at home in a New World paradise: Zion, Bountiful, Mount Pleasant, Orderville. But where the names do not tell the story of biblical exegesis, they occasionally respond to the story penned by water: Salt Lake City, Spanish Fork, American Fork, Springville. Which is to confess that I don't live in the average American suburb, but in what might be more properly called a Mormon kibbutz, a valley of close to half a million people, over eighty percent of whom are Mormon. Though Mormon myself, the borrowed words of history seem as unhelpful as the names in wildflower books since they are merely academic now, clichés that have worn out their utility in making a new home. I am content with where I live. I am tired of moving. I don't want a frontier or a chance to start over on the other side of the country. I need new metaphors and new names for old places. I need to know where it is I find myself.

So I had hoped to be able to start here at the headwaters of this watershed. In my mind's eye I had imagined that I would find some spring pouring out of the base of a fantastical peak rising above the clouds. A sublime and primordial beginning. This idea was no doubt influenced by those paintings of Thomas Cole of the Garden of Eden, boasting jagged crags striking the sky while tiny Indian figures in the foreground raise their hands in praise of their New World garden. There is something perverse, I know, in this proud desire to start over, since I have hardly earned the right in a few short years to feel tired of the predictability of life where I live. But there is something about how stories—like so many rivers—run channelized and harnessed and in disregard for interdependence that has chased me up to these heights.

To my surprised delight, the Lord God seems to have confounded the language of water, spilling its syllables in all directions, mixing what emerges from stone with what falls from the skies. A good place to start, indeed, because starting, I can see, is what it will always demand. Physical satisfaction runs through my body, but I feel no closer to the river's origins since even this lake's source remains a mystery. A peak looks down in silent irony to the immediate northwest, and off in the distance other peaks stand opaque, indifferent.

Cole's Edenic man would raise his arms in pagan praise of the high canopy of blue or perhaps strip and swim, but I can only imagine how cold I would feel. This is because a desolate wind is blowing forty miles an hour, shaking the pines and chilling my sweaty skin. Below me, the dead wood and its graveyard in the lake's shallows have become mute, like some silent motion picture in slow time. I become increasingly aware of my strangeness here, not so much because I feel unwelcome but because the indifference of this staggering beauty leaves me doubting that I know myself. Would the climbers of the Tower of Babel have exhausted language and finally stared at each other in silence? If they were lucky they would have known something beyond words. Still intolerant of a dissolving self, I suppose, and addicted to human society, I am pleased at least to know that had I gone biblical, no one would have seen me.

Driving back down the highway to Kamas, I stop for a beverage at the corner Chevron.

"Howdy, howdy!" the woman at the counter greets me.

Even after almost ten years of living here in my adulthood, I can't shake the bias from my teenage years in the East for the more distant and respectful way of greeting: silence. "Hi," I say, entering sheepishly in my running clothes. Around here, more people experience the outdoors in wrangler jeans and ATVs than with REI labels on wicking shirts.

Passing down an aisle more replete with everlasting gobstopping options than Charlie could have ever dreamed of, I find the back wall that contains shelves of Gatorade, soda, Red Bull energy drinks (which are some Mormons' way of avoiding coffee) and the obligatory silver column of beer varieties (which is some Utahns' way of saying "not a Mormon anymore" or "never was and proud of it"). I make my selection and go place my Gatorade on the counter. The woman has been chatting with a customer in overalls about people they both know.

"Will that be all?"

"Yeah."

"That'll be 89 pennies."

She is round, wearing a white T-shirt with an image of a deer in the middle of a bull's eye and sporting a hive of jet black hair that doesn't match the lines on her face.

Taking my dollar, she then counts change into my outstretched hand. "There you be!" She smiles again and I try to avoid her gaze. "You look like you've been real active." I self-consciously wipe my brow and smile.

"Just running in the mountains."

"Gosh, Darnell, did you hear that?" she says to the man in the overalls. "This fella's been runnin' in the mountains." The man shrugs, obviously not taken in by anything remotely resembling admiration. "How do ya feel now?" she asks.

"I feel all right. Not too sore."

"Where'd ya go?" I take a few steps toward the door, to indicate that she doesn't need to feel any more obligation to me. But her eyes shine brightly with genuine interest.

"I was searching the headwaters of the Provo, so I started at Crystal Lake trailhead and headed northwest. It was spectacular."

"Oh, isn't that somethin'. I know," she says, "I know it well. Isn't it just wonderful?" The fact that I had praised her land was apparently enough to endear me to her forever. And I found myself feeling the same for her. "Say, Darnell, isn't that where those two women from Florida were lost?"

"That's right," he says. I had seen a sign with their picture and the word MISSING printed in bold letters across the top stapled to the trail map when I had started my run. They proceeded to tell the tale of a woman and her daughter who, late last September, stepped out of their car at the trailhead parking lot for a brief hike. They had come to Utah for a vacation and decided a pleasant walk in the mountains was in order, something for the sake of enjoying the yellow autumn aspens.

It must have started out as a warm but crisp sunny day at a lower elevation, but with every five hundred feet of elevation change, the temperature begins to drop. I can imagine how as they drove the air grew tighter around them and the sunlight became more penetrating. The mother was in her fifties, the daughter in her thirties. The daughter's husband appears to have remained behind in Florida with the children. He would make an unexpected trip to Utah only after the two women failed to fly home a few days later. Perhaps they hadn't noticed the gathering clouds. Mountain skies have a way of lulling you into a false confidence until they shift to an indistinguishable white and then finally a dark metastasizing gray. And September is one of those months that can violently switch, like March or April, between the extremes of seasons within minutes; mere cloud cover can plummet the temperatures and rattle the bones.

I can see them arriving at the parking lot and opening the doors, the exhilarating cold bursting upon them as they came out of the warmth of the car. There was also the intoxicating smell of high mountain air, precisely what they had come all this way to breathe. As they began walking the trail, a park ranger approached them.

"You folks ought to put on something warmer. Bad weather is coming and you won't like it much," he might have said. Exchanging some niceties about Florida and its differences in humidity, elevation, and vegetation, they walked back to the car, put on another layer, and headed back up. They didn't get more than a few miles, somewhere past Long Lake. Did they lose the trail before the weather turned? Perhaps they hiked and watched as the snow began at first in soft pellets, as artificial snow sometimes looks on television, gently pelting their front, lodging in the crevices of their clothing. They must have thought about turning around, but the snow started innocently enough and they could always turn around and go back the way they had come.

But once the snow got serious, it must have fallen in blinding, intense patches of larger flakes, like cold feathers. Their hands began to ache and their ears burned. Perhaps it was the white sheets of snow that led them off course or perhaps it was merely the repetitive theme of boulders, fallen trees, and uneven skylines in every direction that pulled them down a steep slope on the northern drainage. In any case, as they attempted to turn back, they did not recognize their location. With each passing minute, the ground was filling up with white emptiness, and terror began to settle upon them. Just some flint or a few matches would have been enough to save their lives for one more day.

Weeks of searching came up empty. The husband went home alone to Florida, vowing to return and search in the spring.

"Those poor women," the woman says to me from behind the counter. "I can't imagine what they must've felt." These mountains are full of such stories, our modern version of the pioneer and Indian sagas of the past, only the violence no longer entails hatchets and shotguns, just the brutality and indifference of seasons on unsuspecting recreationists who only wanted respite from modern life. It is one reason why "untrammeled" can be a misleading word for wilderness; it isn't human absence but failed memory that defines the sublime and desolate wild.[4]

"They found their bodies only a few weeks ago, rotting away inside a simple shelter they'd built, just a few miles from the parking lot. All the way acrosst the Weber River drainage, wasn't it, Darnell? Imagine that." Like a silent sidekick, he nods soberly. "They were heading north when they shoulda headed south. Poor things. No fire, wet clothes, and those storms!" I had probably passed within a few hundred yards of their last living breath on earth.

After an awkward pause I make another motion to leave, not having the courage to seem rude after such a story. Although I am feeling a bit guilty about being away from home for so long, almost as an afterthought I ask about other areas in the Uintas I should try. This results in another fifteen minutes of information about trails, springs, rivulets and forks, beaver dams, canyons, and what time of year is best to try them. We look at maps in the store. Buying one seems like the decent thing to do. She asks if I have family. "Well, get yer kids up here," she insists, thinking it a bit odd that I would have enjoyed this all to myself. I promise I will.

In the beginning of middle age and married with four children, I am living in the land of my ancestors. This kind of promise of belonging in the landscape makes me the envy of most Americans, driven by the forces of modernity from one city to the next, one job to another. But the steady loss of agricultural life in Utah makes it increasingly difficult to see how its unique history has influenced the way we have related to the landscape. Our homes and shopping malls, dependence on the automobile, our craving for connection to the world through television and the internet, all make us no different than Americans anywhere. Indeed, we *could* be anywhere, anyone. Something there is, then, about the way these claims of Mormon history feel too easy, too apart from the world, and yet result in no respect for the rhythms of this demanding land.

"Should we have stayed at home, / wherever that may be?" Elizabeth Bishop wanted to know, a poet well acquainted with feelings of exile. Is home your house, your people? Who are your people? Your family, your neighborhood, religion, country? Must others, in other neighborhoods, of other religions, from other countries, always seem as so many obstacles? And what of the land itself? It is by now a tired diatribe against modernity to complain that we are no longer connected to place. In my desperate search for reconnection, and like almost everyone else in Utah, I don't work the land even though I descend from Utah farmers. And while I am in an increasingly small minority who try to take recreation seriously, I do so as a function of my class privilege and generally find that any other human presence disturbs my Edenic fantasies. This is hardly an acceptable alternative to an exclusionary nativism.

But maybe I can find in my recreation some way of reconnecting to my history and community. I must confess that even though Mormonism was founded because of a boy's encounter with God in the woods, Mormon life makes steep demands on my time and does not provide many chances for solitary meditation away from the trappings and idols of modern convenience. So my idylls are stolen moments of restoration, attempts to begin to understand this particular watershed that made settlement possible along the Wasatch Front and sustains life there to this day. If I can but translate the significance of these moments into a language of common understanding, I will have not wasted my time.

I drive home, heading west on Route 32 from Francis, a blink of a town. The road follows the course of the Provo through the deep cut of land below Francis. I pass a lumberyard and a large outlet of water that drops down from the ridge above, directed by culverts and diversions built some years ago to redirect some of the water from the Weber River to help sustain the booming urbanization in Utah Valley and Salt Lake City. The settlement of Utah by the Mormons would have been unthinkable without these watersheds of the Uinta and Wasatch Mountains, and the explosive growth of the population impossible without the innovations of irrigation and water storage over the last century.

Once the road levels, it hugs a series of soft, rusted gray cliffs exposing themselves like dried sponges. A series of crumbling barns tilting one way or another line the road to the left, surrounded by a curvilinear stand of poplars that have followed the flow of the Provo. These poplars, less common than the related cottonwood, have a strikingly vertical shape with leaves growing close to the trunk all the way up to their bushy tops, giving them the look of old, silent, bearded men. This little valley has been donated by a private owner to be preserved perpetually as a wildlife corridor, at least one bit of evidence that sometimes we can choose environmental restoration instead of degradation. The road rises onto a bluff that provides a stunning view of the Jordanelle Reservoir.

Below the dam the river crosses itself in complex braids. Years of mitigation funds have been spent restoring these snake-like bends to the Provo through Heber Valley. Early pioneer accounts of this valley and the Utah Valley below it provide a portrait of a river sprawling across the valley floors in webs of islands, marshes, and deep river bends. Both valleys teemed with wildlife: elk, bear, cougar, deer, moose. It was irrigation that reduced the river to a straight shot of water and caused the wildlife to retreat to higher reaches.

I notice a stretch of young cottonwoods and low-lying willows surrounding the sinuous shape of the restored river, probably planted by someone possessed of impossible love for what once was. Impossible but preferable because our playgrounds ought at least to have no fences. Impossible but yielding to bends, slow pools, and the texture of the bed's erratics, which dimple the water with seams and riffles. Just as the stuff of dreams enters our waking hours, a river assimilates the accidents of chance into the shape of the familiar. The artificiality of a restored river is no more disingenuous than a poem.

Crossing Heber Valley, the entire western skyline is dominated by the muscular Mount Timpanogos and its neighboring peaks of the Wasatch Front. The road winds through farmland that is becoming increasingly dotted with retirement homes the size of small chalets. I find my eyes drawn to the shapes of crests, crevasses, and crags that drape the face of Timpanogos, which at this early season of summer is only slightly white headed. Mountains rise to the south and even though the Uintas are not visible from here, their foothills lie to the east, cradling the green valley in a basin filled with milky blue air and capped by high summer clouds. The road conforms to the wide and lengthy circumference of the reservoir. I can see the unloading docks that have been extended in recent summers with additional concrete as the reservoir continues its drought-caused retreat from the shoreline. A beach park, with benches and awnings, lies abandoned now some fifty yards from the water.

Below the Deer Creek Dam, Cascade Peak rises brilliantly, textured by patterns of rocky waves and dark pine green. The steep steps of stone have sometimes left the highway riddled with broken boulders after summer rains or, after heavy winter storms, crushed under the weight of avalanches that leave piles of dirt, snow, and broken pine trees. The river once owned this canyon, but, now subdued, shares it with a recently widened highway. The drive demands visual focus, especially since no barrier separates me from the trucks pulling boat trailers up the canyon to Deer Creek. I steal glances at the water's surface for signs of rising fish. The season of the stone-fly hatch is approaching and any hints of activity are to be jealously noted. This is not fly-fishing for the faint-hearted. The largest of flies to hatch at any time of the year on the river, the stone fly floats above the river like a nineteenth-century version of a space-age flying machine. Up to two inches in length, its multiple layers of wings give its heavy tan body an indelicate vertical hover above the water. This is one of those seasons of the year when the fish focus on gorging themselves with the intensity of sharks in a frenzy. No such appearances today.

Above me, geological forms of gray slate follow in parallel lines along ridges that call to mind a sagging wedding cake or a sinking ship. Occasional waterfalls pierce the grayness with white streaks that dissipate into rocky conclusions. I come into the valley where the modern patterns of population growth and development have long since outpaced what the state's agricultural beginnings could sustain, making our dependence on the health of this watershed that much more precarious.

I pass a gas station with a food mart the size of a small restaurant, then a large shopping mall, known ironically as The Shops at Riverwoods, with a faux stream pouring over transplanted river rock. On the right lies a gated community of million-dollar homes in an area known as the River Bottoms, once a rundown and sparsely populated neighborhood that the Provo flooded annually with spring runoff. My eyes look south to Mount Nebo which, through the haze of suburban air particulates, appears indistinct and somewhat diminished despite its claim to being the highest peak in the Wasatch Front at just under twelve thousand feet. The deep blue of the Uinta skies has faded here to an unremarkable paleness. The weather is a heavy desert hot, in the mid-nineties, here at some six thousand feet lower in elevation than the mountains from where I have come.

Perhaps it is the haze in the air, but I find the immediacy of the Uintas slipping from the storehouse of my senses. I am eager to write in my journal, but I know I will only tell the truth like a river, in fragments, upturns, and with variable currents and temperatures. All of my being resists the lie of particulate air, suburban sprawl, and concrete that tells me that I could be anywhere. I know well enough that my life depends on this watershed, that this population owes its existence to the faith of forebears in water's grace, and no amount of smoke and mirrors can alter that fundamental relationship. But how to recover that clarity, with what language?

I have never been much of a storyteller. I make a profession as a literary critic, which means that I have an overdeveloped skill for interpreting the dreams of others but an underdeveloped capacity for dreaming. Besides, the idea that one life should have a symmetrical narrative arc has always felt false to me. The consequence is that I speak on the edge of a persistent anxiety, sensing the enormity of what I cannot remember, what I cannot convey, as though I can never really be sure of how close I came to not remembering anything at all. I might be liberated from my anxiety if I simply accepted the rock-bottom reality of inevitable oblivion, but this seems too nihilistic a conclusion. With trust in the idea of beginning again, the work of memory becomes more than mere imagination; it is restoration. Maybe that is why we still like to think that poets might be seers.

The longer I live in Utah, drinking water out of my own tap has begun to demand of me a story the depths of which I will never sound. I know my basic biology, that I am mostly water, that 97 percent of the earth's water is saline and after the icecaps there is only 1 percent left, that freshwater is disproportionately responsible for the earth's biodiversity. So I live on the milk of the mountains as does everyone else here. I know, too, that given the globe's increasing warmth, there is no reason to believe any longer that we will always have enough water in the arid West. The best information predicts a likely 50 percent decline in snowpack over the next fifty years, even though sprawl spreads without slowing.[5]

But these are only bald facts. Tracing the water back to its source and thereby understanding the nature of one's condition, as I have decided to do, is like trying to decipher the meaning of experience merely by anecdotes. It is like gauging how the planet is handling global warming by looking at the backyard thermometer on a particular Thursday afternoon. But I do want to know if it is warm outside, if it will rain this week, and I have seen and experienced a few things I consider worth telling, so that is where I will have to start. If I can't gain reassurance of the mountains' boundless capacity to gather and store the substance of my life, neither can I find reason to lose hope entirely.

Ten years didn't used to be considered a long time to have lived in one place. The nonindigenous folks in Connecticut like to say that you aren't a native of Connecticut until you've lived there at least twenty-five years, and I only lasted nine years there. My pioneer ancestors are buried only a mile from my home here in Provo. My paternal grandparents were both born in Utah, as was I, and I teach at the university where they graduated in 1928. But I have lived much of my life elsewhere, in the green woods of Pennsylvania and Connecticut, ten years in the brown (some say golden, but that is because they have never lived back east) hills of California, three years among the high and dry ponderosa forests of Arizona, and I have traveled to a dozen places in between.

I am a graduate of the Upper Middle Class American School of Travel Arrogance, having once proudly collected pins from nations in Europe. Between age eighteen and twenty-eight, when my first passport expired, I had stamps from more than twenty nations. My birthplace recorded in my passport, of course, never changed, but it also never inspired particular pride. I did receive remedial education from the School of Humble Living when I spent two years in voluntary church service in Venezuela. I have gone to the Caribbean as frequently as I can, including a trip to Cuba where I once danced, entirely sober, in a sweaty rumba frenzy on top of a fortress in Old Havana but was told when it was over by my African American friend: "Nice try, George. But you are still white."

Maybe I got ahead of myself. Maybe I tried too hard to connect to the world before I knew who I was and where I came from. I was reading recently from the work of Michel Serres, a philosopher of science who makes a compelling case for the need for a new ethic that connects the local to the global, what he calls a Natural Contract as opposed to Rousseau's Social Contract: "Never forget the place from which you depart, but leave it behind and join the universal. Love the bond that unites your plot of earth with the Earth, the bond that makes kin and stranger resemble each other." The weakness of needing to feel native is that it can cripple the imagination and make strangers of others. At the same time, however, without the bonds that unite us to place, we are just foolish globetrotters, addicted to the next exotic thrill.

To paraphrase Will Rogers, I never met a landscape I didn't like, or at least didn't eventually come to love. Perhaps it is a strange legacy of my Mormon ancestors to feel that I am a polygamist of place! But then again, maybe I am like Paul Simon's Americans, all come to look for, but never find, America. All I know is that something has shifted, the wanderlust has abated, and now I am drawn back to those places that formed my earliest memories. Cherish home, not exotica, I tell myself. Accept the romance of the prodigal son, I say. And if this is your chosen narrative, don't forget the wasted inheritance, the destitution, the unambiguous offer of a hirsute humiliation, before the son discovered a father of mercy. And don't forget the other son who never betrayed home, the one with whom the prodigal would have to share the land.

As runoff grows more impotent, a heavy pall hangs in the air, threatening all joys, compromising all ecstasies. My hunger for home is not innocent, especially if it is insatiable, so while it is good to look to the past, I know I must avoid the path of least resistance and find instead the way to deep repentance that will turn me again to the future. Here is where I must start. As the poet Rainer Maria Rilke reminds me in his *Book of Hours*, I will never shake off the great homesickness in any case. Perhaps I might learn something about how to assent to circumstance, how to live within the constraints of place and culture, and then maybe I will know the depth of the extended mercy.

I pull slowly into my driveway where my four-year-old son, Sam, is pushing himself in small circles on his scooter with intense focus. As I open the car door, the hiss of our sprinklers greets me. A white mist hovers over green grass in the early summer light. My son continues to turn, seemingly unaware of my arrival. Just as I am stepping into the house, however, he says innocently, "Dad?"

"What, buddy?"

"Where does water come from?"

I sit down on the steps, because this is going to take some time.

Two

❧

"And one last thing, George. If you don't come up here I'm going to go down there and kick your pioneer ass."

This was the message on my voicemail. My friend John said the last word with especially drawn-out emphasis, knowing I would laugh at his feigned threat and at his Mormon irreverence. He knew I couldn't make up my mind about moving to Utah and had even promised to teach me to fly-fish if I would come. It's not like I had a thing against Mormons, I had joked to him. "Yeah, I know, some of your closest friends are Mormons," he rejoined, then burst into laughter at his own humor. I had learned my religion independently, and I just wasn't accustomed to swimming in a school.

One can still find small towns in America with a majority population of one religion, towns where folks still settle after high school. But Utah Valley is no small town. Safe, clean, beautiful, neighborly, but what makes it like no place in America is that the valley is home to close to half a million people, over 80 percent of whom are Mormon. How would my children learn about the rest of the world? Wouldn't I get bored from all the sameness? Employed as a professor at Northern Arizona University in Flagstaff but trying to keep my options open, my wife, Amy, and I had been agonizing for days over an offer to come to Utah to teach at Brigham Young University. When I was finishing graduate school in California, I had hoped to land a job in the East where I had done most of my growing up, but every academic in the humanities knows that one doesn't get to pick a home like some people special order a car or a pizza. One adopts a kind of philosophical stoicism, similar to what I imagine military families have, and learns to make do with the cards one is dealt. That isn't to say that Utah wasn't attractive to me, but after two attempts on the market in the previous three years, I felt a bit stung by the fact that Utah now appeared to be my only choice for something new.

NAU is a residential campus nestled amid two million acres of ponderosas at the foot of a geologically recent volcanic eruption, known as the San Francisco Peaks. The place offered little by way of urban pleasures for which I yearned, but its miles of trails across dry creek beds and through towering, rust-colored trunks of pines, its modest spring runoff, and violent summer thunderstorms, were teaching me a new reverence for place. The campus was in the process of formalizing a commitment to place-based environmental education. As I became involved in a variety of curricular experiments and formal and informal discussions about the environment, I felt as if I was relearning everything—my training in literature, my approach to recreation, even my Mormon beliefs.

I saw insights in literature I had never seen in my previous decade of training in literary criticism. My relationship to a land completely foreign to me was enhanced by every hike, every wildflower, and every Anasazi ruin site. I went on scout campouts with my fellow Mormon youth leaders and the boys and watched while fathers and sons, sometimes three generations of one family, sat around the campfire and talked about trails, lakes, and stream beds like they were talking about their own kin. I didn't know if I wanted to live and work there for the rest of my life, but I ached to learn the art of living sustainably with a strong sense of place.

I listened to colleagues at the university describe the ethical underpinnings of good stewardship of the earth. I learned about what ecotheologians and church leaders around the world were making clear: that religion can teach a chastened human hope that balances an awareness of our human nothingness and violence with an awareness of our deep and special belonging in and responsibility for Creation.[6] One day on a walk, Sandra, a Jewish colleague and friend who had studied ecotheology, asked me about the environmental values of Mormon belief. I tried to think of everything that might be relevant. I recounted that in Mormon doctrine all things were created spiritually before they were given physical form; animals and plants are "living souls" with the right to enjoy their posterity; the earth will be heaven and is already the waiting place for those who have died; and that the Lord expects radical modesty in consumption habits. I mentioned that the Word of Wisdom, the Mormon dietary code that prohibits alcohol and drug use, also commands to eat fruit in season, to eat meat sparingly, and reminds us of the need to procure sufficient sustenance for all of creation.

Sandra asked incredulously: "Is this true? I don't think anyone knows this about Mormons. At least I have never read or heard anything about it. Has anyone written about this?" And then, stopping and looking me in the eye, she asked, "Do Mormons know this?" I don't think her question was merely rhetorical, but it remains a mystery why Mormons know these doctrines but they have not maintained a *collective* and *unambiguous* ethos of committed stewardship, and this despite the fact that probably no religious culture in American history has had such an intimate and sustained opportunity to determine a relationship to a homeland.

Within a week of arriving at our new home in Utah in the summer, the ambivalence I had felt about Utah's homogeneity was gone. It seemed plainly obvious to me that this was a homecoming and my chance to try to live somewhere sustainably and with familiar intimacy according to the principles of my beliefs for a long, long time. I felt a lusty pleasure in exploration, in getting myself acquainted with my new home. But I knew relatively little about the place, except for fragments of what I experienced as a child, visits to my grandparents' home in my adolescence, two brief stints at BYU in my college years, and what little I could remember from ancestral stories. I would need help from family lore, maps and books, and good friends, and my friend John seemed an eager and willing guide. It was early August, the high season of summer fly-fishing. I had purchased my first rod, reel, and waders and I had passed initial training on Hobble Creek near his house. We went to see my grandpa's cabin on the Upper Provo River that first week, so that John could teach me to fly-fish.

John and I had known each other in college in California where he had joined the Mormon Church, but I hadn't known him very well. Part Japanese, part Caucasian, and part Spanish, he married a Mormon girl who befriended him in high school and now, after graduate school, was living on the south end of the valley. He had become a fiercely loyal, if unconventional, defender of Utah life. An artist, avid reader, sociologist, recreational fanatic, political liberal, social conservative, and a religious man who lived on the edge of spiritual risk, he broke every stereotype in the book. He fished with the passion of a mad lover, stealing away during work hours with rod and reel always in the trunk of his car, falsely assuming that his wife would have minded, and hopeful that colleagues would not notice the particular aroma of mountain water or its dark stains that would cling to him, like some tell-tale lipstick.

On the first of what would become weekly trips, we drove through Provo Canyon along the banks of the river. John spoke animatedly about fishing holes he would soon take me to, about someday floating the Provo and the Green, about winter recreation, about western writers I needed to read, about life in Mormon Mecca. Everything seemed sharable—our family's lives, our intellectual and professional interests, our reading and politics, our religious convictions, and our passionate desire to feel a deep belonging in Utah. He was always eager for my opinion and full of generous praise. It was a rekindling of a friendship that took all of a one-hour drive before it seemed that he was the brother I had lost or I the brother he never had, as if our brief friendship in college had been a mere hint of what was to come. This was the way of it, too, with the landscape as we drove, a faint familiarity slowly awakening as we rounded each bend in the river, passed each patch of pines, each spot of scrub oak on the hillsides, upbraiding me for what I had forgotten.

We drove through Heber and turned to the east and over the Jordanelle Reservoir. "Remember this canyon. Some day it will be under water." I can still hear my grandfather saying these words as I looked through the windshield of his white Lincoln while we rolled eastward toward his cabin on the Provo. He had a reckless habit of driving his fat car directly at opposing traffic while he passed slower trucks pulling horse trailers, my white knuckles holding the heavy door's handle in terror. Only after John and I passed the reservoir did I notice the similarity between the road before me and the road of my memory—patches of scruffy poplars, bent and exhausted barn frames, and high green grass. It was not exactly the same, of course. It felt more like the effect of stereo sound, or two voices repeating the same words in a delay.

We rose to the top of the hill and entered Francis, settled in 1865 according to the rotting wooden sign. A vacated building stood with a broken neon sign advertising "Silver Spur Restaurant and Lounge: Now ..elivering.. P..Zza" along with a partial phone number. A few yards beyond, at the Uinta Junction service station where my grandpa used to buy his fishing supplies, I insisted we pull in. It was the same station, with the same old gas pumps with their curved spouts, and inside was the same glass cabinet filled with relics: spurs, guns, and other unidentifiable rusted pieces of metal. The less identifiable the piece, the more mystique it acquired as a possible fragment from the legendary Spanish miners who reportedly left buried treasures in these mountains. And they were still selling worms in their refrigerator. Grandpa would be pleased. With food in hand, the screen door slammed behind us.

All I knew at that point was that John had been raised by his Spanish grandfather and Caucasian grandmother in Seattle. Later that year fishing on Huntington Creek, I learned that his father took him away from Japan and his Japanese mother when he was only four years old and dropped him with a stepmom in Korea who didn't want him. There he was exposed to gang violence. Standing in the clear stream, he propped his rod under his left arm, rolled up his right sleeve, and showed me the scars. Apparently unable to provide a stable home for his son, the profligate father then dropped John in Seattle with the grandparents so he could continue his life of gambling. There John encountered the stability of an LDS community and friends, fell in love with a red-head, and was baptized and married by his early twenties.

A half dozen fishing trips later, he told me that, at his wife's urging, he found his biological mother after twenty years of no contact. He had spent his life believing his father's lie that she hadn't wanted him. But when he found her shortly after he himself became a father, she excitedly flew from Japan for a reunion. She lived for a few weeks with her newfound son, daughter-in-law, and grandchild, and then returned to Japan.

As we drove past Francis, I noticed the small canal that paralleled the road, spilling its irrigation water across the alfalfa fields in places where blue tarps flattened and spread out the water flow like a fan. Primitive and inefficient, but appealing. Appealing too were the towering serrations of the Wasatch Mountains to the west and then the sight of the Cash General Store in the next small town of Woodland.

We passed a bend in the river that came up to the edge of the road along a line of poplars. To the left, a small cliff of stone hung over the road like a partial tunnel. I asked John to pull over. As we stood on the riverbank, I described the dozens of golden trout I had once seen in this stretch with my grandfather. It might have been the summer of 1976, or even earlier. Word was that the river had been stocked, and the water's edge showed for it, lined as it was with fathers and sons. Grandpa opened the trunk of the Lincoln and bent over the tackle box inside it, while I danced in my shoes waiting for him to rig me up. Before he could set up his own, I had returned with a trout. This happened two more times, each one earning me his praise, as if I had something to do with it. But his own eagerness got the best of him and he finally insisted it was his turn. The fish held their position like yellow brush strokes in the steep drop of dark water underneath an overhanging cottonwood. After so many forgotten facts about his life and my own, it is odd that this image remains, untouched and unfaded.

As I opened the gate to Pine Springs, a small neighborhood of cabins, my mind became a kaleidoscope of memories. My brothers and I climbing out of our blue Buick and walking the road to the cabin, looking over a field of sage and yellow wildflowers. Holding my grandmother's hand as we walked along the dusty road beside the giant pines and quaking aspens. Catching garter snakes with my brothers in a pot among the willows. The quarter-mile drive along the dirt road today hardly seemed to capture the size of the world as it was back then. The river's edge, the wooden bridge, walking among the reeds and willows looking for chipmunks, pinecones, snake skins, jawbones of deceased animals, vacated wasp nests and birds' nests. And then there it was, the old 1936 log cabin surrounded by enormous firs and a grove of aspens, and the small tributary flowing behind the screened porch.

Opening the locked door, we walked inside the cabin just to see it. The slam of the screen door dislodged more memories. The two bedrooms with no ceilings or doors, just curtains, the old coal stove, the fireplace of river rock, and the mounted elk head. I explained to John that not one of the Handleys ever hunted but it came with the property and no one ever had the courage to take it down. I could see the crawl spaces above where I had loved to explore and set mouse traps. I couldn't wait to get Amy and the kids up here, to make this place a part of their memories, too.

Outside, as he demonstrated the proper assembly of my rod, John asked if I had read Wallace Stegner's essays on the West, especially his classic essay on a sense of place. I had and we discussed its merits: the mad rush for profit that had emptied the land of its history and chased populations across the western landscapes in search of El Dorado, and the virtues of the pioneers who stayed put. "No place is a place," Stegner had written, "until things that have happened in it are remembered in history, ballads, yarns, legends, or monuments...the kind of knowing that involves the senses, the memory, the history of a family or a tribe." But that felt too academic, I told John. A sense of place is a precious and endangered thing, but does it belittle the idea to say that it is just one kind of human imagining, that it isn't bestowed on us like some crown passed on from father to son? Besides, Stegner seemed to doom John's diasporic soul to perpetual displacement.

It occurs to me now that in a land rife with ancestral stories that weren't his, John excelled at adaptation. Despite the fact that I was the one with a land and a past to reclaim, he seemed to be my teacher in how to belong. Adaptation to land by adoption of history seemed to be his method, adoption of the memories of others when his own were too painful or lacking. I thought that I liked this idea of affiliation: choosing to make oneself a son to another. As if in search of his own reason for belonging, he prodded and urged my memories to the surface like a careful physician extricating splinters and, like a good patient, I submitted because I assumed his caring treatment meant that I, not John, was the one in need of healing self-discovery.

I knew a daughter of Holocaust survivors in graduate school who once joked that she liked hanging out with Mormons because it was the only time when she could be considered a Gentile. That is because Mormonism performs its nativity by adoption, too, rereading and reclaiming the old stories and adding some of its own, calling itself the latter-day House of Israel. Audacious, no doubt. Too much so for some. But it is nice to know that in the end a genealogy of blood will save no one. Which is not the same thing as saying that tribal memory does not matter, but love of body and blood must cede to love of the spirit, love of family to love of community, self to others, perhaps even earth to heaven. After all, in the Mormon universe, this earth will be the site of the celestial kingdom, God's eternal throne. Say it isn't a replacement but an expansion, a building on the first love born of natal contact with the blood of the mother and the waters of earth so that when we return again and again to the physical foundations of love for family and for place, affections become, like transcendent sexual love, an expression of self-effacement rather than of possession. A transmutation by fire.

This is an addition to the old biblical stories found in Joseph Smith's *Book of Moses*: a double-stitched recounting of the story of the Creation revealed belatedly to Moses on a mountain, translated retroactively by Smith. Moses learns that we are born of the spirit, blood, and water. In the Mormon cosmos, this is because we are born first as spirit children with God and then by the blood and water of the womb. But then Moses says it must happen in reverse, to be born again of water, blood, and spirit.[7] This time the water of baptism, the blood of Christ, and the Holy Ghost, a cosmic chiasmus that stitches together the water and blood of the womb and its kinship of family, with the blood and water of a much greater belonging, the kinship of humanity.

We walked across the road and through a grove of aspen toward the steady sound of the water. Nearby was Edmonds Hole where I had fished with my grandpa. I can remember him standing there on some of the dry rocks among the deep green reeds resting his hands on the back of his hips in his khaki trousers. John and I found the spot and dropped into the water. Upstream, a sharp incline rose to the right covered in straight rows of pines. Rocky sedimentary tables covered in moss exposed themselves there like teeth at the edge of the water. A line of topsoil beneath the square stones revealed how deeply the spring runoff had cut its edges this year. All other stones lying about the river's edge and in the water were round, broken and smoothed by eons of time, many covered in dried and flaking moss that comes to life during the spring floods, making the river bed a fertile feeding ground for the fish. Under the water, the rocks were sounding their deep bassoon notes.

As we stood just off the bank, John grabbed a fly from the air and showed me its tent-like wings. "Let's keep things simple for now. Just think about four classes of flies to use: caddis, mayflies, stoneflies, and terrestrials. This is a caddis. We'll get to the others later. Caddis dart and are always hanging out in the willows by the bank." He swatted a few willow branches with his rod and a small cloud of tan flies took to the air. He then put an elk-hair caddis on my line, and I watched him demonstrate the motion of a proper cast. The olive skin of his arms shone in the Western light, and my eyes were opened to the population of flies zigzagging above the copper-colored water like nervous snowflakes.

We stood knee deep on a bed of uneven stones that made every step treacherous, especially if you were too eager to cast and failed to measure your footing properly. Light sparkled across the riffles and in the seams created by the larger rocks that occasionally broke the surface or only showed their presence by an unexpected rise of the water. The smell of the water was metallic, a kind of bittersweet amber mixed with pine and washed by turning breezes. Amid the incessant murmuring of the water, darting birds hunted the same insects as the fish. A pathetic fallacy, maybe, but the world seemed tailor-made for us, so much so that I would prefer to tell a story of two native sons fishing, like the Maclean brothers in *A River Runs Through It*. But neither of us exactly fit the profile, John for his adoption and I a prodigal who left too early to have learned the art of compressing eternity into a moment.[8]

"Don't let your fly slap the water. It has to land unremarkably on the surface. When the fly lands this way it will drift naturally. Otherwise you will see the drag of your line on the water and notice the fly moving faster than the current. Fish aren't stupid. They know some idiot is standing downstream waving his arms uselessly in the sun. The key is the point of release which must show your patience. You can never afford to be overeager. It has to have the look and feel of art, regardless of results. If you start panting like an adolescent in heat, you will never get any action."

Despite the occasional politically incorrect sexual metaphor, John spoke in long paragraphs with preacherly intensity, making sure I was listening carefully to his instructions, as if he were teaching me the morality of religion. He pointed to the surface of the river ahead. "You see how the river has certain channels or seams. The water is never flowing at one speed and never has one temperature." I could see some white riffles coming down between two large stones to my left, but at my right was a flat stretch of water with an almost mirror-like appearance, reflecting the shadows of the overhanging willows. The river seemed a vast complex of change instead of some nameable entity. "Try to fish just off of the faster waters. That's where the food is coming to them and fish can hold and feed without too much effort. The closer you get to the white riffles where the water is churning the oxygen, the deeper you'll have to fish because the fish will be down low. But we'll learn nymphing on another day. Always keep an eye out for a rise on the surface. Whenever you see that, you're in business because they're looking up." I nodded like a young acolyte.

Love's labor lost, I guess, since my first two hours of casting were fruitless. My line got tangled repeatedly and I slapped the water with regularity, necessitating moving forward in the river to try new holes that I hadn't yet ruined. John was a patient teacher, as content to give suggestions or to watch the water as he was to catch fish of his own. And he was eager to praise what he insisted were my "natural abilities" and quick learning skills. The placebo worked: I imitated the motions of a skilled native, some mountain man raised from a boy on these waters and familiar with their every mood, as if I could be the Isaak Walton of the Upper Provo River of Summit County.

John grew animated when he saw a fish rise on the river to our right, so we slipped forward in the water. Eager to get me into my first fish, he talked me through my casts. My fly landed shy and to the side of the rise on my first several casts but then finally it landed just upstream and drifted over the head of the fish. My heart pounded hard and just when John anticipated a strike, nothing happened.

"Aaah!" John yelled, writhing in agony. But the frustration became part of the game. "Do it again, do it again. He'll take a closer look this time, the bastard." With a forceful cast I flung the line forward but my release point was prematurely stopped when my fly caught a branch in the pine tree behind us. John reluctantly took over, showing me how it was done. Within seconds, he had a gasping brown trout in his hands. "Make no mistake. The trout are on the chew," he said.

Once I clumsily tied on a new fly, I was on my own, pursuing the right bank of the river while John stayed to the left. In the afternoon light, I started to get strikes, then on two occasions I felt the pull of a fish for a few seconds before losing it.

"Make sure to pull your line in as the fly drifts downstream," he called from across the river. "Don't let your line slacken on the water like that. You'll never have time to set the hook. They're laughing at you! Matter of fact, they tell George jokes."

Before long, a fish flashed as it rose and turned, leaving a soft, round, upward impression on the water's surface and then a slight splash. Then that delayed realization that this is what I had been waiting for. This is why I had been standing here. It wasn't mere chance even if it felt like mad guesswork. The world had given me its brief notice that I was welcome. As the fish took off downstream and then across the current below me, John watched. I couldn't contain my amazement that below those flowing shallows of bronze and olive, cruising fish hid and hunted their prey. I wanted to say something about this, but all that came out were hoots of pleasure. John started moving toward me to help, yelling serious instructions. "Keep the line taut!! Tip up! Tip up!"

I did as he instructed and by the time the fish tired and floated limply to my side, a pile of my orange line had wrapped around my legs. I learned then and there not to argue with results, even when they come without art. I pulled a fourteen-inch silver Rainbow out of the water.

Patting my back, John said, "Welcome to your home waters, my friend. You know the phrase, don't you? These are *your* waters, man. You will grow old fishing them, and you will know every neighborhood of fish by every rock. Your children will know them, by name! I knew you had to come here. I told you so, didn't I? Can you believe you almost didn't come?" He went on with what I eventually learned were his characteristic monologues of bursting idealism, about pioneers, about the future, about great books, about what I would write and what he would paint, about the palaces of pines that surrounded us. As he spoke, I could feel the monuments rising in me that intimated the sense of place I hoped would be mine. I placed that first fish back in the water, as I had been taught, and held him gently on the tail until of his own force, the dark dorsal carried his brilliant colors back into the shadows. It wasn't his interest in history and literature that made John belong here, I decided. It was this unbounded embrace of water, earth, animal, and air.

Some months later, on a cold October morning sitting in my car after a successful outing on the river, I mentioned to John that I lost a brother to suicide when I was eighteen. I generally didn't make it a habit to mention him at all, since it always seemed to involve having to say and recall more than I wanted to about the past to people I assumed didn't want to know quite so much. But John's friendship was turning out to provide a kind of surrogate sibling relationship for both of us. His gentle and persistent questions were a welcomed opportunity to loosen the recalcitrance of neglect I had allowed Kenny's life and death to suffer. I told him about Kenny's depression, how it struck him hard at the young age of eighteen, and how, in those days, so little was known about the medical basis of mental illness. And about how, as the years progressed, his ability to cope with college life declined. At the age of twenty-two, when I was in the midst of my senior year in high school, he inexplicably obtained a gun from a friend and shot himself on the grass in our backyard in Connecticut.

Maybe the fact that I had told only a few people before was a sign of my lingering hurt and detachment, since Kenny's death itself felt like a betrayal of my faith in the providential recompenses of life. While I spilled my story in a gush of unexpected emotion, John seemed overwhelmed. We fell into silence.

Staring at the foggy window with nothing more to say, it hit me: *This bullet that ripped a hole through his head and through your life is why you crave friendship and why you love this river.*

"Months after my mom visited me in California I got word that she died," John announced suddenly. "She killed herself." No explanation. No note. With suffocating grief he told me that he had recently seen a gray-haired Japanese woman, a leader in the LDS church, in a bookstore in Provo. "The similarity was uncanny. Just the sight of her small body and white hair was enough, was all I could take."

After his mother's death, his in-laws moved to Utah, and he and his wife eventually followed. He had taken to calling his mother-in-law "Mom," but it wasn't more than a year or so later when she contracted cancer and died, not long before I moved to Utah. It didn't take a genius to figure out why he had to say these things slowly and in fragments. I did my best to absorb the shock waves. Much of our fishing during that year was clandestine, our conversations squeezed in during the oddest hours before work or before sunset, and our casts crossing the air like sutures.

I have fished many waters since John and I first drove to the cabin, but I will always prefer the rawness and untamed quality of those upper stretches of the Provo, above the dams and away from the pressure of development. They have indeed become my home waters, a place of return and renewal, a chance to explore and reanimate the imagination of memory, and a way to explore the ever tenuous reasons for my belonging here.

The Upper Provo is also home to a diverse fish population, as their colors and variety show. Brown trout are an especially deep yellow green with piercing red spots; cutthroats have blood red in their gills, an orange slash on the throat, and flashes of silver on the side—like the rainbows—that contrast with the dark purple-green hue of their backs.

Soon after that first day of fly-fishing, I began to dream of fish, unlike any kind of dreams I had experienced in my life. In my sleep swam fish of florescent brilliance—fish cruising in the clear shallows of some mountain spring water, fish rumbling underneath me when I found myself treading water in canyon glades, fish leaping into my hands in quivering silence—and in the gray light of dawn I would awaken as if I had had a revelation. It was the utter physicality of the dreams that gave them their revelatory sensation. But I have had nightmares, too. I have seen long, anorexic fish with oversized heads in still waters, gasping desperately. I have dreamt of a Provo River running dry, the waters receded from the banks, exposing fields of stones and muddy flats, narrowed to a thin, slow current of brown. It isn't exactly the burning pitch of Isaiah's apocalyptic vision, but it is close.

Before they can be apprehended, the internal workings of water's motions pass into the eye of the imagination. Standing in the middle of a river's moving current, the world seems to be an embrace, a song, maybe a dream, full of changing forms and colors that pass before the eyes, continually dying and being reborn. Whoever said that you can't step into the same river twice, however, never fished as a child. So what if one of them is a fiction to which you return again and again? The same substance, the same sensual reassurance of your belonging in the world, and with each immersion, the same mounting conviction of life's blessedness.

It is true and more than lamentable that we misuse, poison, flush, evaporate, and divert water, but we will never destroy it. Water will just move somewhere else in the vast universe where it is more welcome. Time was when rivers were symbols of eternity, the recompense of God's regeneration of this desert world, but their endangerment has made them warning signs of shallow, fragile time, symbols of our own mortality. Our sustainability depends on how we immerse ourselves in the rivers of our imagination. How else to measure the turning and burning of the world?

That's the way of it for me when I stand in that stretch of the Upper Provo. Every time I step off the bank and into the water, the shape of the current is noticeably different. The water has risen or fallen, it is muddied, olive, or amber, the banks carved differently than before. Fixed places in the mind are no more fixed than the contours of this river, but my suspension of disbelief in my own imagination allows me to perceive the world's changes. Entering the same waters over and over again, it is finally the fact that I am a breathing and dying body that strikes me as the most strange. This wonderment at my own biology is the gift of the river, a fire of transmutation, repentance maybe, but never stasis. Home waters.

Grandpa was in his early nineties and living alone in Salt Lake City when I first moved to Utah. Grandmother had died just a year or two earlier after almost fifteen years of mental decline. Amy and the girls and I ate meals with him from time to time (our son Sam hadn't arrived yet), sometimes at the cabin, sometimes at our place or his. He liked to hold the kids on his lap, pat their knees affectionately, and stroke their hair. Otherwise we called each other to share fishing stories, mine the ones John and I were generating, and his from his vast and impeccable memory. He was stunned to learn of the size of fish we were pulling out of the river. And the kinds: rainbows, browns, cutthroats, whitefish, graylings, brook trout. Although he owned two fly rods, he never had a friend like John to teach him how to fly-fish. It had been years since he put a worm on a hook. Hearing that sound of unguarded wonder in his voice was reason enough to seek experiences that I could share with him.

"I'm so happy that you're having such a wonderful time, old boy. I am so proud of you." Archaic and formal but never insincere. It seemed, in fact, his sentimentality was running amok of late, evident in how his voice would grow tight and halting. At his age, he lived with a lot of ghosts: my grandmother, his parents and siblings, his peers, by brother Kenny, and those who had shaped his Utah childhood so many years ago. Nostalgia and loss in old age seem such an unfair price to pay for love and maybe that is why I never knew what to say to assuage him. So I tried to move the stories along at a good clip before he had time to fall into another well of nostalgia.

One day I called him urgently to tell him about the seventeen-inch brookie I caught in the stream that runs behind the cabin. I had been alone, and it was almost dark. The moon had risen in the east ahead of me before the sun had set behind me. This left the air hanging in a vague orange light, enough to see a fish rising tight along a bank of high grass in ankle-deep water. I had to turn the fish in my hands several times to make sure it was indeed a brook trout, which was the first I had seen in this river, and to make sure it was as large as it felt. I described this to him in detail and I could hear grunts of awe and pleasure on the other end of the line as I spoke.

"It sounds like the fellow was overdressed for the party!" The disbelief in his voice was not meant to imply I might be making this up to please him, but he couldn't help it. "I never once saw a fish that large in the stream. I never tried fishing it in all those years. I just wasn't much of a fisherman, I guess." He paused. "You know, George, maybe we could build a platform out across the stream behind the cabin. I don't know what's wrong with these knees of mine but they just won't cooperate, and I doubt my legs are strong enough to resist the current. Then maybe you could teach me that cast in the middle of the water. What would you think of that?" I couldn't bring myself to say that he wouldn't live long enough to justify the effort. A seven-centimeter aortic aneurysm had appeared, and we all knew his days were numbered. What we all loved about him was how he continued to act indifferently to the passage of time. He was usually surprised to read of his friends in the obituaries, as if it were a shock to die at his age.

"That might work, Grandpa. I'll look into it. I would love to teach you. Maybe next summer." Neither of us said anything more about it.

Talking about fishing was a lot better than letting him start on one of his stump speeches about what caused the Depression or how FDR ruined America, or his occasional complaints about minorities. Grandpa never yelled and was an impeccable gentleman who believed in civility, but he could occasionally say things with a smile on his face that were out of date with contemporary sensibility, and for my family, these comments were a source of nervous tension. I always tried humoring him, telling him he was an old man in need of a dose of the modern world. He laughed back—he could laugh at himself to the point of tears—but it didn't stop him.

This was at the end of my second summer in Utah, and John had already left Utah. I had invited John several times to the cabin to meet my grandfather, but there was always some reason he couldn't come. He did manage to spend a day teaching my brother Bill to fish, while I watched and then fell into the river in excitement when my brother made his first catch. There was one more fragment John couldn't quite tell me. He gave me some cryptic explanation about a job his wife would be taking out of state, a leave from his work, but no explanation about why he, of all people, would be so unemotional about leaving his home waters. Despite our closeness, there was always that suspicion that I would never get to the bottom of who John really was. I made myself available to him, but if he didn't want disclosure, I knew him well enough not to push.

By then, at least, I was an autonomous fly-fisherman. In the long summer days, Grandpa would meet me at the cabin to watch me catch fish, but his lack of energy to watch for long periods and my bad luck brought us no results the first few attempts. With the start of the fall semester around the corner, I sensed my chances diminishing. One day I placed a chair under the willows and seated my grandfather among the tall grasses at the bank of the river. I walked downstream and entered the water out of his sight. He came into view when I crossed to midstream. The sun was setting behind me, casting my shadow upstream, so I required several dry casts to cast long. I could feel a chill in the air among the shadows of a tall spruce alongside the bank. Where the sunlight caught the water, at that hour, it turned the surface a pale yellow, highlighting the frantic action of the gnats and mayflies and the occasional splash of water where a trout was rising.

I said a silent prayer and asked for a fish, just this one time. Hadn't He promised He would never give a stone to those who ask for a fish, I thought, with pretended naiveté? I aimed for a spot just off to the side and below a square stone that created two seams of riffles. A strike met my fly and what felt like an electric current of muscled force shot through my elbow, into my shoulder, and down my back. I reeled it in and held the fish high over my head for Grandpa to see. He was too far away and his sight too poor to admire the creature's startling silver, blue, and yellow markings, and the brilliant orange slash on his white throat. But Grandpa raised his hands and shook them in triumph. His mouth moved, but all I could hear was the rushing sounds of liquid amber moving around my legs and a muffling breeze descending from the mountains. He remains there in my mind's eye, too far from earshot, triumphant and joyous. Two weeks later, my uncle left him momentarily in his study where he was writing a letter. When he returned a few minutes later, Grandpa was slumped on the desk, motionless, a pencil still in hand. He was ninety-three.

On the wall of the main bedroom of my grandfather's cabin hangs a magazine cutout. It comes from the June 1957 issue of *The Monotube*. The picture features a man, nicely dressed in a crisp, collared shirt, slacks, and black, shiny shoes, almost identical to the image I have of my grandfather from my early childhood. The man is sitting on the grass, leaning against a tree in a pleasant reverie. The text, entitled "The Art of Relaxation" by Wilfred Peterson, reads:

> Modern man must learn to break the tensions of daily living or the tensions will break him.
>
> He must learn to bend with the stresses and strains like a tree in the wind. He must develop the resiliency of spirit to spring erect again after the storm has passed.
>
> He first relaxes his mind by thinking thoughts of peace, quietness and tranquility. He mentally pictures the placid pool amidst whispering pines and puts himself in tune with nature's calming mood.
>
> He strives to carry an inner serenity with him so that even amidst a whirl of activity he will not lose his poise. Like the old negro he learns "to cooperate with the inevitable" and he accepts life with faith in the ultimate triumph of right and good.
>
> He relaxes his body by imitating a lazy person—a boy on the beach in the sun—a man in a boat fishing. He takes a tip from the circus clown who told that the way he avoids being injured in his tumbles is by making his body become "like an old rag doll."
>
> He exercises—walks, stretches, works in the garden, plays golf—knowing that physical tiredness invites relaxation and sleep.
>
> He knows that confusion is one of the chief causes of tension so he organizes his work, puts first things first, does one thing at a time, avoids hurry and develops a spaciousness of mind.

He uses the soothing beauty of music to calm his nerves. He listens to such selections as Schubert's Serenade, Dvorak's Humoresque and the folk tunes of many nations.

He observes that the face with a frown marks the tense person, and that the face with a smile is a symbol of relaxation, so he strives to meet life with a sense of humor. He learns not to take himself too seriously and to laugh at himself now and then.

He knows that tenseness and shallow breathing go together, so he breathes slowly and deeply to reduce the tempo of his living.

He takes time for meditation. He accepts the wise counsel of Emerson who wrote: "Place yourself in the middle of the stream of power and wisdom which animates all whom it floats, and you are without effort impelled to truth, to right and a perfect contentment."

He recognizes that relaxed living is a way of life and he strives to manage body, mind, heart and spirit as efficiently as he manages his business.

The patronizing racism is hard to take: the "old negro" who learns patience and character because he accepts the "inevitability" of his plight. There is more irony, too, in that this "art" of relaxation is no longer a natural part of living but is instead a staged drama, a pretense of a smile, the "symbol of relaxation" (should it not be a symptom?), or the imitation of laziness in the midst of hard work and industry. In the end, the body and soul of man are managed by the very same administrative acumen that creates the profits as well as the circumstances of stress.

I cannot help but notice how accurately this paints a picture of my grandfather. He had returned to Utah in September of 1957, just a few months after this magazine was published. He bought the cabin in 1966, when I was only two years old, and it quickly became a family getaway from Salt Lake City, which in those days was not so much the choking metropolis it is becoming today. It was an exercise of class privilege to have such a location to escape to, to rest from work, and there were other much larger and more luxurious lots nearby owned by some of Salt Lake's preeminent citizens. At a very early age, I sensed the class difference between my grandfather and the farmers who lived and worked near the cabin, a difference I could feel in the subtle distance in his voice when he spoke of them. The desire to get up into the canyons of Utah goes back far in Utah history; in the early years of the twentieth century, it was a rare opportunity for farmers to take tents up the canyons to fish, hunt, and camp for a few days.

As the oldest, my grandfather worked long hours for his father as a farmhand and brick mason and walked the proverbial six miles to the one-room schoolhouse every day. He remembered only one such respite in his teens when his uncle and cousins took him to this very stretch of the Upper Provo near Woodland in the early 1920s for a week-long fishing trip, no doubt the reason this location later appealed to him for a cabin site. All I remember is that he remarked how cold the water felt to his feet. Before he left for New York City in 1928, Woodland was the farthest east he had ever been. He was hard-headed, hard-nosed, and no doubt a careful strategist in business, and he raised his children with formality, but he always seemed the very model of serenity. He walked in the woods with dress slacks and black shoes, always with a smile, and I never heard him raise his voice in anger.

But hold on a minute. Something here in this magazine article condemns me as well. I might laugh at the walking, the stretching, and the golf, only because I like to think running, snowshoeing, and biking are more strenuous, but these are my adopted forms of stress release, and all of this is necessary because, as Wendell Berry has preached, our society has become unsettled from the land. More rigorous exercise will not stem the tide of our denigration of physical labor. Our bodies no longer serve us as they once did as instruments of our living. Now they are excess baggage, things to be maintained so that we can continue to live as if they were irrelevant, as if we were not embodied biological matter, destined to the same fate as bracken dead leaves and the mound of rodent hair I found plastered by winter's snows against the front stairs of the cabin.

And I cling to this cabin and these waters, as did my grandfather, as my preferred place of spiritual renewal, and although I might not wear shiny black shoes among the pine needles, I wear clothes calculated (or at least advertised) to help me move with the trees, to feel as comfortable and natural in my unnatural East of Eden state. Oh, stream of wisdom and power, will Emerson explain why you have so little of both? Where is your right and perfect contentment?[9]

Grandpa was no farmer when he purchased the cabin. By then he was a successful New York banker despite his humble beginnings. Grandmother's origins are no more notable, coming as she did from a remote (even for

Utah) valley of light and expanse in central Utah in the town of Manti, settled by Danish and English converts. My genealogical charts tell me that two daughters of James Stratton and Eliza Briggs married two Handley brothers on the same day in the Salt Lake temple in 1879. And they were cousins to boot. My grandfather was born twenty-five years later.

"Our own animals that we had on the farm were generally pretty well worn-out animals," Grandpa related one day at the cabin. With my parents in town, he had a captive audience and my dad was in the mood for prodding his memories. He sat on the brown wicker chair resting both hands on the armrests, recalling his one-room schoolhouse in 1918. "But this man, Herman Nelson, came to school every day from down in Midvale and he drove a spanking new buggy with a horse that just stepped out, was just a beautiful animal. And he arranged to stable the horse during the day at the bishop's barn up the street. So he would pull the buggy in, and he asked me to take his horse up to the bishop's place. He came to school every day. He was nicely dressed, always had a well-pressed suit, a stiff white collar and necktie, and he didn't have any of the sloppy appearance that some of the educators have today. He wasn't trying to be so common. He made a real impression on me and I always planted in my mind that he went to the university because he wore a little 'U' pin, a pearl pin, something I assumed that he had gotten as he graduated from the university. I never did talk to him about it but I decided that that's what I ought to do. And that was the thing that stimulated me to ultimately go to college."

In 1924, a cheap rental in Provo became available, and he decided he would pursue a college education at Brigham Young University where he met my grandmother. After flirting briefly with the idea of becoming school teachers together in the White Mountains of Pine, Arizona, the two Mormon children of the land left for New York City in 1928 where he would pursue an MBA and a career in banking.

His father would die two years later in a tragic car accident, leaving him in charge of his family's financial needs. Having worked extraordinarily long and hard hours on farms all the way through college, hard work in the city came easily, and he was rewarded. Eventually he moved out to Long Island, hired nannies and sent his children to boarding schools, and eventually pushed them on to college and graduate school and professional careers. A Utahn uprooted in voluntary exile, like John he was intent on adoption, in his case of eastern ways. They stayed active in Mormon life among a small group of Utah exiles around the city, but as the decades passed signs of muted ambivalence about their Utah roots began to appear. Adaptation, whether for a convert making home in Utah or a Mormon farmer making home in the metropolis, requires the pretense of adoption. The parent tolerates the strange sensation of his own play-acting in order to obscure an unwelcome background in the hope that things will become second-nature for the children. The American way, one might say. And yet no one knows what it is that separates the acting from the becoming or what fire anneals the soul to a landscape and gives it permission to stop its flight and finally be at home.

Utah called, however. It wasn't the land that called but a job that proved too good to resist. My father followed this back-and-forth pattern, arriving in Salt Lake for college, going back east for law school, and then beginning his practice in Salt Lake, where I was born. Grandpa had returned to Utah, he told me during our fishing conversations, largely with regret for what he had given up. On another wall in the cabin is a cartoon, dated September 13, 1957, and signed by a group of friends from Mumsey Park on Long Island, on the eve of my grandparents' departure for Utah. It features a hillbilly automobile, overstuffed with luggage, chicken coops, children, a box with "Home Sweet Home" written on it, and houseplants. A laundry line waves in the wind off the back of the car, with a flying brazier, shirts, and dishtowels. Atop a signpost pointing to "Utah" perch two buzzards, with question marks over their heads as they contemplate this passing circus of a migrating family. So my grandparents' friends saw this as a kind of regression, too, even if relatively benign.

It was unfair, especially given my own ambivalence about Utah, but I wanted to see in my grandfather some measure of Mormon dismissal of metropolitan, eastern norms, some embrace of the regional pleasures that, thank the Good Lord, are lost on a good many urbanites. Not the crude reactionary turn of the hopeless provincial, but the wizened, mature embrace of the prodigal. But like most of us he was too complicated for simple, self-resolving narratives. He remained a loyal reader of *The Wall Street Journal* and watched the stock market with more religiosity than he worried about his native religion. The same man who never sounded happy about having left New York but who purchased this cabin to which he returned weekly in the summer months until the very end of his life, who frequently burst into spontaneous song, singing "Utah We Love Thee" and other songs learned in the one-room schoolhouse, until his voice cracked with emotion. The same man who wanted to build a platform out over the small stream behind the cabin so he could learn to fly-fish at the age of ninety-three.

I inherited his bipolarity. His trips into mountains for respite from physical labor in the early 1920s were not unlike my trips to New York City for respite from the country in the early 1970s. Although less than an hour's drive, the journey from Connecticut was complicated, riddled with potholes on highways with no shoulder, and we found ourselves winding through cement canyons full of the world's people. We visited the symphony, the Met, the Frick, the Guggenheim, and we saw musicals, ballets, dramas, hard-to-find films.

When I wasn't being educated by the world of The City, living in the East meant playing in the creek behind our house or among the tidal zones of Old Mill and Burying Hill beaches. I sought salamanders, frogs, minnows, snappers, clams, anything that could be captured and observed. I was a cautious preadolescent naturalist who benefited from the fearlessness of some of my friends to push me beyond my comfort zone, whether it was attempting to capture a crab to bring home in a bucket, diving off of a sea wall, or otherwise exposing my body to risk and to the elements. I was always happy for the push and almost always rewarded for overcoming my caution.

As I grew older the beaches and woods became places of refuge, of hiding, and eventually of adolescent subterfuge, places where I seemed to be free of moral obligations and free to experiment with my beliefs as well as my practices, to invent a self outside of Mormon norms: smoking on the grass, drinking in the woods, meeting friends at the beach. This was unusual, of course, for a Mormon, and I was aware and ashamed of my transgressions, but the anonymity allowed me to postpone more serious deliberation about my beliefs and to maintain the illusion of radical freedom that the outdoors seemed to offer me.

The visits in the summers to the Mormon West were unforgettable dreams of crisp color and infinite possibility. I hiked mountain ridges, fished streams for trout, occasionally rode horses impossibly fast through forests of aspen, always oriented by the vast mountain ranges within sight no matter where we were. It was there under those staggering skies in the dry air, in the sweet aroma of pine trees and mountain rain, and the stony taste and sound of high mountain water that I was chastened by a growing awareness of holiness. This was a land of some claim on me, a land sanctified by the sacrifice of a believing band of my direct ancestors who sought to convert a state of exile into the Promised Land.

Most immediately, these summer visits initiated me into Grandpa's past. I can't recall all of his stories, but what I remember more vividly than the details of the stories is the feel of his hand on my back gently nudging me toward a past that reached deep into obscurity where names filled me like a Mormon Quentin Compson.[10] Only these were not the names of defeated slave-owners. They were good, or at least ordinary, people who had the unmistakable feeling of holding the roots of my being. I can still recall the feel of his voice speaking benevolently, persistently over my shoulder, telling me to consider becoming a doctor, telling me to wash my hands, to sit up straight, telling me I was remarkable.

He might have included more instruction about how to be a Mormon like many other Mormon grandparents I know, but perhaps it was the fact that he said little explicitly about his religion that made his admonitions seem of a piece with the place and its history. Even at a young age, I intuitively sensed his praise was intentionally premature, meant to illicit my social and academic best to be deserving of such hope.

And the feel of his thick hands slapping my knee in a show of affection. I remember watching them as he pulled snails off his tomato plants in the backyard of his well-kept Salt Lake home. They were deft, showing a pianist's intimacy with ivory, moving gracefully and gently over the leaves, testing the roundness of the fruits of his labors. Back in the kitchen, my grandmother diced their spilling flesh. "You have surgeon's hands," I remember her saying. She, too, liked to work up her grandchildren into fantasies of professional success. I stared at my fingers to divine what she meant. The truth is that I had hands like my grandfather; everyone knew it because my fingers are short and somewhat pudgy, something my grandfather claimed was the sign of farmer's hands. I carried this irony in my first name as well, which comes from a long line of namesakes, my grandfather included, meaning "farmer of the earth." Far from it. The only calluses I collect these days are from computer keyboards.

Maybe geography teaches us the first lessons of being. Or perhaps we project our inner life onto its contours so that it takes on a meaning that makes living in it comfortable, like wearing an old shirt. Maybe we cling to it because we are simply afraid of its radiant indifference.

For me the East was a land of many histories where I learned to be responsive to others, starting with my friends who were Reformed Jews, free thinkers, atheists, ambivalent Catholics, open-ended Unitarians; it was a land of license. The West was a land of a singularly centered worldview that gave me my reason for being, a staggering concentration of my fellow Mormons, and extended family roots that promised unimaginable community; it was a land of repentance. Strange that this was not mirrored by the two landscapes. In the East, the natural world pressed itself upon me with such aggression that I scarcely saw the sky let alone the contours of my own city. A land of gravitational telluric force, a wet, green merger of self and world, drawing my eyes downward and inward, rooting my being below my feet. In the West, the natural world opened me to immense vistas. A land of celestial potency, an arid desert that demanded a recognition of the intrusion of my presence, drawing my glance outward and upward, rooting my being in the contemplation of space itself.

It almost seemed impossible that these two worlds could ever have anything in common. Perhaps for this reason, it took threats and cajoling from others to believe that making a home here would have to be an experiment in proving these dichotomies false.

When I was in college in California and engaged to be married, some friends drew another prophetic and stereotyped cartoon of Amy and me living in Utah with ten children. This was their way of teasing us for being Mormons. I was used to it, but I didn't always like it. Maybe they were showing some restraint by not drawing a few more wives for me, since I was used to polygamy jokes, too. Amy and I have four children, but here we are after all.

There is a woman around the corner and up the street from where we live who is not Mormon. There might be three or four other non-Mormons, but no more, within a square mile of our home. In the first year or so, I prepared myself to show my California education by showing sensitivity to diversity whenever I might meet someone of a different religion, race, or nation. My first day of teaching at Brigham Young University, I made my usual disclaimer that if I mispronounced their names, they should correct me. I had seen my share of Vietnamese, Laotian, Hopi, Indian, and other difficult-to-pronounce names in California and Arizona. Then I began the list: "Bahr, Christensen, Christenson, Hansen, Hardy, Hensen, Jensen..." I couldn't contain my laughter. I wanted to blurt out sarcastically: "Was that *Jen*sen or

Jen*sen*?" It's becoming a more diverse place all the time, with more students every year from Latin America who have been lifelong Mormons taking my Latin American humanities class, so the future looks different. But all I have to do is cast my mind back to those classes of astounding diversity I took and taught at Berkeley to put things in perspective. I was prepared to be sensitive to that non-Mormon who would cross my path, but weeks, months passed and never the twain did meet. So I got lazy.

A Mexican Mormon woman with few English skills, whose hope for legalization had been put on hold by the government after 9/11, lived in the neighborhood. Responding to the lay responsibilities of the church, my wife and I began to look after her. As a counselor to our bishop in a ward with many Hispanic immigrants who did not know English, my mission in Venezuela and ten years of literary training in Spanish American literature came in handy. Speaking to me in her native tongue, she told me that her husband had abandoned her and that she was expecting her third child. This was deep in December, just a few days before Christmas, and he was nowhere in sight. The two older children hoped for Santa. I developed a healthy dose of righteous indignation toward her absent husband and intended, upon meeting him, to bring down the full wrath of the Mormon God upon him for failing in his duties.

On the day his daughter was born several months later, I came to visit the mother in the hospital, and there he was. It turned out that the Mormon God had lost interest in anger because when I saw his young and confused face, I lost the urge to get angry. Instead I sat down with him and, invoking principles and scriptures every Mormon knows well, went against my natural inclinations and gave him a gentle sermon about being a responsible husband, a strong and kind hand of guidance for his children, a force of spiritual good in their lives. As we spoke in Spanish, his eyes welled up with tears. I had been scrambling to find my anger, but it was long gone. We embraced. Two weeks later I found out he wasn't Mormon at all, as I had simply and foolishly assumed, but that something I had said made him want to become one. Which he did.

And I got lazy, too, about seeing the diversity of the Mormon community itself. It took me a year or so living in my neighborhood before the scales fell from my eyes and I realized that in all my experiences in Mormon wards in Connecticut, California, Latin America, and Europe, this was the most diverse group I had ever broken sacrament bread with: Italians, Brazilians, Koreans, Taiwanese, Argentines, Hondurans, Mexicans, Poles. It felt like a new era in Mormon life to see so many multiracial families, but I guess every time I think I am getting closer to hard-earned community, even our own internationalism can be deceptive.

One Sunday, after I had shared a story in church about ancestors of mine, James and Eliza Stratton, the Mexican-American mother of my children's playmates across the street approached me and told me that her children descended from the same couple through their father and were, I think it was, fifth cousins of my kids. And she informed me that James Stratton was buried a half mile from my house. For Mormons in Utah, especially those with pioneer ancestry, it's more like two or three degrees of separation from the stranger waiting at the same traffic light next to you. Makes road rage a little harder to justify.

There are still those moments of unexpected surprise when, after long stints without leaving the valley, I find myself amazed by the variety in physical appearance of people at airports in other cities—the less modest dress, the racial plurality. I laugh at myself silently, as I try not to stare stupidly, like some prisoner let out after years of solitary confinement. Mormon friends of ours in California once interrogated us about not feeling suffocated in Utah. As I stammered something about the value of community and interconnections and this surprising diversity, they mocked: "Yeah, but how big is your community? A block and a half?!" Ouch.

And herein lies my bipolarity: as much as I could laugh at my own circumstances, I wondered why it is considered a rite of passage into urban sophistication to pity those who have found life worth living outside of the metropolis. I am reminded of an essay I often teach by a prominent Cuban poet and intellectual, Roberto Fernández Retamar, who was asked by a naïve European writer, "Does Latin America *have* a culture?" Yes, we have people here in Utah. Oh, and by the way, we have a land, too. And history. Yes, we have that as well. Had it not been for those fishing trips with John and my continuing habit of exploring the Provo watershed, I would not have realized the blessings of a simplicity of elements. Living here, one short step off the front porch can be enough to come into contact with wild beauty and to understand our dependence on mountains and watersheds. I began to understand that this contact is the quintessence of quality of life and the forgotten starting point for any sense of place. I decided, too, that something about the proximity of others here is teaching me to wrestle with particularity, one person at a time, instead of finding reasons to avoid masses of humanity in wide swaths.

It might be the case that Mormons in Utah get too easily offended, but sometimes it seems they haven't taken stock of how deeply offended they should be. In the mad rush to display all the material signs of having arrived, to show we can run with the big dogs, we can run roughshod over our advantages. The results are signs of recent "progress" evident in the stucco developments sprouting like weeds, the golf courses, billboards, climate-controlled homes and huge cars, the big box stores setting up camp, and the titillations of Mormons making it big in the entertainment industry. Maybe we will be a metropolis after all.

Having left the choked highways of California behind me, I was beginning to learn that cynicism and detachment are no better ingredients for building a sustainable culture than negative protectiveness and loyalty. Which is another way of saying I committed to strive to make a home here in this liminal space between water's bounty and the desert, between wilderness and civilization, because doing so would be a more effective resistance to this wretched "progress" than any amount of chafing. And I could only hope that I just might stand a chance of learning something most urbanites have long since forgotten: the only real cure for provincialism is not dictated by our awareness of the size and diversity of the human family alone, but also by our awareness of the staggering size and diversity of the more-than-human community of nature.

Rilke knew something of the false promises of metropolitan life and the need to stimulate biological sensation and experience:

> Ah, how I believe in it, in life. Not the life constituted by time but this other life, the life of small things, the life of animals and of the great plains. This life that continues through millennia with no apparent investment in anything, and yet with all of its forces of movement and growth and warmth in complete harmony. This is why cities weigh on me so heavily. This is why I love taking long barefoot walks where I will not miss a grain of sand and will make available to my body the entire world in many shapes as sensation, as experience, as something to relate to.[11]

The body is the cup in which to drink the world. As Mormon scriptures tell it, in the premortal ether we cried with joy and anticipation at the chance to be in a body, here, now.[12]

John and I exchanged emails from time to time or we called to talk of fishing and Stegner, but I began to feel his interest slipping away, until one day I received a phone call from his wife in Wisconsin. He was in the hospital under suicide watch, diagnosed with bipolar disorder, after his wife had discovered a long series of deceptions. The impassioned and spontaneous fishing outings that had been so full of soulful searching and that had humorously felt like trysts turned out to be a tragic symptom of a perpetually clandestine unfaithfulness. From her description of the lies she had discovered—John wandering the streets of Madison, posing as a graduate student—it was as if his capacity for adaptation had led to an almost pathological confusion of memories. He had kept his stories fragmented for so long and absorbed so many others that he seemed no longer able to discern his own true story or to center his life around one narrative.

Perhaps none of us succeeds fully at this, and perhaps this can also be a human strength, not a weakness. To see ourselves as constituted by more than our own experience might be what we imagine compassion to be and what imagination is for. Cold indifference, static living—this is hardly life at all. But neither is using the malleability of our own memories to the disadvantage of others. John's had become a perpetually invented life where he undermined the stability that his life was gaining with ever new strategies of adoption.

We spoke on the phone on a weekly basis that summer, as his wife made the decision to part ways with him. Perhaps an inherited biological disposition had caught up to him, making him more like his profligate father than any of the good people who had acted as parental surrogates. Knowing this caused him an intensely steep and bitter pain that he was scarcely able to speak. As much as he had prodded me for stories of my past, I realized that he never felt that the uneven path of his life could be assimilated or adopted by others. Unable to confess the entirety of his suffering and his missteps to others, he spent his life switching between abject humiliation and flashes of intense and angry resentment. The only escape from such pain was to invent a new life and then another, each one without a history.

"Please let's not talk about fishing right now. It's too much, you know what I mean?" I had offered a few stories in case they might provide solace and had spoken of a possible therapeutic trip with me the next summer. "I can never fish in those waters again, man. I mean it. That's the only thing that made me feel totally free, and that's a luxury I can no longer afford. I have betrayed everything that land and the church gave me."

"Maybe you could never afford it, John. I mean, who can? Look, some-day you will be back. This is your home. I don't know half of what you know about what it means to belong here. I'm only guessing now without your guidance." I think we both instinctively understood that fishing now had acquired a symbolism too heavy to bear. I wanted him to understand that fishing here again might mean a small step toward forgiving himself and integrating the broken parts of his life.

"George, you don't know what you're saying. You were meant to live there, meant to fish those waters. You've got the pedigree, you know? Man, listen to me, I never felt home there. It was like I was floating above in the air, watching the rivers stream by, like I was some bird soaring high over the landscape, and all of you red-blooded Mormons moved about under me." He wanted me to believe he was a poser. That belonging was always beyond his reach. "But you, you could fish and feel yourself closer and closer to home. It was like watching an archaeological dig, or one of Jesus's men. It was beautiful." By contrast, he never felt like one of the family in the church. "They tried but I could feel their hesitancy to know what to make of me. That cuts deep, you know. That hesitancy and unease that never go away."

Realizing the import of what he had just said, he grew angry, "I mean, what the hell is that about?! What does it take to belong?! Outright disdain in some ways is less painful than that kind of feeble-minded, half-hearted, piss-ant love. Do you have any idea what I'm talking about? I don't think you do because you, man, you have the history, the calling."

Homogeneity can make community happen more easily, to be sure. I live in a neighborhood where siblings are raising kids just houses away from each other, on the same street where they were raised. I have seen extraordinary families of three, even four generations sitting together on the church pew. People around here live up the street from old roommates at BYU, from women they dated in high school or college. Even though I was mostly raised in Connecticut, there are a half dozen or so people with whom I attended church there who now live within a mile of my house. The upshot is that I can't walk a mile, buy milk at the local store, or sit at an elementary school play without seeing people I love, people I have known for decades, people I would trust with my children, enough to fill a room. It is a beautiful thing, really. But it isn't hard to understand why, if the community isn't careful, others might sense a conspiracy to lock them out. As much as I sympathized with John, however, I didn't think it was good for him to nurse this particular wound.

"Oh come on, John. You know it wasn't like that. You were loved. Besides, we aren't puppets pulled on some genealogical string. Why do you assume everyone else feels at one with the world but you?" I tried to describe to him how often I feel like a stranger living here, or how often I feel that way just living in my own skin. "Every time I fish, I turn to tell you something and you aren't there, I mistakenly call my friends by your name, because no one seems as profoundly connected to the river as you were. Call this nostalgic nonsense, but you are the most genuine Utahn I know. It's how you loved the place that made it your home."

He didn't persist in arguing with me, but as the weeks and months proceeded, our conversations were more brief, less emotionally engaged, and fishing, literature, and faith all seemed like a fading flame. He would undergo several months of treatment and years of transition before he settled again, remarried, started a new family. By then our lives and our conversations had found an equilibrium; we spoke of sea fishing in California where he now lived, the spiritual advice his new Presbyterian minister was giving him, and his new family life.

His failure to make his home here is, for me, a tragedy and a mystery, and I can only assume, in part, my failure, too. There must have been something I didn't know how to give him. My brother's suicide taught me the value of perpetually asking myself what it might have been, even though I spend my life without an answer, because acquiescing to such loss somehow seems self-defeating.

It sorrows me to think that just stepping on Utah soil would cause John pain, but I know too that for Bill, my remaining brother who left the church years ago, and a host of friends I love, visits to Utah are rarely without ambivalence. Sometimes the polarization of Utah culture threatens to overrun the healing its natural beauty provides. Utah stories stir him still, however, and we have found we can share our lives again. But I am still awaiting his return to these waters. I continue to fish them with religious regularity. Without John and my grandfather, I find myself fishing with their ghosts, haunted by the passions of a native son and an adopted son alike, not sure which I most resemble.

Three

*

As a teenage boy, Wallace Stegner joined a troop of Mormon boy scouts in 1923 on a fishing and camping trip to the high Uintas. He wrote: "Now and then nature produces a combination of land, water, sky, space, trees, animals, flowers, distances, and weather so perfect it looks like the hatching of a romantic fantasy, or the effort of a nineteenth-century artist to illustrate Hiawatha's childhood by the shores of Gitche Gumee. Every time we go off into the wilderness, we are looking for that perfect primitive Eden. This time, we have found it." John had often told me tales of fishing in the Uintas, of how easy it was to catch fish there. "You could throw a sock on the water and they would take it," I remember him saying. We had often talked about making the trip in honor of Stegner, and it remains an almost mythical reference point for our friendship.

Reading Stegner reassures me that even if more visitors come to the high wilderness than in those days, even if Eden now had longitude and latitude, I might still have a chance to play-act at my primitive game precisely because Stegner and others before me had the decency to work to preserve some of it as wilderness. Stegner's fortune in being welcomed into a temporary community in Utah, his learned devotion to nature and history, and the legacy he left behind as a teacher and public intellectual are no small recompense for what he suffered at the hands of an abusive father.

I got my chance just days before classes began at the university in early September. A friend and fellow professor invited me to accompany him to his personal Eden in the Uintas, a pilgrimage he has been taking with religious devotion for fifty years. Ted was raised in Utah and his family had built a cabin on the northwest slope of the Uintas that feeds the Bear and Weber river drainages. Our aim was the East and Little East forks of the Blacks Fork River—all part of the Green River drainage in the northeast quadrant of the range—and two unnamed lakes that simply showed up as numbers on the map. So even though it wasn't my Provo River watershed and it was a surrogate Eden for one whose childhood in Utah was interrupted, it would suffice.

The Uintas in a drier summer might not look quite so green at this time of the year, but it had been a wet several months and the land looked more like the Northwest than Utah. Green ground cover, dense forest growth of spruce, lodgepole pines, aspens, and still-blooming wildflowers were everywhere. As we drove along an old dirt fire road, logging houses and other signs of human habitation began to dwindle, and the road's contours grew more primitive.

"There were five of us, all age fifteen." With both hands gripping the top of the steering wheel of his black Ford truck traveling over the rough terrain, Ted was in his own reverie. "Too little food. Vague plans. Poor rain gear, if any. Old Army backpacks and a .38 pistol. We roamed for seventeen days, covered over a hundred miles. Fishing sustained us. I have never exhausted those memories."

I expressed disbelief that he and four other boys would have been allowed to hike the Uintas alone, which clearly belied my envy. Did he ever use the .38, I wanted to know? "No. No need. I have never seen a bear in these mountains in all these years. But we did meet a man on a horse in raggy clothes and a scarred face who gave evasive answers to our simple questions. We later learned a man had escaped from jail in Wyoming and was believed to be in the mountains. I am sure it was him."

Ted was a young sixty-five, eager to experience the wilds of the Uintas again after spending several years abroad in voluntary church service, and our only map was his prodigious memory. At the trailhead, we stepped out, smelling the wet soil with its embedded and decaying pine needles. Everywhere leaves were dripping from the rain that had been falling on and off for days. The vistas were all short-range, because the clouds were low, hovering over the green softness of pine forests that covered the mountains like so many soft brushes. The wind picked up from time to time, and since it was only nine a.m., we knew that this did not bode well for hiking.

We climbed back into the truck and ventured toward the West Fork, but Ted was not optimistic because he had fished it before. "About a dozen twelve year olds and I. I don't think I ever managed a cast of my own. They were all high maintenance and complained that we only caught small brookies. It wasn't a spiritual highlight for me." He said this wryly because it is almost a rite of passage in Mormon life to spend days on end with teenagers, waiting for the wilderness to redeem them from their Lord-of-the-Flies morality. Sometimes wilderness isn't enough, or the effects of the balm don't register until years later. That's when you get the weepy testimonies in church from some nineteen-year-old who never thanked Brother Jones for the hell he put him through in the Uintas that backpacking summer of his fourteenth year. Vindication for Brother Jones for those cold, wet nights spent lying in a tent, listening to the plop-plop of rain against the nylon canvas. At the pearly gates, no modern Mormon can compete with the pioneer stories of hardship, but surely camping with boys in the wilderness has to count for something. And who knows? Your recompense might be to have a budding Stegner in the group.

We slowed to the side of the road where we could see a small dale below us marked by the S-curves of an alluring fork in the river. When I saw the water's shape, I felt inclined to give it a try, and Ted was willing.

"I'm sure my method seems crude and uncouth to you fly-fishing types, but I still like to fish with worms." He seemed genuinely apologetic, but I assured him I didn't care.

As we got out of the truck, he wandered through a field of rocks in his khaki pants stuffed into his green rubber rain boots, turning the stones over in search of worms. I headed upstream toward a sharp bend of water where dark shadows of mountains rose behind a gray-white veil of advancing rain. This was a beaver's paradise, and everywhere I could see their burrows along the riverbanks, making for difficulty in traversing the sheet of high grass and sage leading to the water. Ted headed downstream.

Within minutes, I caught four or five small brookies, but instead of feeling discouraged by their size, I was filled with the naïve optimism of every first-time venturer on a new stretch of water. Around the next bend, I saw rises on the opposite bank. It was a difficult reach, but from a small bluff I cast cross-stream to a mixed current that had pockets of still water surrounded by swirling, twisting, and streaming threads. My long and thin leader was working to allow my Royal Wulff to float down a few feet above the surface and land gently, giving the fly just enough time to drift naturally before a current started to pull on it.

On only my second cast, I got a violent strike and then a prolonged battle. I was fearful of losing him because I had no net and I was high on the bank. The wise thing would have been to step into the cold, deep water and lead him to the shallows on the other side, but the temperature was dropping and a storm threatened in the distance. So I simply held the line taut and let the fish tire himself out before I finally landed him. The experience of losing big fish at the last moment is why the body heaves deep sighs of relief and satisfaction races in the veins when failure has been narrowly avoided.

His fat, oval body lay breathing on the matted grass where I had been standing. The hot-red belly, brilliant white splashes on his fins, and deep red marks on his sides made me wish I was an artist. With two hands I picked him up and smacked the back of his head on a small stone three times until his quivering stopped. I don't eat enough of my own catches to have acclimated myself to this part, but there is no denying his pink flesh was a satisfying breakfast the next day. Squatting down in the grass, I paused and felt the pulse of my blood coursing up and down my body. The wall of rain had moved to within yards of where I was.

I looked upstream and could see a line of water dimples where fish were sipping at the surface. There was more in the offing. Sensing I had moments left before the deluge, I stood and threw the line toward the spot where the closest dimple had appeared. The fish took the fly without hesitation, and he felt larger than the previous one and smarter, since he immediately shot under the bank in front of me and stayed there. I held my rod tip over the water to maintain a tight line and again contemplated jumping in to get him out.

A loud crack of lightning struck close by, startling me out of my fever. Winds whipped up into a frenzy and heavy rain was suddenly thudding on my head. Overcome by reason, I broke the line, took one more look at the half dozen or so fish that were still rising and creating sizeable swirls in the rain-pocked riffle, and sprinted back to the truck where Ted had wisely already returned.

We spent the night drying out at his family cabin on the Bear River. Like many Utah family cabins, it is modest, well used, stocked with old mattresses, and full of decades of family lore. Instructions for use and care lay in plastic sleeves on the kitchen counter. Still in the family despite the passing of his parents some years ago now, the siblings and their children and grandchildren share the responsibilities for care and for scheduling its use. No one knows for certain how much longer they can be shared by an ever-expanding web of kin.

By morning the rain had stopped. When we stepped outside into the dripping pines, we caught a glimpse of blue patches in the sky that gave hope for a dry day on the trail. An hour later, we arrived at the trailhead and struck out, with nothing but food, water, and fishing equipment. The trail slowly rose as it followed the path of the Little East Fork, taking us through fields of marshy grasses and dense forest. Along gentle, tree-covered slopes, we saw numerous springs sprouting spontaneously from orifices between rocks, the small capillaries of mountain blood that gather momentum and pour downward to the Great Salt Lake. The trees and willow branches dripped with moisture, but only the winter months would prove if the drought was over. The wet summers at least meant that the reservoirs maintained levels otherwise impossible in late summer. There were early signs of fall as well, what with the smell of decaying leaves and yellowing plants sagging from the weight of their eager and frenzied summer growth.

Ted kept an aggressive pace, and we arrived at an opening where several small spring streams interrupted the trail. Flat stones placed across the patches of dark mud provided our pathway. To our right up the hill was a large spruce tree, underneath which we stopped for a snack. Ted was almost euphoric. He had been anticipating the tree for about a mile, and now he was confident we would find the lakes.

"This is it. Strange how things can feel so familiar after so much time. And yet it all seems different. I remember eating red licorice under this tree when I was a boy." We hadn't seen anyone on the trail, and he liked it this way. We put more distance between ourselves and any chance of encountering others by free-scrambling our way up the steep slope behind the tree until we found ourselves on what seemed to be a deer trail.

"Does this part look familiar?" I asked with perhaps just a touch of doubt in my voice. But Ted was fully engaged now, hiking with a sense of mission, guided by the powerful scent of memory. Our feet slipped often on the steep trail and our hands pawed at the soft mixture of soil and pine needles between the stones.

The slope leveled and then began to slide gently downward, causing our bodies to stand more erect. We arrived at the edge of a deep, black mountain lake surrounded by tall grasses, ferns, and moss. Blades of tall grass lay strewn across the still water along the edge, evidence of a moose having had breakfast in the marshy banks. Across the lake, stretching straight up from the water, was an enormous boulder field of pink granite, covered in lime-green lichen. Neither of us spoke, but the inner exultation was extreme, almost to a breaking point. It wouldn't be too dramatic to say it was akin to the spiritual ecstasies of a Teresa de Ávila or the sexual giddiness of pawing lovers, if it weren't for the fact that there is a reason that such emotions, when made public, seem downright indecent.

Ted wisely headed off to find dry wood to start a fire, since we were wet inside and out and the temperature was not exactly temperate. I sat down and with shaking hands tried to set up my rod as quickly as possible. I could see deeper, more interesting waters on the other side, so I crossed to the left where a stream entered the lake and fished on the moraine that had spilled down from a steep climb of rock behind me. The cliffs the rocks had fallen from were ensconced in low clouds that made the lake feel like a small room. I managed four or five more catches of mid-sized brookies with almost ruby-red bellies and alabaster splashes of white on their fins. I kept thinking that with such brilliance they ought to be easy to spot under the surface, but the wriggling dorsal greens and blacks on their backs kept them moving like ghosts.

Ted emerged from the wood after warming by a fire, and we spoke across the water. With the low clouds, the surrounding rocks, and the glassy water between us, our voices traversed the space with barely a breath behind them, as if we were standing next to each other. All of a sudden the clouds parted, and at first it looked like a temporary arrangement, but after another thirty minutes or so the skies had cleared almost entirely, leaving us basking in high mountain sunlight for the rest of the day. It was still relatively cool, but the intense rays of the sun penetrated our skin and illuminated the shadows of fish in the water, intensifying the outlines of everything around me. I could not stop staring at the pink boulders beneath my feet sprinkled florescent green.

Ted insisted that paradise was still up another five hundred feet in the direction of the tiny stream I had crossed. We were already at close to eleven thousand feet, and our legs were tired after four hours of climbing, but we scrambled up a large moraine of erratics that separated the lakes.

Grabbing boulders with our hands to hoist ourselves onward, Ted suddenly stopped. Our breathing was heavy. After a few seconds, he said, "Several years ago, I was hiking in this very spot. I can't explain it but I spoke with my dead parents. They were both right here." He pointed at our feet. Not sure if I should prod further for more details, I hesitated to speak. But I couldn't help myself.

"Do you mean you actually saw them?"

"Well, it's not like that exactly." He said nothing for a minute. I was starting to feel that my question was impertinent. "You know how you feel when you jump in a lake and you know the bottom is near. And your feet stretch out in anticipation?"

"Yeah," I said.

"It's like that."

It wasn't enough for me, apparently, because then I said, "What did you talk about?"

"Oh, I don't know. It was like they were on a hike of their own and didn't have all day to catch up. So we said the essential things."

He didn't want to say more, obviously, so I didn't press, but after a few more minutes of scrambling ahead of me, he yelled back without turning around, "They loved me and approved of my life, that much they said."

At the top of the moraine, we saw a large, sprawling lake bordered on the right by a semicircle of a rose-colored cirque, an amphitheater of stone. To the left where the lake hangs on a precipice of ancient talus lay a deep valley carved by the East Fork River and a series of repeating cirques that seemed to dissipate in the distance. This was the Ur-space of the high Uintas where the slow work of glaciers and the freezing and thawing of rocky springs bursting from the crags work away at the propulsions of land that giant plates of earth have thrust skyward. The sharp edge of the cirque told a story of such labors too ancient for words. Intermittent dimples rose over the entire surface of the water.

Ted broke the silence. "In all these years I've never taken a photograph and I've never seen a single person at this lake. I'm not sure what I would do if I did, to be honest. I think I would be afraid someone else wouldn't appreciate the spiritual strength of the place. It's a paradox, really, because I can't keep it to myself. Once I was here by myself and I was so elated after three or four huge fish that I had to share it with someone. I had to stop fishing. Sat by a quartzite boulder over there and prayed to the point of tears, and all I could do was show Him my fish."

Quaking from the sunny pleasure, we began fishing from one side of the lake to the other. We both caught plenty, enough to find us sunning on the south bank after a few hours of satiated fish lust. There was little room on the edge for soft ground because of the sloping talus behind us and the tundra-like patches of abbreviated green between the stones.

After a few hours, we made our run for home, this time slipping down the precipice directly to the valley floor below not as the crow flies but as water falls. We knew that as long as we followed the gathering stream, we would hit river and then the truck. When we arrived at the East Fork, I couldn't help myself and fished some more, pulling what appeared to be small Bonnevilles from the water with virtually every cast. I was almost drunk with giddiness by now, exhausted but renewed. Gorgeous little creatures, with the

parr marks along the side—yellows, reds, and sky-blues—like wild finger
paintings, extravagant and superfluous. It was exhilarating to wander the
slope with the flow of water as my guide, and the fishing gave me an excuse
to get rest.

The entire world was there for the sensation of it, a real, palpable presence. Poor Wordsworth, I thought, sitting on his rock wall looking down on
the lands remembering his youth,

> when like a roe
> I bounded o'er the mountains, by the sides
> Of the deep rivers, and the lonely streams,
> Wherever nature led.

Yes, his memories brought back "sensations sweet / felt in the blood
and along the heart"—memories of nature to keep him alive in the cities—
but why did he assume that the time of his adolescence and its "glad animal movements" were past? Anima, animus, animate: the animal is the soul,
the soul the animal. Spiritual health without nature is impossible, but poetry
alone is not sufficient to bring back childhood. We need to keep recreating,
in both senses of the word, to perform the conditions when the soul can express its animality and find anonymity in belonging, when it has

> no need of a remoter charm,
> By thought supplied, nor any interest
> Unborrowed from the eye.[13]

It would be four hours before we found the truck, and Ted showed no
signs of tiring. I had the sneaking impression he was hiking faster than we
had all day, that the happy boy lost in the mountains had become the father
of the man.

Autumn

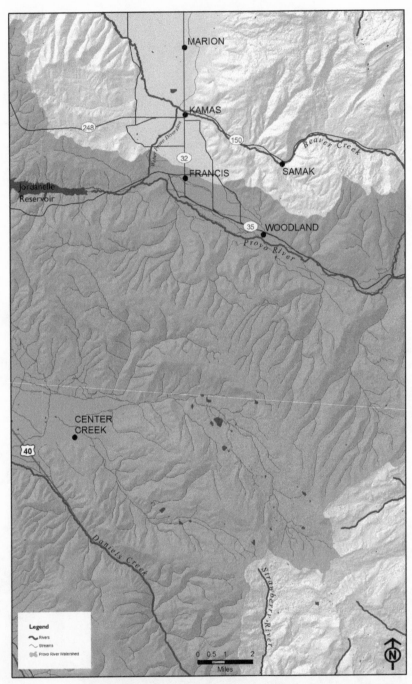

THE UPPER PROVO RIVER, BELOW THE UINTAS

Four

*

I ALREADY FEEL I MUST START OVER...DEFINE MY SENSE OF PLACE BY RE-
turning again to the beginning, and then open my eyes, one more time. The
greatest solace and the greatest truth begin with the rebirth of the senses.
Home is apprehended, not inherited or owned. So I must refuse the peace of
ancestry, family trees, and printed maps, and explore my own *terra incognita*,
try my own primitive hand at cartography. As Rilke says, sensation is what
one needs. These mountains have never been seen before, at least this is what
I will have to convince myself if I am going to touch this earth with immediacy, with sensation.

I won't take much convincing, since the way the sheets of rain pelt the
surface of the lake creates an illusion I have never witnessed, as if some commotion from below the surface were causing the water to boil some twenty
feet or so ahead of me. What is most startling is that there is a clear demar-
cation between the boiling water and the flat plane of the lake that extends
out to the shore where I am standing. I am not sure at first that it is, in fact,
raining, but my nose detects the fragrance of a high-elevation squall, and the
wind carries a light spray that gently laps my face. And that gray wall of water in front of me is starkly real, shrouding the gray hills and dark trees behind it, even if I have never stood so close to the edge of rain.

The voices of children call me back to my place on the sand at the edge of
Lily Lake in the High Uinta Wilderness. They are my children, sitting with
my wife in the car, waiting for me to give a weather report about the chances
for a dry hike. They have opened the windows to experience that same
strange sensation of approaching rain that is only feet away but which leaves
you dry. In this sensation of the headwaters, I almost forget that I was the
one who brought them here to touch the wind, the stones, and the water.

The bright sunshine slowly and steadily deepened the sky's pale morning
blue in all directions when we started out at daybreak to follow the Provo
upriver to the Uintas. Sometimes the river was to our right, sometimes to

our left, and never as straight as the roads we were traveling. Had I been told it would rain this hard, this soon, I might not have believed it anyway because I still haven't learned to expect the unpredictability of mountains. The Uintas receive sixty inches of precipitation every year. The valley where I live gets only fifteen, half of what is needed to grow grass. I am resistant, too, to what it requires to be truly prepared, which usually involves carrying clothing for all types of weather. Which isn't the worst of sins, except for the fact that I dragged my wife and kids into the elements for an innocent, short hike to Wall Lake when the deluge began. Wall Lake, I told the kids, feeds a stream that reaches lakes below and then eventually reaches the Provo River and our valley.

We had started off at the same trailhead where I had done my run previously, but we headed up an east fork. Cobalt skies hung to the south and west, but a hub of cloud-cover began to darken to the north and east where we were headed. We could hear lightning in the distance, but I figured chances were just as good the wind would take the storm out of our path. Was it one mile per second between lightning flash and thunder, or one-tenth? Or something in between? My wife and I disputed the point for several minutes as we continued to hike.

The terrain around the trail was layered with leafy bushes, watercress burst from the ground wherever there was spring water, and abundant reedy grass thrived at the edges of small ponds. The dark pines were painted with hairy moss, too, which, along with the lime-green lichen on the stones, all seemed poised in resistance to their inevitable journey to dust, creating a world of green reverberation. I tried hard to keep the children distracted from the rising wind, which whipped the tops of the pines with a low moan that mingled with the sound of distant thunder.

The elements had me feeling an ecstatic joy, making concerns for safety seem like some unwanted mosquito in my tent. We may not have gone more than a half mile before the rain began to fall in torrents, leaving us completely exposed. We hadn't even brought rain coats, and so we tried to sprint back to the car. Lightning flashed all around us, and hail began to hit us hard. We sought shelter among a grove of short trees and waited until the downpour slowed enough to run again. White balls of ice bounced across the hard stones, ricocheting in all directions. The ground was becoming white all around us, like some careless spill of Styrofoam packing pieces. Looking up to the indifferent skies, all I could see were white threads streaming down from an invisible gray source. Small clumps of pine needles floated about our feet in brown puddles.

Paige and Camilla cried in the protective arms of their mother, their blond hair turning brown and limp in the rain. Our toddler, Sam, hugged my neck in terror, making it difficult to breathe. Our young teenager, Eliza, was able to keep her fears in check, but the emotions of her siblings had her on edge. Her blue eyes darted nervously between me and her mother. Amy gave me that look of maternal disapproval. "Isn't this incredible!" I offered with an exuberant smile. No one said a word, and the tears continued. "We'll be fine," I said, a little more soberly. I felt stupid for my stubborn insistence that we keep going on the trail as long as we had. My problem was adolescent: every turn in the trail, every new expanse that came into view, pulled me forward and I felt like pouting now that we had to leave all of it behind.

Once back at the car, we drove farther up the mountain with the heater on, until the rain stopped and we found ourselves here, by Lily Lake, where the rain seemed blocked by an invisible wall of glass. I stood waiting for the rain to hit me, perhaps hoping that by willingly exposing myself to the elements while my family watched I would have paid penance for my hubris, or perhaps I would have shown them how thrilling nature's force can be when faced directly. But once it became clear that the rain was receding rather than advancing toward the shoreline where I stood, I climbed back into the car. Welcome back, nature boy, Amy's eyes seemed to say. We continued driving around until we found another hike.

As much as I chafe at my wife's maternal caution and as often as I try to chastise my children for excessive and irrational fears, I am deeply ambivalent about the adventures I seek. It is a lasting legacy of my brother's death, because while I want to overcome my own fears and desperately don't want my children to be crippled by their own, I cannot tolerate even the thought of causing them unnecessary pain. This is not a strength, I know. Children need to develop resolve to face the physical world, and I won't make them the last children in the woods by coddling them in their fears.[14] I generally achieve this kind of tough love when it seems necessary, but it always requires a herculean effort to go against the grain of my deepest, most intuitive, overprotective urges. Maybe I would have had those urges anyway without the violence of Kenny's death, but there is no doubt that I go through life permanently haunted by the prospect of those I love facing sudden pain and intense fear. After that hike was over, the look of terror on my young son's face haunted me for weeks and overshadowed the sublime moment of thunderclaps, whipping wind, and streaming hail.

The only cars at an elevation of ten thousand feet were filled with families like my own, seeking recreational restoration, to no avail. We wanted nature, but perhaps not this much. This required more respectful distance than we had bargained for. We caught glimpses of each other's shadows through the fogged-up windows of our vehicles as we passed on the shining wet mountain pass.

Last year around this time there were cars lining the highway on both sides, as hundreds of people came to help search for a twelve-year-old boy who had disappeared near one of the many mountain lakes here. A group of Mormon families had come for a campout and some fishing in the days prior to the beginning of the school year. These were hardy people, well seasoned by Utah's high mountains, driving in their large, four-wheel-drive trucks, pulling trailers filled with Costco-sized food packages, Dutch ovens, fishing rods, and bait. And rain ponchos, no doubt. These were the kind of Mormon families I had encountered in Flagstaff, well grounded in the landscape of home, hearty outdoorspeople, spending their nights sitting around the fire, sometimes three generations at a time, filling old tin cans with embers and placing them by their feet while they shared stories of the outdoors.

This trip was extended for weeks because of a boy's inexplicable disappearance almost in plain sight of his family. It was early morning. The boy and his father were fishing on the edge of the lake when the boy fell into the water. His shoes were wet and the mountain morning temperatures left him shivering. He asked to return to the campsite some two hundred yards away to change his socks. The father offered to go with him, but he said, "I can do it." He was twelve and a boy, after all. "I'll be right behind you," the father replied, as he began to gather in his fishing line. Turning to make sure the boy knew his way, he saw his son aiming in the wrong direction. "Not that way, son." He pointed in the direction of the campsite some forty-five degrees to the right. The boy corrected his course, and the father turned back to his rod and line, which had become entangled during the exchange. I'll be right there. Right there.

And he was. Only a few minutes later.

He walked into the campsite to check on the boy. Anyone seen Garrett? An innocent question that turned to quiet panic, and then terror spread through the camp in an ever-increasing pounding of the human chest.

Scattering in all directions, the family ran frenetically, calling "Garrett! Garrett! Garrett!" until they were hoarse. Even his bones have yet to be found.

I read the story one morning over my breakfast. Volunteers gathered to help a coordinated effort to walk as many square feet of the area as they could in concentric grids of five hundred square meters. Hundreds came at first, then dozens, and by the time I finally committed to help on a day in mid-October at the tail end of the search, five, maybe ten, came at a time. The anxiety was no longer about the boy's being alive and in pain, of course, but about gathering him before the impending snows would grind him into the very stuff of mountains. This is civilization's greatest ambition: to preserve our human difference in the face of the indifferent law of decay and regeneration.

Just when the boy's dissipation into the dust of the earth almost demanded that hope shatter, the human difference announced itself in bold and admirable outline: the father's faith seemed as beyond reproach as it was beyond my capacity to imagine. A man whose life experiences have taught him that God hears and answers prayers, he believed He would not give him a stone for his lost son. It was a simple enough request. Closure—to give the boy a proper burial, as they say—that was all the father wanted. He spoke with a broken, raspy voice. "We just want...we need...to find Garrett and bring him home." He was speaking on the news, now several weeks into the search, standing in the high mountains in the dark while a steady rain pelted his poncho and hit the microphone. "Each searcher helps. We can only do this together. Thanks to those who have come here and helped."

I knew this man, I suddenly realized. Not closely, but the demand for volunteer service in the church had brought us together briefly on Sundays for a few months. Sometimes reading the obituaries here is almost like reading the gossip column or a Christmas form letter from a distant relative. Which means that it is beyond obvious here to point out that no man is an island, especially if you and he are Mormon and in the practice of calling each other "brother." As I have so often experienced in the practice of my religion as part of a lay clergy, what initially posed itself as a theoretical question about what I would do or feel became personal and immediate.[15] I was ashamed to admit that my religious ties to the father, however tenuous, were needed for me to feel our common humanity more deeply, but at least I got up, searched my calendar, and set apart a day to go.

I started to think of my own children, Amy, my parents, my brother Bill, and I also remembered how in my adolescence my oldest brother, Kenny, had disappeared from this world just as suddenly and illogically, and that it caused a similar anguish: Where did he go? How did we lose him? What do I have so that I can still hold on to him? We may never make up for personal losses, but certainly we seek recompenses in the healing bonds of community, bearing the burdens of others, and in the wordless solace of nature. And I noticed my own attitude shifting from anger to hope. So many had poured out their hearts in prayer in the first few hours and days of the boy's disappearance, and if God ever answered one prayer, I wondered, why would a God of miracles turn a deaf ear?

But as I prepared to go into the mountains, I found myself admitting that, platitudes aside, time, truly deep time, contains mysteries of forbearance and suffering. The man of God "knoweth nothing yet as he ought to know."[16] Paul had it right, suggesting that it is more valuable to act and to feel than it is sometimes to have knowledge. Garrett's father seemed to know how to act out of an instinct that told him to reject the inevitability of things. Perhaps some Greek dramatist would connect the boy's death to an innocent mistake of the father, but there was no hubris here, no tragic flaw. His intent searching might have seemed inconsistent with religious submission, but in addition to the thousands of people from many faiths who ended up aiding in the search, the boy's family raised over sixteen thousand dollars to build a school in Ecuador in his name.

The forging of community bonds or the building of a school can't take away the pain, but I started to think that some strange chemistry was at work, like the time I sang the "Hallelujah Chorus" at my high school concert only two nights after my own brother took his life. The pain of losing him—his gentleness, his brilliant intelligence, even his dark periods of silence—was a measure of my love. I learned for the first time that I could feel pain *and* inexplicable comfort and that perhaps they were one and the same. I still don't know if I cried more of sorrow or of some as-yet-unnamed joy.

At the trailhead to Ruth Lake on the Uintas' north slope I met up with only five others, a woman from Salt Lake who was new to Utah and Mormon culture and new to the search as I was, and four men who all appeared to be retired and of unidentifiable religion. I assumed at first that they were family, but none was. "We are now," said one in his checkered, red flannel shirt and wrangler jeans who had been volunteering for weeks. He had come to love the father like a brother, "and that includes how brothers can drive you crazy sometimes," he said with a smile.

The weather that day was spectacular. The morning hours were quite cold, of course, since it was October, the coldest air I had felt since the previous spring. Patches of spring water everywhere on the trail were covered with ice sheets, creating striations that looked like basket-weave or bronze stained glass. Hiking through a meadow of thick, dead marsh grass, my feet crushed the thin, icy layer and sank into soft soil beneath. To my right wound a slow-moving body of water in deep oxbow curves. Beneath the ice I could see brook trout gliding with just a hint of panic at our movement. With the exception of such flat openings, most of the terrain was rocky with thickets of pines and bushes, reeds, moss, occasional fields of pink granite rock, and consistently uneven and unpredictable surfaces.

Searching for a human in a more-than-human world required absolute devotion to a straight line in a world in which such lines did not exist. But this, I quickly learned, was also how the contours of the land can best be experienced. I wondered how much of the variegated surface of the planet I had bypassed in my need for ease. We charged over rocks, down steep drops and up small faces of stone, and literally straight through bushes. Only a lake turned us from our chosen path temporarily. We regrouped into a straight line to move parallel at the opposite side of the lake, guided at both ends by the two men holding GPS devices. Between long silences, the man in the flannel shirt who held the GPS to my left, spoke out loud from time to time. "Come on, Garrett. Today's the day. Today you come out of hiding. Be a good boy, now." The trees and rocks grew monotonous, as if the mountain had run out of ideas.

Our pace was very deliberate and slow, so that we had time to look into tightly formed groves of trees or bushes where a cold and frightened boy might have hidden. As the morning sun rose and shone more directly down upon us, I could feel my body beginning to sweat. I paused to shed some clothes and brush the salty sweat from my brow. I felt guilty stealing glimpses of the castellated peaks of rock, the broad meadows and high grasses, the variegated limbs and trunks of trees, living and dying... or dead, the strange, wild world that had stolen this boy.

Looking at the incipient soil of a dead tree, tragedy seemed a feeble human concept in such a world. But I looked around at these men and this woman who had no connection at all to the family or their faith, acting on their commitments, and I knew that my heart had to refuse this peace. I would have to think of beauty as a distraction because the smallness of human love and loss can't win against the expanse of the physical world's incomprehensible reach. Maybe this is what Pablo Neruda meant when, despite his lifelong fascination with the sea, he insisted that man is wider than the sea. Maybe he never convinced himself. But at least he learned impatience with nature's mute indifference. The dark passage of faith that took Abraham and his son to the altar does not seem so anomalous in light of the acquiescence to the law of death that nature seems to demand of us all.

The sky above us was unrelenting in its openness. Small bursts of white, streaking clouds interrupted the drumming blue, and as the day wore on and the feet grew sore, the relentless variations on the ground seemed downright monotonous. No boy, only stones, trees, sky, and water. We found balloons, an abandoned shoe that didn't match the boy's, a bag of dead fish, a bottle of nasal spray, and the occasional beer can. This was only one day in an effort that lasted for two months with thousands of man-hours, but I now had a better sense of the weight of all that effort.

It seemed the boy literally walked off, or into, the face of the earth. Even the next spring, when the snows receded and the family organized one last push to find his remains, they only found animal bones, other shoes, other socks. Hunters, campers, hikers, wandering the oblongs of the earth, all believing themselves alone and beyond the reach of human society. Something about the endless shifts of forest trees, mountain slopes, streambeds, and spring creeks appeals to wanderlust, a need so unsatisfied by the conveniences of modern living that men, women, and children clamor for the chance to risk disappearance.

It was what drew a young teenager in the 1930s, Everett Ruess, away from his California life into the wilderness of southern Utah, year after year, until he too disappeared. Recently discovered bones were thought to be his, after decades of mystery, but they were not. Instead, they remain at large in the vast universe of dispersed matter. "He who has looked long on naked beauty," he wrote in his heartbreaking journal, "may never return to the world, and though he should try, he will find its occupation empty and vain and human intercourse purposeless and futile. Alone and lost, he must die on the altar of beauty." I myself couldn't escape the temptation to come back with my fly rod and wander off trails seeking unnamed lakes to catch wild trout.

As indifferent as it is, the mountain wilderness holds no guarantee of escape from humanity, however. The idea of a humanless world is the intoxication of American rugged individualism, whitewashing the West of its native populations just for the chance to play Indian to civilization's cowboy.

It was astonishing to consider just how human the place felt despite, or maybe because of, the boy's invisibility. So I wondered if it was because of our humanity that we come seeking nature, and even in losing ourselves, if we need wilderness to finally confirm our suspicion that we are unique. Was it our humanity that persisted in desiring to escape from our condition? We seem born to die in such confusion.

A proper burial. I like the idea of my body joining the drainage, the idea of dissipating into water and soil, becoming fish and plants or quaking aspen green. That would be a homecoming, but I don't say this to sentimentalize the boy's disappearance. Accepting death may always be a matter of finally admitting our biology, but it isn't religious energy that is misspent in denial of the bloody facts but rather the energy of our hurried, automated lives.

The real question is why, once one death has been absorbed, we can't accept the fact that no death should rise above any other in significance. I remember being in the hospital in Connecticut where my brother had died and staring out the window onto the highway, astonished at the moving traffic. Who hasn't lost a mother, a sister, a brother, or a child and not felt betrayed by the continual march of humankind and the spinning of the earth along its indifferent course? If biology were a sufficient explanation of myself, I would not continue to keep at bay the pain of a lost brother with so many frenetic and pitiful stopgaps.

Nature's peace? Perhaps. If the beauty of the world offers such peace, it is only acceptable when it comes to the afflicted as revelation, and that is not mine to receive, which is why I won't insist on knowing why God would not grant that family the chance to find the boy's body. I don't like to think about nature's end any more than the end of man, but as I walked in straight lines I thought that maybe trust is possible, trust in some promise that will catch and connect us all after all this waiting, changing, losing, and searching. The sorrows of the body are what remind us that we are individual and idiosyncratic. But I think it is when we are surfeited by the body's ecstatic joys in the vast physical universe, our capacity for sorrow signifies something much more, that we are human and alive, with no end of companions. We are impatient with history, it is true. But it isn't the history we have lived in the land that should define us, anyway. The past that should define us is the history that the land hides, that we keep searching for with desperate and abiding human love. These are nature's recompenses.

Our search party reached a small ridge, below which we heard the calm lapping of mountain water before we could see it. I wondered who these sounds were for. I listened to the hollow wind as it blew through the branches of desperately rooted trees which leaned into the mountainside in their pretense that they would always be able to resist the heavy pull downward. From such heights it seems impossible that anything ever remains standing. Seeing slant and drop in every direction feels as if the world is a protruding island, a thrust of denial in the face of the inevitable death of all things piercing the clouds and the blue sky in one last hurrah of stony resistance to the law of gravity. Which only seems to suggest that death is the lie, even if it is the rule. If it weren't for such protrusions, there would be no concentration of precipitation, no purification of water, no riparian worlds of vegetable, mineral, and animal, no human community. But if there were no protrusions and all the earth were a sea of glass, we would know exactly where little Garrett lay hiding, along with every other lost son or daughter of the human race.[17] So the fact of the earth's uneven surface, its infinite variety, is the ultimate tomb of all human dust even as it is the womb of all human possibility.

Five

I HAVE COME TO THE CABIN TO DO SOME READING AND WRITING BEFORE we close it for the winter. It has been a mild fall, so there is time still for a day at the cabin. I have made a conscious decision that this place will be my home base, my place of recollection, and a site for gathering new family memories for my own children. I know this is a romance, really, not to mention a stroke of good fortune, since my father purchased it from his siblings after my grandfather passed away. I think he likes the idea, as I do, of making new family memories for me and for my brother Bill. Coming here in the late summer is one way to prolong the pleasure of fall by catching it early, before it has arrived on the valley floor, following it down with each passing week, until finally you are still enjoying the brilliant colors, the smell of decaying leaves, and the first slant light of winter, well into the first week of November.

Now that I am here, I can't help feeling I am blind. Shrouded at best, hoping at least for some small new strangeness to be revealed. Today the water runs like silk past the cabin, the aspens display their changes unevenly, some more like lime green, some prematurely brown, but plenty in full naked yellow, sending reflections in all directions and making even the ground glow. I am not one to believe in the radical need for disavowing all modern life, but here at least it seems that the veil of the world is thinner, and I am always yearning to push through the surface of what I see, to feel a hand on the other side.

Might not the angels also wish for the same, to reach back into us, to feel the pulse of our blood and to feel the swirling of the earth's breath around them, to veil their minds again with the blue sky and green canopies of trees that are our home? Yes, I think they envy us. I am with Robert Frost: "Earth's the right place for love." Or with Rilke: "Hiersein ist herrlich" (to be here is glorious).[18] It is an old and tired argument that religion is for those who can't face the reality of death. Ever since my brother died, the most paradoxical gift my belief in life after death seems to have afforded me is a penchant for weeping at the transcience of beauty. Whoever thought that the idea of eternal life meant we could disparage this fleshly life never finished the hard work of belief.

It seems to me that when my son, Sam, announced one day upon entering my bedroom, "I want to be an animal," he was expressing the spirit's unique impulse to explore the dimensions of physical experience. "Which kind?" I asked. "A lizard, a fish, and a bird." When pressed for his reasons, he was equally deliberate and forthcoming: "To be fast, to swim, and to fly." Precisely because the life of the body is so thoroughly enjoyable, it surprises me just how often I crave the chances to be startled by those small discoveries that I am something more than flesh and bone. Emily Dickinson was right: doubting keeps belief nimble, and doubting the ultimate reality of my biology seems only to intensify the simple pleasures of the flesh. Which is why I am drawn to this place at the side of a river in the mountains.

I must at least admit this to myself: earth is an odd place to find myself and the oddness of it is precisely what makes it so intoxicating. This is a one-time affair, never to be repeated again, and I want all of it. Children pulsating and growing in my arms, this aspen half-dressed in yellow, with that dead black branch extending itself into the air for no one, this compost with its nuggets of pine tar, under these feet, here, now. Even without Moses striking the rock, God's hot pebbles on human lips, or stones illuminated by His finger's touch, who can miss the earth's glow?[19]

I meant to say that I caught and released about five fish earlier today on the tributary above where the beaver dams used to be. Before they were bulldozed this past spring to help protect the cabins from flooding, they were so numerous that this stream of ankle-deep water ran three or four feet deep in long stretches. The deep pools the beavers had created were hard to reach because of the unexpected cuts of water through the high grass and thick groves of trees.

When she was only nine, I took Paige fishing along the shallow water above the dams. A child willing to spend painstaking minutes separating her mushrooms and peas in her stew just because they are mushy or peeling the red skin off of her new potatoes with a surgeon's precision because of their texture, I fully expected her to recoil from the mud and bugs and demand that we return to the cabin. But something in the idea of the hunt pulled her forward, even though her sandals sank into the beds of sediment under the water and the water touched the hem of her shorts. As the light around us scattered to a gray twilight, I watched her closely. With her thick hair tied behind in a pony tail, her blue eyes hardly glanced anywhere while she nodded intently at my gentle instructions. I tried not to draw any attention to the spider webs hanging from the branches or the prospect of snakes and leeches. Her persistence was rewarded when, after almost a half mile of missed opportunities, I yelled for her to set the hook but I was too late. She already had done so after landing her fly just above where a dimple had appeared on the water's surface.

"Nice job, Paige!" I congratulated her enthusiastically.

She held the animal in her hands and set it back in the water. Not one to emote like her mother, she grinned and said decisively, "That was fun."

I was alone once, too, peering through an opening in the vegetation at a large fish feeding in the slow-moving water, much too slow to have waded without spooking him. He was making his occasional start for the surface, circling around and holding for his next morsel. There was no room to cast behind me, so I cut and shortened my line, retied my terrestrial—a small beetle pattern made of black foam and red thread—and held it in my hand like an arrow while with a bent wrist I leaned the rod forward into an arched position. With one quick release of the fly, in what felt like one motion, it flew through the opening, landed on the water, and was taken by the fish who was noticeably excited by its unexpected appearance.

The fish fought me admirably while I scrambled through the brush trying to keep the line taut and get close enough to net him. I couldn't hold the rod high enough, and the two large cottonwoods at my sides with their rough hewn bark didn't give me room to steer him from one side or the other. He darted under some exposed roots around which the soil had been eroded by the rising waters of the dams, and the line broke almost immediately. Crouching down in a pant, fishless, with my heart knocking against my ribs, I didn't know whether to cry or pray in thanksgiving.

Now the water is ankle deep throughout the upper stream where the dams had been. I thought it might be worth exploring the same waters again, since perhaps the fattened fish in the beavers' waters had remained behind or had returned after the trauma of the bulldozers. I was not disappointed.

The air in the cabin feels wintry, so I start a fire, using the leather billows to stimulate the sparks on old copies of *The New York Times*, which despite my family's western relocation remains the newspaper of choice. As the sparks begin to flame and the wood crackles, I feel a pang of hunger and reach for my bag of peaches. Perhaps the greatest consolation for the end of summer in Utah, next to yellowing aspen, is the fall season of peaches. You see the fruit stands on the side of the road, or more jarring still, in the middle of sprawling shopping mall parking lots, filled with baskets of bright orange, yellow, and red fuzzy balls. There are the ears of corn, too, lined up vertically in their green striped suits.

The peach arrived in the New World as a weed. It was growing in the Americas in some places before settlers even arrived, evidence of the speed with which seeds travel in the mouths and feces of birds, perhaps giving the Europeans the impression of wild welcoming parties of familiar sweetness. The book of Nephi in the Book of Mormon records Lehi's dream of a fruit, sweet above all that is sweet, that a father feels compelled to share with his children. A line of people forms and stretches into mists of darkness as they feel their way toward the tree and its offering—most likely, I am compelled to believe, a Redhaven peach.[20]

Wiping my mouth with my sleeve, I sit down on the wicker chair and open the files I have brought with me. Like virtually every other Mormon of pioneer heritage, I have carried for years old copies of family trees, copies of brief life stories written by descendents of prominent ancestors, and photocopies of old photographs. Stories of these pioneers are shared at family reunions, recounted in Church meetings, and celebrated with mythological grandeur in Utah every July 24, Utah's designated Pioneer Day. The truth is I wasn't raised to be well versed in this history, but it seems that if I am going to come to terms with living in this watershed, I can't rely on my poetic urge alone to soak in this present earthly beauty. I will need to wrestle with whatever claims the legacies of my ancestors have on me, legacies of hardship, persecution, and unspeakable faith but also the legacy of making the desert "blossom as a rose."[21]

One would think that, scion of Mormon pioneer stock that I am (on both sides of my family, no less), I would know my pioneer stories well, that they would form the very root of my identity. But raised back East by not the most orthodox of parents, dinner conversations focused no more on my Mormon past than on things I learned at the Seders of my Jewish friends and the ancient language of their fathers they repeated at Bar Mitzvahs, the storytelling of Native American and African American writers I read in high school, or the experiences we had in museums and concert halls in New York City. When we did talk about our Mormon past, it was with respect, but not devotion. I don't suspect that this was due to any shame about our Mormon heritage but because my parents were afraid that heavy doses of Mormon exceptionalism would make it harder for us to appreciate the value of other cultures.

Maybe I went too far in the other direction. By the time I finished my undergraduate and graduate education in the Bay Area of California, I was pretty accustomed to the utter invisibility of Utah history and Mormon experience in the American mind and largely ignorant about it myself. Utah was the repository of my strangeness as a different kind of American, and it hardly seemed possible that Utah and the rest of America could ever be part of the same imagined community.

I am told that it only takes twenty generations before you can link any two human beings on earth by DNA, a little more, it turns out, than it takes to be connected to Kevin Bacon but enough to justify caution in assuming exceptionalism. It is a strange thing, this search for roots. It usually leads to dead ends, which would suggest that they aren't roots at all, at least not tap roots that go straight down and deep. Which has always been a cause of wonder for me, since what is known in Mormonism as the spirit of Elijah is foundational to Mormon identity. You never know when it will happen, but at some point in your life you will be swept up in a desire to know your forbearers, to visit their lives, and to feel after them in the dusky remote rooms of the past.

Maybe we are simply too linear in our thinking, and while we are busy thinking about parentage and lines of descent, we take our eyes off siblings, aunts and uncles, and the myriads of cousins—those contemporaries to whom we are brothered by a shared past. There are simply too many tangentials and too many generations in the past that must finally exhaust us and be arbitrarily ignored in order to create the impression that families are "lines" at all and not wide webs, connected below the surface of time like that grove of aspen trees out my window breathing in the same nutrients through their shared root system. There is such pretension to singularity in the way each tree bends, shoots out branches, colors distinctly under the pressure of decreased temperatures and with variable intake of water, battles for light and real estate by the river bend, and ruptures and boils on the surface of the bark according to the wounds each has received. Variation is the appearance but subterranean unity the rule.

So maybe the mission of the spirit of Elijah is to get us to the point where we no longer have to depend on or be determined by the past, where we are finally free to live in the interest of new futures. It was only a few years ago before moving to Utah, after years of doing research on novels from the plantation histories of the South and of the Caribbean, family histories far different from mine, that I found myself wondering about my mother's father, a soil engineer who died of a heart attack at age fifty-six while trying to push his car out of the mud on a remote hillside in California. My mother was only nineteen at the time and hadn't even met my father yet. In a long-distance call, Mom fed me fragments of memories—his gentle kindnesses, his quiet reserve, his hard work in various towns in California and Oregon wherever opportunities arose.

In the mail, later that week, I received photocopies of a small handful of letters he had written her when she was at college, letters that expressed a moving tenderness for his oldest daughter. One letter gently chided her for not asking for more money, thus explaining why he had included in the letter more than she had requested. Hard not to like a quality like that, and I felt a bit more keenly his absence in my life. She also sent to me a manila envelope of other materials she had been able to collect about remote ancestors on both sides of my family. The stirrings of interest didn't last long enough to even begin to read those materials she sent, however, at least not until I finally moved to Utah where so many of these stories had taken place.

So here at the cabin I reopen the envelope. James Stratton, son of Barton Stratton and Susan Vyse Stratton, born on December 22, 1824, in Hertfordshire, England. Simple enough. Worked as a freight carrier in his early teens, moving rum and sugar from the West Indies and spices from Asia to northern counties above London. His contact with ports and ships opened up the outside world to him, and he had left for New York City by the age of nineteen. After roaming the eastern seaboard performing a variety of odd jobs, he joined the U.S. Navy and sailed against Mexico on the eve of the Mexican War.

He later returned to England, in part to recover his health (he never mentions his specific ailment), and it is there in the spring of 1850 that he hears for the first time the Mormon missionaries, who had been seeking converts in England for almost twenty years. "At the close of one meeting," he says, "I was asked if I wished to be baptized. I told them I didn't know if I were a fit subject, remembering that the Methodists had their subjects on trial for a time. I was asked if I was a sinner, and I said I was. He said it was sinners he wanted. I said I was willing to be baptized. So on the 3rd of August, I was baptized by Elder William Goats. On the following Sunday, I was confirmed a member of the Church of Jesus Christ of Latter-day Saints by Elder Heart, and received a new birth. For I was born of the water and confirmed by the Spirit."

I find the humility endearing and the prose searingly simple and under-stated. One picture shows a small, hunched man with a gray beard and sunken mouth, a sure sign of missing teeth. Another, what looks like three generations of a family gathered outside a red brick home, at one side a small grandfather with a crumpled hat and the same sunken mouth.

I get up to put another log on the fire. The elk head on the wall stares blankly back at me.

James soon receives what was known as the "spirit of gathering" and leaves for America again, this time to learn more about his new religion in Salt Lake. He is with his "companion," Francis Clark. On the first Sunday of the voyage, the Apostle Orson Pratt marries them. 1851.

Within short order, at least that is the impression from his brevity, he is living in Salt Lake Valley, raising a family, helping to build adobe homes, and assisting from time to time with the defense of crops and settlements against Ute Indians in nearby Parley's Canyon. He is sent on a few military missions during the Walker War against the Indians in Sanpete County, several days' journey to the southeast. Did he kill anyone? Only a few words about the joy of hearing the apostles preach.

It is painful to have so much and yet so little. I can place him in my mind's eye in that vast Salt Lake Valley, scarcely spotted by development. May-be a few sinuous lines of gray smoke emerging from encampments by creek beds but no carpet of concrete, highway, and malls. My mind's eye has been fed by old Bierstadt paintings and early daguerreotypes with blurry edges, showing open vistas of land surrounded by piercing mountains. There is a remarkable absence of visual depiction in his story, even though this was presumably written toward the end of his life when his own posterity might have already thirsted for knowledge of that primal encounter with the wil-derness. What anguishes is that he died when my grandfather was three years old.

I can't blame James. Can't blame anyone. I am uncertain what I could convey in five pages of the essence of my life. By the time I am finished telling my genealogy, my geographical movement, my occupations, and the names of my wife and children, you would know nothing about me. And you, too, gentle reader, would want to get up and eat a peach.

Which I do. And then decide to go for a walk.

The porch door with its spring hinge slams behind me, clanging wood on wood. The sun has gone behind some clouds, and the colors of the leaves, the alternating deep and light greens of the pines on the mountain slope across the river, and even the taupe road under my feet have all lost their brilliant distinctions in the absence of direct reflection. I try to enjoy this sensation, but it becomes too chilly. Even if the sun were shining, it would be hard to find warmth on this stretch of the river because of the steep mountainside directly to the south and the many towering pines along the banks. The shifting sound of pebbles and dirt beneath my shoes is the only human sound within reach of my ear. It doesn't feel like solid ground, never has. Too many echoes, strange recollections and sensations of long-ago visits here as a toddler. Someone's large hand guiding mine, immense trees bending to greet me. Soft wind. The tall grasses hiding garter snakes.

Hard to imagine pioneers here, too, but they were. And Indians. But now it is a neighborhood of rustic family cabins. There's too much I can't get past...or to.

A marmot stands frozen in his question-mark pose as I approach. Perhaps he thinks I can't see him if he remains still, the thought of which makes me laugh. Below him, a small ridge of layered and lichen-draped stone hangs over the river, casting a dark shadow over swirling deep water behind a subaqueous bump of accumulated rocks. On the far side of the hole, there are competing currents that make it almost impossible to land a fly there for more than a few seconds before it starts dragging across the boiling swirls. There are simply too many oppositions surging from beneath for the line to lie invisibly on the transparent surface. I have tried casting with my arm high in the air to allow excess line to land next to the fly, buying myself a few seconds before some current starts pulling out the coiled line. And I have tried the opposite approach of landing the fly with no line touching the water at all so that with the motion of my arm I can allow the fly to appear to drift naturally. I have used droppers, too. I always feel compelled to give it a few casts. Some holes are like that. I am convinced it is just a matter of time.

Half a mile of walking straight east parallel to the river, the road bends along with the river to the north. This is where a south fork meets this central artery of the Provo. To the south I can see the canyon that produces this fork and to the north the opening of Pine Valley where the Provo comes down from the Uintas. This is also the site of the vanished bridge, washed out by the floods of the early 1980s. I remember crossing it when I was scarcely old enough to reach the railing and glancing down below to what seemed to be violent raging whitewater. A spring-fed water pipe used to line the underside of the bridge but now emerges alone and naked from a swath of deep green watercress on my side of the river and crosses to the other side, ringing to the sound of its inner flow.

Below the pipe is a swimming hole, close to ten feet deep, of swirling, translucent olive water, foam patterns sketching Sanskrit on the surface. There are a great number of fish in this hole, arguably the most within miles. I know this because once, at dusk, John and I stood chest deep in the water watching it boil with fish feeding in a frenzy on the surface. As the sun set, in the black air we continued to throw our entire arsenal on the water—blue wing olives, elk hairs, caddis emergers, humpies, cripple patterns, parachute adams, stimulators, any size, any color—without a single take. A humiliating experience that is hard to admit, even all these years later. The hole has been a curse ever since, never once revealing more to me than it did that night, and though I catch fish here from time to time, it will never be enough.

My wife and I waited until our first child was born to find out her gender, so we had to have two names at the ready. I thought I deserved the privilege of innocence in naming my children, I suppose, innocence from the weight of the past, and yet I remember the feeling that such innocence is more power than I wanted. After little success looking through borrowed ideas in name books, I found myself looking over the papers my mother had sent, including a family tree, like one might search through old city maps for a nice street name. I hadn't read the stories and had before me only bare bones: full names, dates and locations of birth, dates of death, so much rubble of living settled into a tree of names, each name like myself, a knot of time and flesh, holding forth momentarily but ultimately powerless to resist the great diaspora.

I saw one Elizabeth Clark Handley, the mother of my grandpa's grandfather, and then two or three other Elizabeths. Too many syllables, we thought, and besides, we didn't know anything about these people. But the first part of the name, Eliza, seemed to make for an indirect tribute and an opportunity for a name of our own making. It was later that I noticed there was an Eliza as well, so I felt that maybe the choice had been fortuitous. A few weeks after Eliza's birth, I held her with outstretched arms and open palms and prayed to God, joined in this naming ritual by the similarly outstretched hands of the men of her extended family in a circle.[22] I told God that we intended for her to have this name and that we wished to give her a blessing of health and wisdom. Such prayers are offered with clean hands, as clean as we can make them, I suppose, to mediate between the forces of parental will and of whatever it is that providence has in mind for the child. The child's will became evident soon enough, but lying in the palms of my hands, with a half dozen or so others joining me in offering her upward toward heaven, for a brief moment Eliza felt like clay, responsive and vulnerable.

I find myself back in the cabin after my stroll, a little more eager to read. Eliza Briggs Stratton, the mother of my grandpa's grandmother and James's second wife. Time to get to know her story. As I sit again on the wicker, the fire now glowering in red embers, I feel heat leaving the pores of my body. I can look forward to maybe thirty minutes of equilibrium before I begin to chill again and another log becomes necessary.

1856. Two companies of pioneers, the Martin and Willie handcart companies, both with over five hundred persons each, in Iowa City waiting to begin their trek to Salt Lake by late June, but the handcarts are not ready. Handcarts were a lower-budget method of travel, one that necessitated greater care in deciding what was absolutely essential to bring along. In the rush to get on with their journey before the onset of cold weather, both companies departed in the last weeks of July with handcarts made from green wood that was not properly aged and treated to be able to withstand the duress of the trip. After a brief debate in Nebraska about whether they should continue and risk encountering the arrival of winter, they determined to move on into the storms of tragedy. Winter would come early and hard. It was only October 19 when they were overcome by massive snowfall, a symptom of one of the wettest cycles the West has ever seen, but their faulty handcarts required frequent repairs thus slowing their progress and draining their supplies.

Eliza was the nineteen-year-old daughter of John and Ruth Briggs, parents of six children, including Eliza's younger siblings Thomas (thirteen), James (eleven), Mary Hannah (seven), Sarah Ann (four), Rachel (three), and Emma (eight months). By the time the company would arrive in the valley, John had died of starvation trying to ration supplies to his children; Thomas died a few weeks later, and Mary Hannah was gone on November 29, only one day before the company arrived in the valley. Ruth would pass away a few months later. Eliza lost parts of her feet and would never walk again without difficulty.

She was only fifteen when she joined the church with her family in Lancashire, England. They left four years later for America at the beginning of Eliza's young adulthood—her heart beating with excitement as she wondered about the adventure that lay ahead. She was filled with concern for her young siblings but appreciative of the significance of such a decision on the part of her parents. America was warm and green when she arrived, for she had not yet crossed the hundredth meridian into the high, dry, and bitter air of the vast western landscapes. But the new lands and new faces intoxicated the young woman, who would display the fiery resolve of a true convert to the end of her life.

Over the last several days her father had become insufferably angry and despondent. He was the one pulling the cart, filled with some five hundred pounds of food, blankets, pots, and other necessities. It had been his conversion and faith that had entered her own heart like a warm, welcoming fire. He was always a hard-working and decent man, but after he was baptized he had become buoyant, even silly at times. (Do I know this? Of course not, but the sparse details leave me no choice.) Eliza responded like a face in the mirror. She felt his joy, wanted to embrace his world and see to it that his faith was not in vain, that his posterity would be grateful to him for generations. She ached inside her belly for children to name after her mother and father, to see their posterity spread like sand across new lands of toil and possibility.

But now they were walking across bitter lands of unmerciful wind and biting cold, their handcarts falling apart, and supplies running short. What had begun as an impatient rush to Zion was slowly turning into a horrific, drawn-out nightmare of unrelenting hardships. God had seemed a warm, close insider to their family's dreams and the land welcoming, like loving arms. It was He who was quilting their story, but just when their hopes were tantalizingly within reach, just when they could start to imagine plowing soils near winding rivers, it seemed now He had given up and gone elsewhere and the promised land of bounty had turned bitter, alien, and indifferently wild.

She knew her father well enough to know that he would refuse to see his own fortitude. He had been too proud and optimistic about their plans to respond to such a sudden turn of fortune with anything but deep shock, leaving him disheveled, drudging through the muddy cold of early winter like a broken, budless twig. But he was self-sacrificing to the end, which taught her to see his shock as a measure of his hope. One night Eliza noticed her father's hand shaking in the firelight as he served their meager dinner. James was hungry and began to cry for more. As her father slumped back against the handcart in the dark, she told James stories to keep his mind off the hunger. When the stories lost their effectiveness, she retired behind a wall of sagebrush, dusted lightly by the snow, to be alone.

Something soft in the air awakened her under the cover of the stretched canvas just as the sun was rising. It was the coldest hour of the day, to be sure, but the light was pink and inviting and peaceful. They were at least two hundred miles from help and the rate of their journey now had slowed to just a few miles a day. She heard the softness again and this time recognized it as the voice of her mother, whimpering like a muzzled bird. She rolled over and saw her mother outside, lying across her father's stiff chest, her body shaking gently as the tears flowed. Eliza rolled a quarter turn back to stare at her sleeping siblings.

It seems unfair to have to resort to fiction, despite so much documentation of a remarkable but historically insignificant journey lived so many years ago. Maybe with enough research I could put all of the facts in their proper place and make this story shine with even greater vividness, like some massive stage design, and provide the needed epic glory the story deserves. To really make it an American story, perhaps. But something in me doesn't want that. They wouldn't, either, I suspect. Not because they don't want gratitude for taking those first horrifically difficult steps across an unforgiving land, but somehow I want to honor the fact that their faith was a tough and bitter and ennobling choice, not something natural or inevitable. I want them alive, fleshy, frightened, guessing and groping for reason and hope. I don't want the smugness of monumental memory. I want the horror of uncertainty only because this seems to be the best way I can honor that incomprehensible moment in which they chose faith by submitting to the choices cruel circumstance had left them.

It is the kind of faith that borders on madness, and would be, if it weren't for the fact that quiet choices of the heart, like so many ripples on still waters, expand through time, transforming and extending the reach of their bounty. And just as ripples always move away from the place where the stone disappeared into its liquid grave and are mere secondary echoes, it is impossible to return to the first cause. The amnesiac core grows in direct proportion to the passage of time and to the growing significance of the event.

I don't know what kind of madness Eliza endured, what labyrinths of panic and terror her mind took her through, before she apparently decided not to be afraid of death and pain. Shallow minds, usually minds that have not dared the depths of faith in their own lives, cannot possibly understand this as anything but inevitable heroism or, just as bad, a kind of blind fanaticism and folly. These acts of fierce determination were not performed before an audience of millions of appreciative believers; the only audience was the bitter cold of wind and hunger that attacked without mercy or respect of persons.

Eliza arrives in Salt Lake in the winter of 1856 with badly frozen feet. Brigham Young instructs the Saints to take in these weak fellow citizens in the household of faith. James and Francis take in Eliza, while the rest of her family is sent to live with Francis's parents. It is not clear if the intention all along was for James to marry Eliza, but Brigham Young shortly afterward requests that those men who have taken in single women marry them. "I became very fond of Eliza," writes James laconically, "and when President Young asked that we marry the young women we had taken in our homes and given them a permanent home, I asked Eliza if she would consider marrying me into polygamy. She accepted and we were married."

The afternoon light has begun to cast an orange glow through the trees, exposing the flittering caddis flies which, like whimsical snowflakes, dart among the willow branches and tall grasses. I stand to look at the surface of the water through the window. The flies are indeed hatching. I can see slaps on the water from the small cutthroats in amateurish training, impetuously eager to prove their aggressiveness. I step out onto the back porch and sit on the stairs to listen to the water and watch, still occupying in my mind that distant landscape and moment in time.

James watched as the sunlight lounged about among the shadows of the peach trees, creating the sensation of so many beings, all drenched by the sun and cooled in the shadows of the straight lines of the orchard. I suppose that afternoon brought the greatest solace to James because he felt less alone among the long pews of peaches all in worship and thanksgiving. The harvest was fast upon him and his sons, and there was little time to waste for the peaches were beginning to sweat their sweetness into the air and might soon be lost for good. The aroma left him almost intoxicated with nostalgia. It was amazing to consider how the desert soil seemed to blossom in response to the harnessing of the Provo. Each spring the entire orchard was aflame with lines of cottony blossoms, making the trees almost tangibly sweet before the fruit ever arrived. It hardly seemed possible that he had struggled to survive in this valley in only a mud house when Eliza had first arrived at the age of nineteen, almost thirty years before, when James was in his early thirties and already raising a young family.

She was a beautiful girl, with a slight asymmetry to her face that made it hard for him not to stare. She was weather worn and carried a frightful darkness with her, but as the days passed, and as she was fed and warmed by the fire and her feet recovered what use they could, light began to return. It was an extraordinary moment when she first smiled, a real smile that no longer was a feigned attempt to hide her deep sadness but an emission of inner light. It had been a small thing, as James recalled, something to do with the pig that had got its snout stuck between the fence poles, but Eliza smiled and then laughed. James couldn't have felt more delighted with himself for having restored this girl to her humanity with the help of his wife.

It was Francis who had taken to her first, to be truthful. James kept a proper circumspect distance from a girl who was more beautiful than his wife and whose story of immense loss and deprivation could stir an affectionate pity in the most cold-hearted soul. But James loved and honored his wife, and he believed in his duty to keep his mind and soul on things of God. He did this without hypocrisy or pretense. He began to worry, though, when he noticed how deeply attached Francis had become to Eliza. There was talk of Brigham asking the brothers to marry up the stray girls, to welcome them into their lives. James did not care for the thought of another wife, but he did care for Eliza. At first it was almost a paternal affection, but as Francis's affection for her grew, he felt safer in his own attachment to this forlorn one. And then Francis approached him with the idea of marrying her. "I think we should take her in, James," she had suggested. "She is so dear, and I can tell that you like her. I won't be jealous. It would be the right and Christian thing to do."

Once Francis had raised the topic it was no longer possible to look at her with distant attachment. He began to long for her, noticing her slender waist, and watching her red lips when she spoke passionately about her father and brothers and sisters in the winter light. He couldn't escape his conscience then that bore down on him like a gun barrel, accusing him of hoping that God would reward him for his carnal desires.

One night at the conclusion of the day's labor, he found himself walking along the bends of the Provo bench a few hundred feet above the whispers of the river carving its sinuous and interwoven path along the valley floor. The late afternoon light brought the mountainside into sharper focus, the rusts of early autumn jumped to life, and James felt that he could hold onto himself no longer. He thought he might lean over the hillside and catch the cool breeze's destination—to be something, anything other than a man, with a heart, and a mind, and a body as hopelessly emptied as his of contentment. It wasn't entirely clear to him if what he felt was passion for life or a desire for death, or if he understood anymore the difference.

The orange light illuminated the small bump of a home he had left behind. Francis would wonder where he was since it was almost suppertime, but he could scarcely breathe in that house anymore with the smell of Eliza's sweat mixed in as it was by now with the smell of the earthen walls of their home. He had lain at night now for weeks in their hovel smelling the air thick with Eliza's steady sleeping. Next week he would be married to Eliza, having received orders directly from Brother Brigham.

James walked home in the dusky light, occasionally catching his toe on the roots and rocks that poked out of the dusty trail like a cryptic text. By the time he could see his home his only eyes were his feet feeling their way along the uncertain terrain, hugging the ground beneath him. His only certainty was that sensation of footwork.

Can I really imagine this as some kind of happy arrangement, one sought for by the first wife? And why do I imagine this scrupulous self-control? It's because I don't know what to do with these words I find in my family papers:

"Francis felt sorry for this lonesome girl and wanted to share her home with her. They got along nicely together and made a pleasant home."

But, of course, when were those words written? In 1956 by Anonymous Proud Descendent. Case closed, it would seem. Just another case of family pride.

But who started the rumor? Was it based merely on how the story turned out? The strained efforts of some Mormon apologists? Polygamy is indeed the oddest of historical facts, stranger than any fiction. Strange facts have a way of making strange bed partners. Apologists and anti-Mormons deserve each other, I say. Like an unimaginative and ideological historian, they are paranoid. They have to be. That is their job. They have to anticipate outcomes, which in the end must not be surprising. Surprise must remain a mere illusion, the product of ignorance. Which is to say they often aren't very interested in history after all, since its bald facts are intolerable.

All I know is that Johnson's Army arrived to put pressure on the Mormons to cease their polygamous ways. James's family moved to Provo in 1859, just a few years after the first Mormon settlement on the banks of the river and the Battle of Provo that saw the end of the Ute dominance in the valley. They came to seek refuge and to start over, but the family soon found themselves in financial straits. Francis had certain talents as a seamstress, so she took her baby and four-year-old son with her to Camp Floyd, on the western side of the Jordan River where Johnson's Army lived, to sew. Eliza's account tells us that "away from home and without proper influence, Francis became infatuated with a soldier and then the company of soldiers were released and went back East to their homes, Francis went with the soldier taking her two children with her. Louisa, her eldest child, about seven years old and James, about three years old, remained with their father and Eliza." True to form, James's account is much more terse: "Francis went back east with the soldier of her choice. Our baby, a boy, passed away before he was two years old. I never knew where his little body was laid to rest."

It is almost dark now, the mosquitoes are out, and I promised to be home before the kids went to bed. The least I can do is respect Amy's kind understanding. I enter the cabin, check everything one last time before we close it next week, grab the broom for a quick sweep of spider webs on the front and back porches, and stir the remaining embers in the thick pile of ash in the fireplace. I pour some water on them just in case and close the wire screen. Nodding to the elk, I bid the place goodbye and turn off the electricity outside.

I drive with caution for fear of deer crossings. There is no reception yet on the radio. I can make out the reflections of stars on the glasslike surface of the Jordanelle reservoir. It maintains appearances, invulnerable to the whimsies of seasons and the caprices of water. The dam was an exponential leap from the days of irrigation. Donald Worster aptly describes dams as making "the difference...between holding an umbrella over your head when it rains and making the rain go somewhere else. The first is a momentary defense, the second a concerted attempt to control and defeat a threat once and for all." Once you have modernized the system to become invulnerable not only to flooding but to provide unqualified recompense in the desert. Worster notes that "all mystery disappears from [water's] depths, all gods depart, all contemplation of its flow ceases."

Maybe it is nostalgia for what we were destroying that explains why we began to build cabins when the damming began. It's as if we have believed we could order time in a straight and sequential chain, belying time's surfeiting fluidity, as if the past is not also our future, the dead our living. Dams have created the impression that water is manageable, fixed, and immutable. While this feat of engineering makes living comfortable, it elides reality. And the danger is that as we distance ourselves from those places where water is born in surprisingly rocky crags, our safety makes us indifferent to its fate. As if all it took to make something liquid and drinkable were the turn of one's wrist.

Water's ancient story goes underground, in so many buried canals, still working upon us and nurturing the present, but we are no longer aware at what cost, at what distance it comes to us, or to what extent it still shapes us. Elizabeth Bishop was haunted by a river's intimations of a history that cannot be translated:

(As if a river should carry all
the scenes that it once reflected
shut in its waters, and not floating
on momentary surfaces.)

It would be easy here to pick a favorite institutional target—schools, churches, government agencies, the entertainment industry—that dam history like a river and complain that if we could just rid ourselves of their institutional restraints on our imagination, we would be free from the past's monomythical claims. One might enter the battlefield of historical memory itself in order to counter myths with still more historical fact, and one would at least find comfort in the company of friends. Mormonism and its many enemies have spawned no shortage of amateur historians aspiring to get it right. But this would miss the point: no one is responsible for my imagination except me, and while institutions are often guilty of historical distortion and intentional error, and while historical inquiry is always valuable, I can only blame myself for failing to understand that I am always in time's flow and that historical memory is always rhetorical. I don't need fewer myths, only better ones, spawned under the conditions fate has allotted me. The only potent thing is imagination.

Say it is true that Francis liked the idea of polygamy. Say her husband lacked the emotive and impulsive qualities she craved. Say she saw them in Eliza and then in another man for whom she fell idiosyncratically. And that she made an impossible choice, one that haunted her for the rest of her life. Was she surprised at her rising jealousy of Eliza? Perhaps. Did she try to convince herself that polygamy was strange, or perverse? Perhaps. But this was not without ambivalence because sometime in either the late 1880s or early 1890s, when James was close to seventy and had been a widower since 1871, Francis took the long and solo journey from the East to seek forgiveness and reconciliation. James asked his church leaders what he should do, and he was told that it was up to him. "I forgave her," he explains, "and felt sorry for her, but I could not accept her as my wife again. She returned to the East and I never saw her again."

He spent his elderly years gardening and living in the houses of his children. He apparently loved flowers and haunted the local cemetery, making sure that on Memorial Day, the children and grandchildren gathered wildflowers among the sage and placed them on each grave.

"I saw thousands of fish being caught by hand....I could buy a hundred which each weigh a pound, for a piece of tobacco as large as my finger. They simply put their hands in the stream, and throw them out as fast as they can pick them up." The words of Parley Pratt in 1849, speaking of his first visit to the Provo River. Despite its blue-ribbon status today for fly-fishing, the Provo is not stacked with fish, let alone natives. The Mormon settlers were starved for protein and in 1849 they had come into the valley—a land that for all its beauty appeared to be nothing but "sagebrush and desert cobble rock," according to Pratt—with the hope that the Ute Indians would be helpful. Initially it appears they were. James earned an early living making adobe homes and trading rope made from the rushes he gathered by Utah Lake. But trading for fish would not suffice for settlers intent on staying put and growing.

Only years later, after Eliza had died giving birth to her last child, James and his sons would irrigate from the river, helping to create the first canal fed by the Provo, and then plant peach trees. It was not uncommon for fish to find themselves stranded in furrowed rows, becoming fertilizer by happenstance. The first harvest was in 1892. What Francis would have seen in her prodigal return was a stark contrast to what she had left behind in the 1850s: red brick homes, orchards, wildlife scattered to the mountains, and Ute Indians noticeably absent in the valley since the creation of the Ute Reservation a hundred miles to the northeast in the 1860s. After thousands of years, the transformation of the desert had begun, all in the name of desperate survival.

Take a step back, then, and imagine one more piece of the puzzle. Take James and Eliza out of Utah Valley, a climate of four seasons, each challenging and beautiful. These were not individuals roughing it on the frontier to discover their American individuality. These were members of a community who acted in concert according to their faith in the church leadership. With one broad stroke, Brigham Young had already changed their lives with permission to marry. Then he called James and Eliza to the Muddy river Mission in a desolate and isolated region of southeastern Nevada in 1868. A land of naked red rock baking like pottery in kilns. Bent juniper and pinyon trees, sagebrush, and caked, water-starved soil, with one lone spring-fed stream. The ultimate challenge to the cause for Isaiah's desert elations. Ninety miles from the nearest settlement, St. George, sixty miles from any timber, and entirely inaccessible by roads. Summer temperatures as high as 125 degrees, to say nothing of evening temperatures unpleasant enough to force settlers to sleep on top of their mud homes under wet sheets.

The settlement was in its fifth year when James and Eliza and their seven children arrived, and there was an atmosphere of resentment among those who already lived there. Over half of the 158 who were called along with the Strattons left within three months. It didn't help that, shortly after James and Eliza settled in, Brigham Young made a visit and declared the place God-forsaken, demanding to know who had advised him that this would be a good place to colonize. Once it was discovered that the territory belonged to the state of Nevada and the colony was consequently subject to new state taxes, the mission was disbanded in 1871.

Eliza was pregnant by March of 1870 and became very ill. Just months prior to the call to return to their homes or to settle new areas, James urged Eliza to return with him to Provo where he would be better able to care for her. "No," she is reported to have said, "the President of the Church called us here and we will stay until he calls us back." She died only two days after her last child was born and was interred in the hot sands of what is now Overton, Nevada. The mission is now buried beneath Lake Mead, an ironic watery grave for a desert wasteland they worked so hard to make blossom. A few months after Eliza's death, James traveled with nine children, the oldest fourteen years old, back to Cedar Fort and eventually to Provo. James tells us that it took some five years before they were all recovered from malaria and other illnesses contracted in the heat.

With the invention of air conditioning and the irrevocable drift toward an economy of shopping outlets and grocery stores stocked with tropical fruit and slabs of pink salmon shrink-wrapped on ice, the area near Muddy river is no longer so foreboding. Suddenly the land of red stone, fantastical geological colors, and staggering vistas of desert sun and expanse have become a mecca for artists, retirees, and golfers. It is tempting to wish that the beauty of the place might have offered them a balm to soothe the wounds of living in such want, but that was a luxury they simply could not afford.

"Behold, I will send you Elijah the prophet before the coming of the great and dreadful day of the Lord; And he shall turn the heart of the fathers to the children, and the heart of the children to their fathers, lest I come and smite the earth with a curse." Every Mormon knows these verses that close the Old Testament in Malachi, words repeated by the angel Moroni to the boy prophet, Joseph Smith.[23] Hearts not so inclined, Malachi tells us, will be "stubble" when all is said and done and left "neither root nor branch." Words that announce the latter-day call to seek restoration of knowledge of the scattered family of God, one family at a time.

Not raised by threats and not one to respond to them anyway, I guess I preferred to repent when my heart turned of its own accord rather than behaving as if the fate of the earth depended on my study of my genealogy. No inheritor wishes to bite the hand that feeds, especially when it is a hand of desperate and devout suffering, but might this suffering feed a perpetual martyr complex? There will always be those who can't see the humanity behind the stories, who reject them out of hand, simply because they seem to be stories of religious fanaticism. But perhaps there will also always be those for whom such stories inspire nothing more than indignation at the vile persecution and betrayal of American values that chased these unwanted aliens into the desert.

And now some environmentalists are saying that Mormons are antiecological, that they continue an ancestral pattern of destruction of the native qualities of land and water until it is all dammed and transformed. It doesn't help, of course, to read, as I did recently, about the proposal of a massive water park for river rafting and surfing in Mesa, Arizona, a city of no small percentage of Mormons, and the remarkable local support for the idea. Because, the architect remarked, he couldn't imagine his children not having the chances he had had as a child in far wetter climes, to engage in water sports. I guess moving didn't occur to him. So his heart is turned to the children, but to what end?

Does this modern biogeographical arrogance have its roots in the likes of James Stratton? I don't buy it. He at least had to honor the seasons, the times of flood and of drought, and he had to worry himself about soil. He was more Adam—working for his redemption by the sweat of his brow—than the most ardent environmentalist. But I also won't defend his story just so that I can keep circling my Mormon wagons, licking my Mormon wounds, and further contribute to a disregard for ecology. The humility of James's story moves me—its particular humanity, and the prospect of a new world that there is still a chance of discovering and suffering for.

If I can get to those human moments in the past before they become monumentalized, perhaps I will discover what the Cuban poet José Lezama Lima once called "the conviction that what happens to us, happens to everyone," which suggests that a belief can never be of service to the world if the stories of its origins only reinforce its peculiarity rather than its universality. The fact that no belief began without the human stains of particular people, places, and times is what Mormonism's critics and apologists alike find so unpalatable. The history is too recent, the stains still too fresh in the soil, for anyone to remember that Mormonism can never be relevant to humanity without them.

I live in brief moments of constriction, like some napkin ring holding together fanning folds of cloth expanding outward above and below me in time. Descended from converts in the days of Joseph Smith, and with polygamy on both sides of my family, I suppose some people would expect me to have been born with a tail. It is a tight constriction, to be sure, but brief, because history is not dropped down some funnel into the bottles of our memory. I didn't want to feel trapped by obligations that are not of my choosing, but I have learned that genealogy does not determine my choices. This is because in being remembered, the past is remade in my image. Memory is a selective and a forgetful thing, after all. There is nothing to be done about this but confess it, and I confess it. Every story wants to be made flesh, but every time I pick up the broken bones and clothe them in costume, the past is betrayed. I must learn to accept this because impatience with the elusiveness of the past only repays with nostalgia and regret.

I think what Elijah teaches is to honor the past but to learn to play house with it since what you really want is to build a home for the future. Seeing relics lie limp and discarded once in a while like old ragdolls helps to keep believing in the past nimble. No matter how much I think I know, my knowledge of the past is based on the broadest of generalities, the shallowest of detail, and hopelessly myopic blurring. Deep affections for place must be nurtured by this humiliation. Because then it becomes obvious that promised lands are never permanently given, only provisionally loaned. Otherwise, like patriotism, such affections go beyond their utility and fuel passions for homelands with well-protected borders, like so many silly gated communities. Those with the "wrong" forefathers, or worse, with insufficient evidence of where they came from, get burned. Turned hearts are soft and malleable.

Fly-fishing has changed the way I see rivers. I wish I could wade them all, to feel that familiar resistance to my efforts to move upstream just as I will resist its will to pull me down. Standing still in the middle of a rapid passage of water, sending out those incessantly hopeful, wriggling lines, there is the temptation to lie down, to give up resistance and float down where the water seems so eager to take me, to finally rejoin the fate of the earth's arteries. But, like so many mossy stones, I have decided that I will steal my chances to hold my ground, to see what I can catch. In so doing, I feel the weight of time and I catch glimpses of its elusive electricity. It comes to me, passes through and around me, and leaves me changed, nurturing the inescapable suspicion that I was never temporary.

Six

Days of monotonous gray light have stretched into weeks, deepening in their density to the point where I sense it is unhealthy to go for a run outdoors. I don't know if I noticed it much the first few winters I lived here, but this valley's seasonal inversions have become hard to miss and more distressing with each passing year. When pollutants get caught in the inverted air, aided by the geography of a ring of mountains surrounding the valley, we have air conditions that are among the nation's most polluted. Breathing these spikes of smog over a lifetime is the equivalent of being a lifetime smoker, costing a year or two of our lives.

In my ecstasy at finding myself finally home in Utah, I accepted the almost moral imperative to try to love everything about this place, but it has not always been easy. As I have learned in marriage and in my lifelong membership in the LDS Church, the initial euphoria of commitment can make it easy for disappointments to feel like betrayal. Although baptized at age eight, I wasn't really converted until age eighteen, and it was after a decade or so of service in the church and the proverbial seven years of marriage, I found the unambiguous pleasures of these relationships wearing off. In my neglect of honest self-analysis, I instead noticed the weaknesses of others, whether it was the occasional overbearing or materialistic Mormon or the sometimes emotional distance of my wife, and each seemed like a personal affront to the sacred commitments I had made.

This pollution feels like betrayal, but I am wise enough now to understand that I am no less at fault than anyone else. I might just have to learn to endure. At least these colder winters have portended forgiving snowfall, for which I generally can't complain, but with the colder temperatures of a waning autumn, all it takes is a brief dry spell for inversion to take hold. The first day the light seems a milky blue, slightly dissipated, but as the days pass, the mountains disappear, and we hunker down, conserving emotional energy, awaiting a storm to clear the air again. It is delusional, really, to place all hope in some act of God to wipe our human stains clean as long as we are unwilling to repent. While beauty and bounty are our most ancient desires, sometimes the recompenses of our own pollution are what we deserve. In a state highly dependent on coal for its electricity and not yet weaned from the automobile, we will pay the price for many years to come for our refusal to move aggressively toward clean and renewable energy.

Everyone here knows that there is nothing quite like what a morning promises after the first snows of autumn. The crags of Squaw Peak and "Y" Mountain spotted in white, the tree tops billowing like low-lying cumulous clouds over the neighborhood, and the glistening streets melting into clarity in the piercing and warming sun. When we are socked in by this kind of hazy man-made light, though, I could be anywhere because the world seems a prison house of stasis. I know I have to get above or away to encounter the sensations of clear light, air, and the singular surface of the world in some remote place.

Necessity is the mother of invention, as they say, so I have taken up some new forms of recreation. I can never forget that December morning a week after intense snowfall had arrived with a fury, breaking the back of the drought. I went with a group of friends up to the top of Squaw Peak, three thousand feet above the valley floor, all of us feeling perhaps the same desperate need to stir the stillness of the soul as the inversion had started to gather.

When we met that morning at five a.m., there was enough light pollution in the valley even at that hour to make the mountains glow in a ghostly white, an effect enhanced by the abundant snow on the valley floor and draped on the crags of the mountain. The west face of the Wasatch generally doesn't remain covered in snow for very long because of the lower elevation and because of the direct light that burns on the mountainside every afternoon. The effect is a season-long shift in color and texture created by the different degrees of snowfall. When the snow is completely melted from the face, you can see the brown earth rising at a startling angle from the basin floor, while behind the ridges, still higher peaks stand ominously in white robes all winter long.

This canyon displays the effect of a split caused by two sinking plates and the work of spring runoff that flows through the mouth and into the pipes in my neighborhood. It isn't the water of the Provo, but it used to join its braids of water on the valley floor in the days of the Indians. Timpanogots, or so the Ute natives of this valley were known, means simply "water emerging from the rocky mouth." Water born of the mouth of stone, and here we stood at the lips about to be tasted by its tongue. The glow refracted off of the snow and the serrations of the rock face. The effect was a display of faint rust, orange, yellow, and white that made it hard to believe that Rock Canyon was indeed stone; it looked more like autumn leaves on a windy day, or with foreboding black above us, like a violent fire licking air.

I stared at those tessellated teeth of jutting stones held in relief by the surrounding snow. Faint, falling snowflakes pierced the purple shadows like diamonds. We ascended in the dark for some time with headlamps, but it wasn't long before the glowing light of the morning revealed the backside of the mountain we climbed. House of the Gods. For the Timpanogots, at least. We Mormons have a House of the Lord just down the hill. We could see the brightly lit bronze Angel Moroni atop the temple blowing his trumpet behind us just before we made our final turn into the heart of the canyon. But it was all of a piece. The canyon was the reason for the temple's location.

And the reverberation: "These are the generations of the heaven and of the earth, when they were created, in the day that I, the Lord God, made the heaven and the earth, and every plant of the field before it was in the earth, and every herb of the field before it grew. For I, the Lord God, created all things, of which I have spoken, spiritually, before they were naturally upon the face of the earth."[24] Joseph Smith's revelation about the creation is a re-creation in two senses: the story needed to be told again and the world needed to be created twice. And so chiasmus: imagined before it was spoken. Spoken before it became flesh. Sensation of the flesh inspires words, and words, the life of the spirit. Deeper still in the heart of the temple, the creation of the world is commemorated as a reminder of the care with which the Lord created diversity. And of how our own hands and minds played a role in honoring the world's beauty. And before it is gone, how our hands might still have work to do.

By now our hiking party had gone far enough that looking back to the west we could see the lights of the valley and the peak's strange shadow angling now from a completely different perspective. We would lose sight of it altogether as we climbed up on its back. I can see the peak from my house, and I have often thought I should learn to paint it, like Cezanne's Mont St. Victoire, over and over again in all its seasonal dressings.

When mountains take on iconic form, they are emblems of our sense of place and belonging. Historian Jared Farmer suggests that this isn't an entirely innocent process. When Mount Timpanogos to the north became the favorite peak it is today for the valley's citizens, it was a choice among others and was a symptom of a whitewashing of history used to forge a white, Mormon claim to a "native" homeland. Mountains as landmarks belie what any hiker—or anyone with the eyes of an impressionist—knows, that a mountain never retains the same shape. There are as many mountains as there are steps it takes to climb them, or as there are angles of the sun and shifts in weather. Would the faith to move mountains include willing feet and keen eyes, since all mountains move, every one? Recreation and art can keep us honest about the contingency of home, to learn to see it otherwise. To give the lie to a static sense of place was the energy behind Cezanne's mania to paint as many Mont St. Victoires as he had canvasses, even if he remained rooted in essentially the same point in space.

No one knows for sure when the Timpanogots arrived but it was several centuries before the Mormons. We know at least that their lives revolved around the water cycles of the Provo watershed (which was initially named Timpanogos after them), that they wintered on its banks and gathered in the springtime to celebrate the end of winter, to dance in honor of their ancestral bear, to catch fish and to begin the great gathering of food that would take them up the canyons and into the mountains in the summer and fall months, hunting big game. Bulrush, pine nuts, Bonneville trout, June suckers, whitefish, rabbit, elk, deer, antelope, mountain goat, water fowl. My bones ache every time I read about the quantity of fish in the river and in Utah Lake, to say nothing of the indigenous population that the Mormons pushed out to make their home. The harshest months were those before the break of spring when the Indians could only hope their winter supplies of dried fish, pressed fruit, and seeds lasted long enough. Living in the mountains means never knowing how long winter will last. Some years I can hike behind the mountains to nine thousand feet and find little or no snow in May, other years I may have to wait until June or July before the ground has cleared.

The name "Provo" had stuck by the time the Mormons settled along the banks of the river in 1849. Some twenty years or so before, a man named Etienne Provost passed through this valley and up into Salt Lake Valley seeking furs. The Timpanogots didn't give his men resistance but when he passed the point of the mountain to the north, he found himself surrounded by Shoshones who were seeking revenge for trappers who had stolen their horses the year before. Unaware of their plot for revenge, he was invited to smoke a peace pipe.

They sat in a circle around a fire in the nippy October air. The vast valley of Salt Lake lay to the north in the gathering afternoon light. Mount Olympus towered above them to the east and reflected its gray stones and deep pine strokes in brilliant variegation. The chief signaled that it was against custom to have metal objects near a peace pipe. Did they speak in broken French? English? Or did they communicate with hand signals the best they could? He knew enough about Indians to understand the importance of showing respect for their odd customs, so he immediately ordered his men seated in between Shoshones around the circle to place their guns at a remove from the fire.

"Are you sure this is wise?" one of his men asked under his breath.

"Go on, just do it," he answered.

He looked carefully into the chief's eye in order to detect any dishonesty, but the chief smiled broadly in appreciation. As the pipe made its way around the circle, the muscles in his face and in his back finally began to relax. The chief raised his left hand briefly and in an instant, he saw next to him his friend's neck slit as he fought off an attack from behind him. The cries of dying men filled the air as others screamed, "To the guns! To the guns!" Provost reached his first, shooting one Indian in the leg as he sprinted away from the circle. One, two, maybe three others followed—the accounts differ—as he made his way down the bluff toward what became known by the Mormons as Jordan River to seek protection from the arrows that showered them. One grazed him in the calf. The rest of the party, eight or so, lay in their own blood in the circle Provost had left behind.

Such experiences were perhaps well known to men like Provost, but the sudden and seemingly unwarranted violence of the encounter must have shaken them. He and the other survivors made their way back toward the mountains where they knew a crew of trappers had been encamped. Was it there that he learned of the revenge the Shoshone had sought? Provost would return the next year to Utah Valley, steering clear of the Shoshone. In 1836 the Jordan River appears as Proveau's Fork on a map, but the Mormons would call it Jordan. The name just migrated south to Mount Timpanogos to make room for a more Biblical narrative to the north. Eutaw. Ewtah. Utah. Proveau River. Provo River. Provo City. These names would come with the translations of time. Like all names, they slid into repose by accident, but once accidents become historical they seem as natural as the unchanging canyon walls.

By the time we scrambled through stands of aspen and pine, through deeply buried meadows, and a thicket of scrub oak, we were close to the top, and the sun was nakedly shining. At the summit, the white world around us refracted the slanted, hot light without compromise. The entire valley lay ensconced under the cover of inversion, which looked more like a naturally deep fog than some gaudy human pollution in the land. Out of the haze emerged the ringing horizon of mountains, standing bald and indifferent to the human world they no longer had to witness. My friend Chip brought a thermos of hot blueberry soup, a drink we passed around to each other in congratulations for the effort. For all appearances at this height, a healthy world of mountains, light, frozen water, and satisfied hearts.

One year when I took Paige and her friend snowshoeing at the cabin, the inversion was so bad we had to drive all the way to the overlook over Jordanelle Dam before we were clear of the soup that had enveloped Utah Valley, the entire Provo Canyon, and all of Heber Valley above. It was reportedly worse in Salt Lake, but that didn't seem to provide much comfort. The world was inverted, so instead of encountering colder temperatures as we ascended to seven thousand feet, it grew warmer, hovering just below freezing. When we arrived, we were walking on top of snow almost as deep as they are tall. The girls spilled across the field below the road with abandon, arriving at the frozen ice over the stream by the cabin. The water beneath the ice was only a few inches deep, but it still seemed to them audacious to cross over to the cabin.

Later, as we walked along a stretch of the Provo, we stopped to stare at the surface of the snow, which in many areas in the shade had developed several inches of impeccably symmetrical ice crystals that looked like small fans or wings or church windows. I could run my hands over the top and hear the small shards shattering. The girls compulsively scooped handfuls to eat at every chance, calling these special crystals the "tasties."

We saw evidence of what I had read in the paper about the successful return of the bald eagle—one flew south following the river above us, the first I had ever seen. The girls grew tired from the depth of the snow and rested where a spring still fed green watercress strangely moving in the water like clovers in the wind, surrounded by white stillness. On the drive home, the girls mentioned that a sixth-grader had formulated a project for the upcoming science fair to test the pollution levels of the snow in the valleys and compare them to those of the mountain snow.

Snow is grace to any westerner. Water experts and farmers alike are known to cry at the sight of deep snow pack. I have learned gratitude for seeing the waters moving slowly, giving off their winter steam, in the stillness of the mountains through the long months of forbearing accumulation. I have seen the source of Noblett's Creek that feeds the south fork of the Provo, a green mouth opening in the side of the mountain, a headspring spilling out of rock and over moss, surrounded by deep grooves of aging snow. In the summer this is bone-chilling water but here it looks like hot lava, melting a gaping hole for its exit into the air.

In the neighboring woods, I have heard the muffled cries of the numerous streams under deep covers of white powder that renders smooth the unruly edges of the earth. As I have searched for the origins of the milk-blood under the high mountain snows, I have been reassured that the small tributaries that gather to feed the Provo don't stop in the cold, still world. This instills hope, against my natural inclinations, because the mountains extend time in winter, which comes earlier and leaves later than it does in the valley. Snow's silent oblivion masks a deep pulse that beats quietly, steadily until the riotous days of spring. I like what Pablo Neruda wrote:

> Perhaps the earth can teach us
> as when everything seems dead
> and later proves to be alive.

Acclimating myself to the cold and escaping inversion before winter officially arrives, I have learned, help to fill reserves of sensation that I will need for the long months ahead. On another such effort, I invited Taylor to explore the watershed behind my father's cabin. Taylor, approaching fifty even though the only sign of age is his white shock of hair, is a former employee in Silicon Valley who retired early so that he could enjoy creative, recreational, and educational pursuits with abandon. We started on a road east of the cabin that follows the "Little South Fork" of the Provo. Directly to the north, the main stretch of the Provo flows from the Uinta Mountains to join forces with these waters gathering from the gentler mountains to the south. We faced a series of small rounded hills covered in pines and bald aspens, disguising the higher ranges behind. At first, the snow was a marvelous light powder that moved aside and blew through our snowshoes with each step. It hardly seemed possible that winter hadn't quite officially arrived. Underneath we could feel the more firm and dense snow of previous days, but since my poles had no baskets, I frequently found them slipping all the way to the ground, some four feet or more below in places of drift. Eventually we reached the end of a trail that had been created by others before us, so we blazed on by ourselves taking turns in the lead.

It became a moment lived in contrasts, the sun bright and spectacularly clear breaking through the dark green cover, light and dark playing on the surface of the snow, and temperatures wildly fluctuating between the warming, sunlit openings and the bone-numbing pockets of shade and canyon-guarded crevasses, the cold wet of the snow melting on our hot hands and steaming bodies whenever we stopped or fell. An hour passed, then two, as we broke through the trees from time to time to catch a glimpse of the opposite side of the ravine. Eventually the slope seemed to ease up, and we found ourselves walking parallel to Little South Fork, running untamed under the snow and occasionally exposing its dark stains in the open air as it emerged between mounds of snow cover. We could see that the snow was wont to aggressively accumulate here since even the trees appeared stunted by the weight.

In the spring, the earth's thirst would take the first few feet of snow underground but the generous remainder would be runoff for the Provo, for the rest of us. I have seen the violence that this portends at this altitude when the river spews downstream past the cabin in one long shot of water the color of milk chocolate, with the whipped cream of foaming waves twisting and contorting. When the water is that high, I can stand at the edge— where I normally would step down a good six feet to enter the gentle curves of the current—and see the water already pawing at my feet. I can't help thinking about the fish beneath, holding deep and close to the banks, hoping to survive the deluge.

Taylor and I noticed a line in the fresh snow crossing perpendicular to our chosen direction that bore the mark of a heavy, wide-bellied animal and then found bighorn sheep scat at the stream's edge. As my eyes followed the creek upstream, it appeared to dead-end in a ring of hills that surrounded the area, all providing spring water and runoff to the Provo. As we walked up an opening in the trees where a road no doubt passed, the aspens were covered with an offensive display of graffiti, carved by visitors from as far back as the 1970s, according to their mania of recording years, names, and obsessions. Several of the offenders seemed rather eager to lay claim to this territory on a number of occasions over several years. We must have seen the carved names of "Tip Allen" and "John Lee" and "Rod Fitzgerald," among others, a dozen times or more. There were also a few pot pipes crudely rendered and the repeating motif of a naked female torso. Taylor and I joked that one of the "artists" seemed to prefer a more shapely figure than the other. In fact, his Matisse nudes served for some time as our map to keep us on the path when the clearing and the blue diamonds on the trees had disappeared. I thought, too, of those secret signs for the mother lode of gold that legends say await the happy traveler in the Uintas.

In obscure history books about irrigation, I have seen black-and-white images of men working in the high Uintas, withstanding the intense mosquitoes and horseflies that abound in the ponds and lakes, during the months following winter's demise. In one image, a man stands with fists on his waist, standing proudly in the middle of the lake's stream that pours out into the forest below. They haul out corpses of trees cleared for the construction of small walls of stone. At the top of the wall one sees the headgate wheels that would increase or decrease the flow of water at the dam's bottom by means of a shovel-nosed blade that slid along the pipe's opening. White spume bursts out under the pressure of the swollen body of water.

In the early decades of the twentieth century, dozens of lakes were shored up with these small-scale dams to allow their levels to rise during spring runoff. With each lake's holding capacity increased significantly by some 30 to 40 percent, the mountains became a collective reservoir that farmers all along the Provo watershed could tap during the dry summer months. These elemental irrigation efforts of the early twentieth century compare favorably to the hubris of the later massive dam projects, so it is easy to be bitten by nostalgia's bug. Intoxicating images of the Stratton orchards flourishing on the Provo Bench on the northern end of Utah Valley, for example. Blossoms and bees swarming the air with sweetness and light. Day laborers, usually young men from the valley, hooting to each other atop creaky ladders, and a far cry from the haunting sounds of Utes hooting in the night around the small fort built on the banks of the Provo in 1849.

But then consider this. The Utes were friendly enough at the beginning, but their own economic desperation and a series of misunderstandings later cause violence to erupt. The peace of the orchards is facilitated by fiat from

President Lincoln who pushes the Utes east to a reservation in the Uintas. When the settlers get a taste of a river-fed life now that it is vacated by hungry and desperate Indians, their irrigation efforts increase. Now more aware of their dependence on the distant Uinta Mountains, it suddenly looks like a mistake to have ceded so much of the watershed to the reservation. Word had it that the government was growing impatient with the Indians' refusal to learn irrigation on their new reservation and the Mormons thought they might try their hand on higher ground. Even with a shorter growing season at higher altitudes, there was talk of using the idle canals on the reservation and damming the small lakes of the high mountains in order to build up storage for the valley.

August 1905, only forty years after Lincoln agreed to leave them in peace: half of the reservation is opened to homesteading by whites, thousands gather in downtown Provo for a lottery that announces the new homesteaders, the first a lucky Ray Daniel of Provo. The crowd explodes in jealous celebration. Swedes, Icelanders, Danish, and British, these were men less familiar with Indian life than their own fathers and grandfathers who had seen the Indians throughout the valley only a few decades earlier. Opportunity mixed with ignorance has more dire, even if less violent, consequences than direct intercourse with an alien people. Their arrival on the Uinta basin would bring them into contact with Indians soon enough, and most would learn charity and peaceful coexistence. But their march up toward the Uintas was also a march forward for modernization in the valley.

By 1910, high mountain dams are being erected, and some sixteen thousand acres in Utah Valley and to the north in Salt Lake Valley benefit. The Strawberry Project, the Bureau of Reclamation's first in the state of Utah, in 1902, channels the waters of the Colorado Plateau to the south of the Uintas into southern Utah Valley, laying the foundations that would enable the desert to blossom first as an agricultural and then as a suburban rose.

Only recently granted statehood in 1896 because of the end of polygamy in 1890, Utah was eager to seize the prospects for a more Americanized future. Some felt eager to leave the hard-scrabble pioneer life behind for educational and professional opportunities in the East, like my dad's father who became a banker, or in California, like my mom's father who became a soil engineer. But most remained in Utah to modernize the agricultural foundations of the pioneers. I have no small number of distant cousins among them, as became evident when I moved here. "Congratulations," the DMV clerk said behind the counter, as if this were his favorite Utah joke, "you are the sixth George Handley in the state." I didn't believe him, so to prove it, he swiveled the computer monitor so that I could see the six names flashing in neon green letters. One was my grandfather, but the others? Still haven't met them, except in the mirror.

Utah would remain the heartland of Mormonism despite a conscious shift away from "gathering in Zion" to "building the kingdom" wherever you lived. Joseph Smith's visions of urban development, which Brigham Young tried assiduously to realize, followed in the tradition of Thomas More's Utopia and Jefferson's dream of an America of the small farmer, twenty acres a lot for Smith in close proximity to one another to foster communitarian values and shorten the distance between urban and rural cultures. Brigham Young agreed to explore the Uinta Basin for irrigation potential to help stem the growing tide of urban development in Salt Lake City, which he thought was eroding Mormon values. The report he received was that the Uinta watershed was a "contiguity of waste" and only good "to hold the world together." The Mormons went anyway.

Homesteading on the Indian reservation offered 160-acre lots and encouraged the kind of prospecting Smith and Young seemed to want to control. But if this is the beginning of the dramatic transformation of the watershed, it seems odd that today one sees these few remaining family ranches of the Uinta Basin as swaths of land that do more than hold the world together; they hold the memories of the land that are all but gone in Utah Valley below where suburban blight rules the roost. The distance between the more urbanized Wasatch Front and the rural flavor of these highlands is greater than mileage can measure. I feel it every time I drive by irrigation water spilling across the fields of alfalfa under the Wasatch Mountains to the west and at the feet of the Uintas to the east. Every time I buy gas at a local station and hear the strange sound of my accentless English or feel conscious of my economy-size Japanese car.

Family farming in Utah resisted the industrial pull toward larger-scale production in places like California, as is evidenced by the farms still in operation here at the feet of the Uintas, and agriculture still lays claim to the majority of the state's water supply. But small-scale agriculture is certainly an endangered species, always threatened nowadays by the encroaching demands of suburban housing and recreational homes, everyman's *coin de terre*. But at least at these higher altitudes, suburban spraddle is hard to imagine. Thank goodness.

Farmers aren't extinct, not yet, but it seems you have to interview an octogenarian to know anything of such life anymore. It wasn't long ago that you could hear the wistfulness in the voices of elder Mormon leaders who would sometimes speak allegories of, say, feeding pigs, or jumping the old irrigation canals, but if Mormonism was going to save traditional values and retain a sense of community, it was going to have to focus on the individual family household. Sermons about the vital connection to land that was presumed to sustain those values went the way of the farm itself. Maybe that's why I feel like a fish returning to the spawning grounds, resisting the downward drag to stasis. It was here in the Uintas where life in the valleys below was made modern. Not an innocent beginning, to be sure, but a beginning nonetheless and a dependence on a watershed that we could stand to relearn.

In my need to explore this watershed, I am not alone. A small number of descendents of early pioneers continue to spend their lives looking in vain for the lost mines of colonial Spanish gold bricks reportedly hidden up in the mountains. Brother Brigham wouldn't approve since he preached frequently against the dangers of the earth's treasures, but legend has it that Young's emissary, one Thomas Roades, was shown gold mines in the high Uintas by the Ute Indians, mines believed to have been created by the Spanish in the 1700s with Indian slavery. The secret to their location is believed to have been buried and resurrected again and again in a series of mishaps, lost maps, premature deaths, accidents, and Indian resistance.

Testimonials of God's hidden purposes abound: perhaps the Mormons couldn't handle such wealth, or, my favorite, maybe Spanish gold fueled the Mormons out of financial misery in the early twentieth century. There was the deathbed map drawn by Roades's son. The maps stolen from Roades's great-great-grandson, Gale, after his death in 1988, and the empty briefcases found on the debauched sofa in his spent trailer home. Gale wasted twenty years blasting through tunnels all over the Uintas, dying divorced, cigarette-sunken, and poor.

Somewhere along the line the missing mines became known as "sacred," at least to those who cared. One man claimed he had found them but couldn't come up with a sufficient explanation for why he continued to work at the local grocery store and drive an old Chevy truck. At gas stations in the Uinta Basin, one can find copies of self-published books about gold mines in the mountains written by modern mountain men. One such book (okay, I confess that I bought one) shows a man dressed in full regalia:

he holds a shotgun on his shoulder and looks wistfully off into the distance (even though he is clearly inside a studio), wearing a chamois and Indian jewelry, with animal skins draping his chair. He writes of secret signs carved on trees and rocks, providing the reader initiation into occult knowledge that will tame the threat of wilderness and provide material recompense beyond all imagining. These are the Harlequin romances of the hard life of ranching country, the fantasies of generations whose fragile existence in the high drylands of the Colorado Plateau never found sufficient stability or trust in a modern government that catered to increasing numbers of professionals.

No doubt that local community is a value, but if it comes at the cost of trust in civic society, the wagons are circled and the world outside turns intolerably strange. Even teenage graffiti of nude women and pot pipes can be imagined as a lost Spanish language of orienteering. Rock art, rather than suggesting a depth of history that should humble the onlooker, becomes an invitation to exploit. Abandoned mine shafts are so many fragments of an unknown past, hieroglyphs whose decoded meaning passes from father to son. Once a source of humility and awe, nature's strangeness is reduced to a cartographic paper-and-parchment deed to genealogical rights of freedom from all cares. This is the pornographic version of Isaiah's promise. Pictures fill the pages of the books, leaving these poor sots and their hapless readers no peace as they fill themselves with toxic nostalgia for the mother lode of the past.

The fragments of the West's past could stand some reassembling but not because a coherent memory makes a man rich. Coherence isn't what's needed—it isn't a coherent history anyway—but rather the imagination to bring the land's strangeness into close familiarity again. The odd east/west trajectory of the Uintas across the Colorado Plateau, their drainage into the Green River and into a dead sea in the Great Basin—this geography was an empty and largely flat space on maps for close to four hundred years, a veritable *terra incognita*. The progression of images from the 1500s starts with a continent that looks like a small embryo, in the shape of a seahorse, morphing into its satellite shape; first sprout the southern regions of Baja, California, then northern Mexico, New Mexico, the Sierras, and the California coastline. Not until the late nineteenth century do we begin to see the geographical reality of the Great Basin.

It was a hard truth to swallow. The space was filled with myths of watersheds flowing to the Pacific, which was the great hope that had chased

Escalante across the southern stretch of the West in 1776 and later Lewis and Clark to the north in 1803. For almost a hundred years in the eighteenth to the early nineteenth centuries, rumors of a great river grow and spread. The Rio Buenaventura, the River of Good Fortune, was believed to extend from the northeast where the Uintas now lie to a large saline lake, the western limits of which were not known. The hope was that the river continued westward to the sea. Was this Good Fortune the Green River? The Provo? The Weber? The Bear? In any case, it did not offer the sought-after passage to the sea. The most mountainous region in the country and yet one of the driest, much of Utah was once a great lake of staggering proportions and before that an ocean. Now we erect civilization on an ancient raft built by silt and floating on disappearing water tables.

The Great Basin would be the promised land to that long line of Mormon pioneers who left the outer limits of the United States on foot to found their own kingdom. It seemed more than mere coincidence that they found themselves in a desert where a river connected a saline sea to a freshwater lake. The world, it turned out, was a mirror, divided by wide seas. New World metaphors would not suffer the existential anxiety of the Old World because this land could hear its own echoes. Let there be Jordan River, and there it was, a reversible world, a dead sea to the north instead of to the south, and let exile be a prodigal return, and they saw that it was good.

Seeing a satellite map of the Great Basin, you notice the lines of mountain ranges that move across its floor like so many waves, pages turning through time, belying times when the earth was still strange, when man didn't need outer space to conjure images of strange beings because home was strange enough. There is something profoundly truthful in these cartographical fictions, these pre-satellite attempts to imagine and name rivers and mountains. But this wouldn't be the first time fiction is more truthful than history. Take enough steps back in time and no river, lake, or mountain range retains its shape, a geological reality refracted in the imagination of mapmakers who, with the ever-changing flow of empirical knowledge, took the clay of the world into their hands like some god on the sixth day and declared the world good, and known.

Take the explorer Alexander von Humboldt, for example, who has a river named after him despite his having never stepped foot in the Great Basin. In 1809, Humboldt draws two lakes—a Salt Lake and a Lake Timpanogos to the north. In subsequent mappings of the region by other explorers, this will change—the Salt Lake will appear to the north and Timpanogos to the south, and sometimes they appear on maps as the same lake. Might Timpanogos be Utah Lake, fed by the Provo? On Humboldt's map, we see a mountain range to the east and the words *Yutas-Tabeguachis Indians*. And then the stunning declaration next to the freshwater lake: "This lake, the limits of which are imperfectly known from the journals of Father Escalante, is perhaps the Teguayo Lake, from the borders of which, according to some Historians, the Azteques removed to the river Gila." Lower, in what is now southeastern Utah, we see the word *Aztlán*. The heartland of the Aztecs in Utah? At the confluence of the Green and Colorado, perhaps—that seems more likely, according to most historians—but Utah Lake, homeland now to tens of thousands of Mormons, homeland to the largest population of Icelanders outside of Iceland, Scandinavians of various stripes, Welsh and English descendents, all contracting skin cancer in the high thin air of the Mountain West at alarming rates? But also the gathering place for one of the fastest-growing Hispanic populations in the country. So why not?

The Dominguez-Escalante expedition coming up from Santa Fe was led by two Indians, a father and son he named Silvestre and Joaquin, who hailed from the shores of Utah Lake. They traveled down what is now Spanish Fork Canyon named in Escalante's honor and contemplated a thriving ecosystem rife with wildlife, fish, and ample freshwater supplies. A few years ago the Mormons erected a Catholic cross on a bluff there to honor the expedition. Escalante thought Utah Valley might sustain a population as numerous as Mexico City. He called it Valle de Nuestra Señora de Merced de Timpanogos. Careening into this new century, we can only hope he had no prophetic gifts. Their expedition was originally planned for July 4, 1776. Spanish explorers aided by Indians honored by Mormons and echoed by the arrival of contemporary Mexicans. Sounds more like Interdependence Day.

Mexicans and other Latin Americans who come to these Edenic shores today arrive too late to witness its wild offerings of 150 years ago, but they still hope for a Promised Land, a blossoming desert as their recompense, and perhaps belatedly fulfill Escalante's broken promise to return within the year. The fictions of history suggest that their arrival in Utah is a homecoming. If the Aztecs migrated from a territory to the north prior to their establishment of the city of Tenochtitlan in 1325, it suddenly seems more than coincidence that Anasazi ruins throughout Utah and the Southwest indicate a disappearance at some time roughly corresponding to an Aztec migration.

In Mexico City, I have seen the sacred codex that depicts the migration, a figure of a woman carrying a wrapped cloth on her back that grows into a child, while small footprints move relentlessly from left to right. A large tree is chopped down, and underneath its roots protrude small, anthropomorphic feet. That the Ute and Hopi languages appear related to Nahuatl has given some credence to this theory. How far north the migration began remains a mystery, but, who knows, it might have been Utah Valley, the Great Salt Lake, or the Uinta Mountain range.

So I wonder how a Promised Land can be a land for everyone. Armando Solórzano, a Mexican sociologist at the University of Utah, posits the idea of "Aztlan-Zion," a hybrid imaginary that connects the mythology of origins for Mormon, Mexicans, and Native Americans. This seems like a step in the right direction. The default solution so far has been to wish history away, especially any history that is not part of your own genealogy. But if genealogy teaches anything, it is how narrow and contingent our understanding of kinship is. The stories of Native Americans, Hispanic immigrants, the tales of Mormon pioneer faith and suffering, and many more deserve an equally compassionate ear. Disinterest in the human dignity of one group of people in the interest of the dignity of others hardly seems an adequate response.

Perhaps the lives wasted in pursuit of lost treasure can serve as a warning. Their treasure seeking is a manic search for deep, singular belonging that will be complete by answering the riddles of the land and of ancestry simultaneously, not to mention the freedom from responsibility to community that the treasures will purchase. The riddles of the human past are more interconnected than we often remember, but even more importantly, the riddles of the land belong to everyone who drinks the water of these mountains, and they will not be solved within the limited scope of any one particular tribal memory.

Like spawning fish pushing our way up our distinct tributaries, the water will eventually bring us to the same genesis. One has only to consider what happens when the whole landscape is turned into a hieroglyph of the story of one's exceptional liberation, when the land is a veil hiding the materialization of one's individual wishes. As much as I might try, I cannot convert these mountains and this Provo River into a sign of history I think I want to honor. What rides on these waters is the stuff of the past, to be sure, and it arrives on banks under my feet, but their refractions are too innumerable for me to ever be sure of where I really am. And that's the peace they afford.

Taylor and I had turned to the east and were looking for another turn to the north to form a loop around the mountain, but it occurred to us at some point that we had not seen a tree carving for some time and had lost the trail altogether. We turned to the left again, rose up to the top of what felt like a mesa, and headed toward where we believed our car would be. We did not anticipate how the increasing cloud cover would scatter the light indistinctly in all directions nor how the undulating hills and turning ravines would defy our confidence in knowing where we had already been. Of course, we knew that we could always follow our trail back exactly as we had come, but we had reached the point of no return, since going back would likely get us to our car after dark. Snow began to fall heavily, erasing any hope of human memory in the landscape.

I pulled out my compass to orient us, hoping to overcome the mountains' deceptions. It was deep enough on this mesa, I told Taylor that for all we knew the snow was covering the Matisse nudes that had been our guide. "Good," he said, "it was bad art anyway." I didn't disagree, but it would have been nice to know someone had come this way before, that this was not unmapped, unclaimed. At one point, the snow beneath us suddenly shifted and we froze looking for a telltale crack somewhere around us, as if we might begin surfing at any moment. We weren't on a steep incline, so there was no immediate danger of an avalanche, but the varying density of snow layers beneath us left the ground unstable. The movement was accompanied by a loud hissing, as if a large and gaping air pocket in the middle of the snow had just expired through some small hole somewhere. This happened several more times as we crossed the top of this small mountain, each time stopping us in our tracks and making our hearts race.

Eventually the ground beneath began tipping downhill as we had expected. The descent was steep, dropping at some forty degrees through a dense forest of pines. Fallen trees hid themselves beneath the snowpack at unpredictable intervals. "Be careful," said Taylor. "A friend of mine snapped his leg on one of those skiing." After taking a few more seemingly eternal detours left and right, we were rewarded with the trail that runs along Little South Fork at the mouth of the canyon. The bad news was that it looked like we were a good hour from the car, and my legs had nothing left. Taylor seemed eternally chipper, and as we climbed some of the last hills, I told him I could no longer converse until we were on the final descent.

We finally arrived, of course, but significantly later than we had hoped, and all of a sudden my evening's obligations fell heavily on my mind. I drove frantically to a phone to excuse my absence from dinner and from some church obligations I had that night. Amy didn't seem bothered, but then again, I had learned that didn't always mean she wasn't. She was determined to be supportive of my need to explore, but I had to worry if it was starting to take a toll because it was unlikely she would tell me in time to make needed adjustments. We had hiked for over seven hours in deep snow, and I had seen far more evidence of the power and depth of mountain precipitation and had experienced far more sensation than I had bargained for. Maybe it was my Mormon propensity for domestic guilt, but when I returned home to Amy—busy and unreadable as usual—and my house abuzz with the usual evening activities of piano and violin practicing, chores, and bedtime routines, I couldn't escape feeling selfish both for the pleasures I had experienced and for my utter exhaustion. At least I knew that I had purchased some emotional fuel to push me through the coming onslaught of December's long dark. That night Amy and I were both too tired to talk much, but lying next to her warmth in bed, I could still feel my blood flushed to the edges of my skin, healing the muscles, warming the extremities, and working to assimilate my deepened awareness of the snowpack.

Interlude

I HAD BEEN PRETTY METHODICAL ABOUT MY TRIPS, WORKING MY WAY down from the upper reaches of the Provo River watershed to my home in Utah Valley, but I couldn't resist an invitation to move in the opposite direction and drive in the depth of winter out to Robert Smithson's *Spiral Jetty* on the north shore of the Great Salt Lake. This would be an opportunity to compare the heights of the watershed in winter with its ultimate culmination at the depths of this New World Dead Sea. The goal was to arrive at the site by dawn, so my friend Tom and a scholar from the Getty picked me up before five a.m. This was my first descent, since moving to Utah, to the shoreline of the Salt Lake, and I was eager to see the saline stillness of the water that begins on the western half of the north and south slopes of the Uinta range and gathers force from the Wasatch Front.

On the drive, we discussed the deep inversion we have been trapped in for a few weeks, a topic on everyone's lips these days. I mentioned one expert's claim that depression at this time is not due to seeing gray, polluted light and breathing dirt for days on end but simply to the longer nights of winter. Suffering myself from an unprecedented and growing suffocation, I mention that it seems like insisting on the technicality that it was pneumonia, not cancer, that killed the patient ravaged by chemotherapy.

After more than two hours of driving, we left the highway and started west until we arrived at Promontory Point. Glances in all directions revealed no sign of people anywhere, just open space surrounded in the far distance by rings of mountains. From there we ventured south on a ranching road for what seemed like an hour, driving over rough terrain in what appeared to be about two feet of snow. The sky above us was already glowing from the dawn light, and the car indicated that the temperature outside was hovering around zero degrees, at one point reaching as low as six below. Fortunately we were in a Jeep that managed the snow well. We hit patches of intense fog on and off as we drew nearer to the lake, never having the assurance until we finally arrived that we would be able to see anything at all.

As we got out of the car and walked around a corner to the shore where we could make out the jetty, the sun had just started to rise over the peaks to the east. The air was shockingly clear this far north of any human habitation. Looking directly south, we could make out the dense, inverted air hanging over the southern and eastern shores of the lake. I found myself standing at different angles from the jetty along the shoreline, confounded by the synchronicity between the turning lines of the jetty, the serpentine shoreline, and the pink cloud line above us that obeyed the contours of the shore. The striations on the crystallized floor of salt joined in the rhythm as they widened in concentric lines outward from the spiral.

Built in 1970, the jetty was once a casualty of floods in the 1980s but is now a gauge of the drought since it recently resurfaced and became visible again. The scholar of Smithson from the Getty was like a child at a dinosaur museum, giddy at the prospect of seeing in real time and space a work that has been submerged for so long. What impressed me more than the jetty itself was its reemergence into a staggering environment that appeared to have reclaimed it. The water had receded to the point that only a small and absolutely still pool of water remained in the centermost circles. In the clear air, however, the water seemed somewhat opaque, like colored glass. Only inches deep, it lay on top of a salt-crystal floor that resembled white marble and reflected the pink light of the sky.

This stood in startling contrast to the jetty itself, which was sealed in a white diamond coat of hardened salt crystals, shining like fragile snow powder but maintaining the texture and solidity of stone. The crystals reached to just an inch or two above the water, leaving a gap and creating the appearance that the jetty was hovering. It seemed that in the delicate equipoise between drought and flood, between bounty and deprivation, the spiral jetty had found a temporary and precarious balance between liquid and solid, earth and sky, humanity and nature. A way of accepting what sometimes feels like the fickleness of the Lord's recompenses.

The air held absolutely still, the water showed not a single ripple of change, while the hard bite of the cold began to numb the feet and hands and to tear the eyes, requiring me to rock back and forth as I stared at the scene. If Smithson had intended a work of art that merged with the entropy of nature and eventually led to the disappearance of his human hand, then he succeeded fabulously. As the earth artist Andy Goldsworthy says, "Total control can be the death of work."

The *New York Times* story about restoring the jetty struck me as a ridiculous and self-defeating project, its proponents clearly having no appreciation for the extraordinary beauty of this place and the sculpting power of the lake itself. That was no new irony, of course, at least when it comes to perceptions of Utah and the West. In the metropolitan narratives nothing really happens here until the gaze of the Eastern Seaboard arrives with its patronizing appreciation. If it is true that Smithson himself may have been vulnerable to this kind of metropolitan bias and picked the lakeshore because of his penchant for ravaged and discarded places, he may have made a fabulously fortuitous misjudgment of this spot. He claimed that he chose the location because it was a dead and wasted sea, and he sought the red tones of the water as his blood pigment. Dead and wasted, maybe, but not without regenerative powers, because there was little doubt that the lake had become the proprietor of the jetty and fashioned it after its own image and likeness, an irony I hoped Smithson would have enjoyed.

It is a strange thing, art. Recreating the conditions upon which an initial shock strikes the soul, reformulating the elements of the world into a new world, only to have to acknowledge that the world never needed our impotent praise. Smithson claimed he didn't owe his existence to anyone, but no one can make this claim with impunity. Call it God, the divine light, or simply the numinous, but the subject's subjection is the rule. Joseph Smith called it Christ and saw it everywhere, even in the light of the sun, making our perception of things a discovery of our answerability:

> The light of truth is … [t]he light of Christ. As also he is in the sun, and the light of the sun, and the power thereof by which it was made. As also he is in the moon, and is the light of the moon, and the power thereof by which it was made; As also the light of the stars, and the power thereof by which they were made. And the earth also, and the power thereof, even the earth upon which you stand. And the light which shineth, which giveth you light, is through him who enlighteneth your eyes, which is the same light that quickeneth your understandings; which light proceedeth forth from the presence of God to fill the immensity of space—the light which is in all things, which giveth life to all things, which is the law by which all things are governed, even the power of God who sitteth upon his throne, who is in the bosom of eternity, who is in the midst of all things.[25]

Light is, at first, a metaphor of Christ, of truth, but then we are told that this truth is both "in" the light of the sun and moon and moreover "is" that light and also the power by which it was made. The metaphor loses its shape entirely when this light of Christ becomes the very light by which we perceive the physical world around us. I always learned that metaphors were a way of dreaming of likeness between two unlike things, but now I find that the world is inverted, that differences are the real illusions and that metaphors are a way of imagining them. Like that flash of lightning in a kiss, that sudden discovery of ourselves as physical phenomena, as if we are surprised to find ourselves here, now on this earth, in individual bodies. Which only suggests that we spend a great deal of our time sensing that we inhabit something more than a body even if this feels uncannily like home.

Joseph Smith seemed to be saying that the discovery of the physical world is not a discovery of our alienation from the divine, or a second order of our being, but rather, as the men on the road to Emmaus learned, that the divine has place in the very stuff of our physical existence. Only two verses later, he states simply that "the spirit and the body constitute the soul of man." It is not insignificant, even if seemingly contradictory, that this ubiquitous divinity would be found in a theology that posits the physicality and situatedness of God. Smith's name for this place, Kolob, is also the name of a canyon in Zion National Park, and anyone who has ever been to that canyon won't argue the point that the name might not be merely metaphorical. The rub is that we see only light's reflection, not light directly, so perhaps we are always having to turn around only to be denied the ability to look directly into the source of our ecstasies. Hope is believing that if I keep turning and absorb enough of light's reflections, I will hold the substance of the whole within the inner eye.

Is the jetty on the verge of disappearing again? The snow fell later that week and the inversion cleared, offering a faint glimmer of hope for the end of drought and the prospect of its burial again. The elements inspire the spirals of our minds, but once set free into space, we no longer control the turning. It seems we are asked to learn tolerance for a world that erases all trace of our art, or at the very least so thoroughly recompenses so as to erase the divide that separates us from the unfettered wild. After the floods of the 1980s, millions of dollars were spent, far more than it would have cost to compensate individual homeowners for losses sustained in the flood, to build huge pumps at the edge of the lake. These pumps, built to direct overflow water into the nearby Newfoundland Basin, stand unused and at a significant distance from the shoreline after years of increasing drought. Given recent global climate prognostications of a possible 50 percent reduction of snowpack over the next fifty years, it seems unlikely the pumps will ever be useful enough to have justified their cost. They are the anti-art, the utter intolerance for the natural ebb and flow of a watershed and for the mounting evidence of the human hand spiraling out of control in the very workings of the climate. Signs, then, of impatience at finding ourselves in these particular bodies, in this particular and strange home.

I think what Paul meant to tell the Hebrews had something to do with the fact that faith is a principle of action, that labor on behalf of what is anticipated helps to bring another world closer to the surface of the visible. Faith is not waiting for revelation but anticipating it by working to make flesh the world of the imagination. When you begin to believe you see the Promised Land in the works of your own hands and lose your sense of comparison with an unseen world, faith has ceased and you have crossed the fine and dangerous line between art and idolatry. The city of God becomes Main Street, USA.

Hedonism is a denial of the uncertainties of mortality and the unpredictability of nature. If religion hopes to be the antidote, it must not lose patience with these contingencies. Then we lose out on those blessed intimations of heaven on earth, the radiant, burning heat of life that is our gift and His revelation. We lose our humanity. Among other things, the Mormon account of the creation teaches that we can identify spiritually valuable and ethical uses of natural resources only after our perspective has been informed by a sense of wonder regarding our spiritual kinship with the whole of the earth.

There is no room in this theology for believing that whatever we choose to do to nature is holy simply by virtue of being able to do it. Only those acts that respect our kinship with the creation are holy, redemptive, and provide the recompenses of a fortunate fall, a fall into blessedness. Acts that decrease wonder, teach us that nature is mere dead matter, stop our growth of understanding, or insist there is no way to act in our human self-interest *and* in the interest of the web of life, are profane, tragic, and therefore provide the recompenses of the unfortunate fall into man's profound alienation from God.

There are two kinds of millennia: one in which God destroys the works of humankind and replaces them with His; and the other in which civilization more and more resembles the City of God until it is no longer possible for God to withhold Himself. Just another example, I suppose, of how we are always choosing between fear and love.

I wasn't able to resist the temptation to touch the briny water, even if it meant that I sent rings of ripples outward, shattering the mirror that linked heaven and earth. My hand burned. So this is how it ends, I thought, cupping its liquid form in my hand in defiance of the freezing temperatures. The solidity of all things is the lake's pretense until someone arrives to disturb its shores. So you know its secret. Big deal. Even if the oblivious tendencies of water are a mirage and even if you can't dance your way into disappearance, there is art in imagining otherwise.

Winter

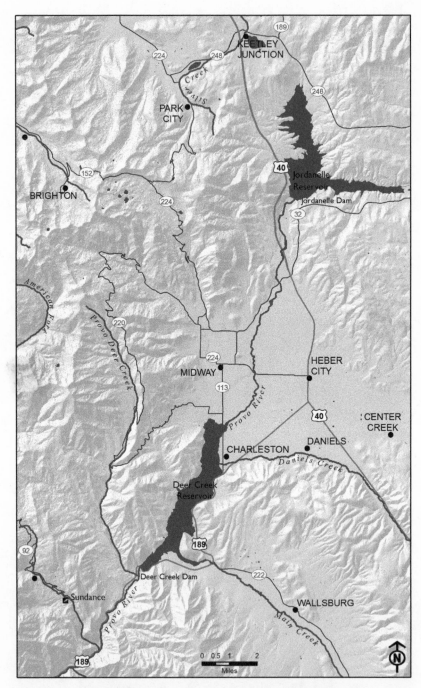

THE MIDDLE PROVO RIVER IN HEBER VALLEY

Seven

LIGHT CASTS SHADOWS ACROSS THE WHITE SURFACE OF THE TABLECLOTH, giving the appearance of weight to the cooked flesh of some fowl, life to the juicy grapes in the basket, and fluidity to the undisturbed water poised in the goblet. Caravaggio's beardless, almost adolescent Savior raises his hand in a declarative that seems to say, Here, now, this moment of the flesh is the eternal substance, the restored life of things, everything as it once was, as it will always be.

On a university stint in London, I found myself transfixed by this invented image of the supper at Emmaus, hanging on the wall of the National Gallery, a fictional representation of a story repeated through the centuries of a meal shared with the resurrected Lord, the moment of revelation, this "here, now" as restoration after our patient waiting. Luke says that the Lord ate with two men but Caravaggio adds a third, a man standing over Christ's shoulder in the shadows who seems intent on fixing his eyes on Christ, trusting that his senses will eventually tell him how to react to what he has seen. The disciple seated to the left pushes off of his elbows from the impact. His gaze is focused on the food as if the event has transformed his relationship to the task of feeding himself. The man seated on the right throws his arms out as if to try to take in the whole of it, staring indirectly at the entire scene of this Immanuel at this small table. Caravaggio will spend the few years that remain for him still making the attempt, I think. I wonder if art gives substance to dreams or if divine revelation confirms the reality of illusions. The senses mark the bodily limits of our knowing but perhaps, too, they are the portals of contact with the spirit.

Mormonism is a religion of restoration, not reformation, which is a bit like saying that its motion is not with but against the grain of the ripples of water a pebble stirs. It seeks to go back to that moment of impact when spirit first moved upon the face of the waters. This is the faith of all forms of knowledge, the trust in what Marilynne Robinson calls the "law of completion." It is to believe that moving water can tell the story of its rocky origins, that somewhere in the microcosmic structures of its flowing particles, somewhere in the play between the sound of its splashing surface and its gurgling undertones beneath, is the genetic code of the cosmos itself. It is to believe that stillness wants motion, and motion wants stillness, that sands and silt as broken shards are already and always the stuff of the whole, still earth.

If Christ is the cornerstone dropped in the pools of time, restoration becomes a reckoning with the fragmentations that his earth-shattering contact with the human and natural realm of this life has caused. It is to be about the business of gathering the broken mirror of human experience in order to imagine in its rough assemblage the face of the divine. If there is no thought that remains forgotten and all things ever imagined some day will come to remembrance, revelation is a restoration of what was always known. This is, anyway, the hope of art and the faith of religion.

The man looking on is mesmerized by the glistening sweat of the grapes, by the way the circle of light refracts through the carafe of water, spills onto the tablecloth, and reflects again onto the glass, the way the surfaces of all things refuse opacity. All this in the presence of a God in the flesh. He is struck, as I am, by the oxymoron of eternal transience. It is the work of restoration to have the eye of a William Blake, in his "Auguries of Innocence," a poem I return to again and again:

> To see a World in a grain of sand,
> And a Heaven in a wild flower,
> Hold Infinity in the palm of your hand
> And Eternity in an Hour.

And I wonder if this feels like a kind of repentance, an awareness that time inevitably runs short. Perhaps what blinds us is a homing desire for stasis, control, for nature as commodity, a refusal of atonement. As Blake puts it simply:

> A robin redbreast in a cage
> Puts all heaven in a rage.

The scarcity of water makes home vulnerable, of course, but as the most fluid of nature's offerings, water is also the most defiant of attempts to hold it still. Red canyon walls throughout the deserts of southern Utah are stony, palpable memorials to the invisible, sculpting hand of the water that has escaped. Everything I see is really only a museum to a great ocean floor, shells crushed into stone at seven thousand feet of elevation. Arid country requires an imagination of the not-there-anymore, but once the scales fall, cascades drop before the eyes and tremulous, aching arteries quiver beneath every step. Then it becomes a matter of keeping your head above the water.

It is certainly a lot easier to remember the rule of water after an intense winter storm. Winter semester was a few days off, the kids were restless, and we had just received a spectacular storm on New Year's Eve. The next morning presented a chance to explore Heber Valley and the Middle Provo. Assembled into the car first thing in the morning, we drove the forty minutes to Midway to rent snowshoes near Wasatch State Park where we could hike in the deep powder. Amy and I had only been snowshoeing a few times before, but it was a first for all of the children. We were most unsure about how Sam, just days away from turning five, would handle it. But the store had snowshoes of all sizes, some small enough, it seemed, to fit a large doll, and Sam was game.

The sky was a mix of departing storm clouds, hovering mists wrapped around the foothills, and cobalt blue expanses with bright sun piercing the clouds and radiating on the intense white surface of the snow. Large billows of snow hung heavy on tree branches drooping into the street, its surface finally warming and melting after a seemingly unstoppable storm had shut down the area's residents for the past two days. Portions of the air filled with still-falling snow wherever darker clouds still lingered, creating the impression of Turner's sublime brushstrokes of white density falling from a dissipating threat in the sky.

The eastern face of Timpanogos towers over this valley from the west, and yet it was shrouded almost entirely by the clouds, only hinting at its presence. I had been in this valley many times, but it looked entirely new and strange, which is the paradox, of course, of intense snowfall, since the monotonous sameness of white can spread across the world and make it seem reborn and perpetually strange.

We stopped in a plowed clearing where a handful of cars were already parked near the entrance and put on the shoes. As we entered the park, we immediately found ourselves in deep powder, deep enough to exhaust the hips from the high stepping such snowshoeing requires. We went in order of weight and height, I first, then Amy, Eliza, Paige, Camilla, and Sam in the rear, so that the snow would be increasingly packed down for the smaller kids. Even so, the snow was so dry and light, as it often is in this climate and at this altitude, it felt as if we were just temporarily clearing downy feathers. Although we made several efforts at a formal fight, snowballs were virtually impossible to make. The cold was unrelenting, the kind that pierces the lungs, burns the eyes, and aches in the bones, but as the trail began to ascend in the deep powder, our bodies exerted enough energy to warm us up.

By the time we had gone only a quarter of a mile or so, we were shedding coats while steam seeped through the edges of our clothing, off of our necks and faces, and into the winter light. The kids groaned a bit at the beginning, so Amy and I worked up a few games to keep them distracted. We formed a starting line and I timed foot races. Everyone paired up against everyone else, running until we were exhausted and giddy. Occasionally, we ventured away to explore ravines, willow groves, and the protection of large pines that could be shaken to create the stage effect of a blizzard. We pulled a sled to provide a break for anyone who needed it.

Amy and I had drifted to the back as we watched the kids tumble their way down the back side of the loop we had taken. After a teenage life of meandering passions and questionable choices, an abrupt shock at age eighteen with the loss of my brother and my awareness of my mortality, and some prolonged soul-searching and repentance, I finally found myself living a life of faith and by my early twenties in love with this woman. The self-disgust and frustration with my imperfect self-control has never entirely left me, and it remains a temptation to sink into despair at the thought that real change—a new creature with a new heart—might be an illusion. But now I have four children, new lives brought into the world, and an entirely new set of human horizons to worry about.

There is redemption in this work and play. It is not that I couldn't have had different children and a different life or that no other happiness would have been possible for me, but I tried haltingly to express something of my gratitude for the particular life we had forged together and for the particular joy of these children here in front of us, all of which was made possible by her willingness to love someone who had been off the beaten path of traditional Mormon clean living. I reminded her of the conversation we had when we were dating that had pierced me to the bone. Many years ago now, she was telling me about a conversation she had with two of her girlfriends when they were in their teens. One of them had taken a rather dogmatic view about former sins she would never tolerate in a future husband, and Amy and the other friend had tried to soften her attitude.

"Even if he fully repented?" Amy had asked.

"Yes, even if. I just don't want that baggage."

"Then you don't really believe in the Atonement," the other friend responded. Amy told me this story before she knew of my particular past mistakes, and it was a godsend. It gave me the confidence to believe that even though repentance doesn't make things exactly as they could have been, it is only by forgiving ourselves and others that we give change a chance.

Stopped by a tree where she could trace animal tracks in the snow, Camilla announced:

"I want to be a biologist, or a veterinarian. I think it would be fun."

"You would make a good one. You are always gentle with animals," said Amy.

We both remembered a similar moment when she was even younger, squatting down and pouring red sand through her fingers in southern Utah on a family hike. "I love the desert," she had said, all of five years old and sounding like a monk in meditation. She has always been a quiet, reflective child, one given to moments of surprising verbal clarity. For her sake, I wish pets and farm livestock were not all that remains of human/animal relations in a hemisphere that saw no pigs, horses, or cattle until the advent of Spanish explorations in the sixteenth century. These waters provided sanctuary for elk, moose, bobcats, and lions, and sustained native whitefish, Bonneville cutthroat, mottled sculpin, and other fish with histories that dwarf any of our documented human ancestries. The big game have adapted to the higher reaches of the surrounding mountains, and the waters are now overrun by brown, brook, and rainbow trout, smallmouth bass, carp, and a host of others; these are the species introduced from other areas of the Americas or Europe that mirror the majority of the American population's deep history of transplantation.

There is an inescapable feeling of having been cheated or of intentionally cheating myself whenever I have caught introduced trout in high mountain lakes and streams. Helicopters fly over the high Uinta range and drop fingerlings into the lakes for fools like me seeking their Edens. A hatchery lies just a few miles from where we were snowshoeing. Their fish are recognized most often by one clipped side fin. But only 1 percent of all stocked fish are dropped in the high Uinta wilderness and 6 percent into the streams; 93 percent go to the reservoirs which are increasingly the recreational attraction.[26]

While the majority of these fish are not native to Utah, without the hatcheries, no protection of native species would occur at all. These kickback benefits come from strange parasitical branches of the government, quietly trying to undo the damage of reclamation. These hatcheries have the difficult task of cleaning up after the government as a government entity, protecting endangered species while trying to meet the demand for sustainable recreational opportunities. It's not exactly a politics of moral purity, but then again, what is? Ever since we decided in favor of Gifford Pinchot's model of management over John Muir's notion of preservation, we have worked in the interest of commercially defined species and separable territories and made the task of restoring the well-being of systems a steep mountain of repentance we need to climb.[27]

I like to think that such repentance is happening right here. From above Heber Valley that day, Amy and I could see the Provo wending in uneven and dark braids across the white surface of the valley floor. Although it appears wild, it is the careful work of bulldozers, engineers, biologists, and landscape architects, a kind of ecologically sound version of the English landscape style of Capability Brown. What is so moving about these restoration efforts on the Middle Provo is not the prospect of a perfect restitution but a performance of re-creation. Unlike continued recreational pleasure at the expense of a sense of place, of which there is no shortage in these parts, these performances are a turning back against the tide of our oblivious tendencies, an imperfect but respectful learning of what our presence in this place has meant and an acknowledgment of the dynamic force of autonomous life systems.

Science is our best source of information, but we all know it is insufficient. We wouldn't act on science without faith, faith that acting self-consciously and according to good principle even with incomplete knowledge is still the right thing to do. This is not what it means to dismiss science in the interest of religious dogma. It is to admit that we act on the basis of what we think we know, knowing also that we take human, moral risk. Better to discover our humanity in the effort of restoration than to insist on a humanity defined by its deafness to the cries in the wilderness.

A restoration in Christian theology is also deeply eschatological; it signifies the end of all things, the great gathering and reconstitution of the broken body of the earth and of each living thing. It is a shame, really, how abused this concept has been with regard to environmental degradation. It is as if some Christians anticipate and welcome the destructions prophesied in the Bible, as if it is their Christian duty to hurry along the end of things with their own destructive behavior. God has promised a new earth, a new heaven, so no point in preserving what we know is destined to die, or so the logic goes.

But there is a shifting tide in Christianity—Baptists, Lutherans, Catholics, Evangelicals, and others joining the conservationist chorus—which would suggest that eschatology does not have to cause apathy. The prospect of an end to things might instead imbue the physical world with a deep and abiding ambiguity. The world *is* but it is also *not yet*, and to believe in an end dictated by a Creator is to see that nature's particulars flirt with what could be, which is not the same thing as arguing that nature is a microcosm of the foretold fulfillment. Nature is not yet perfect, not always beautiful, always just beyond our full understanding, and it might benefit from our best efforts to restore it. A going back, a repentance, is also a going forth, a movement toward fulfillment whereby we remake the fragments of experience into a quilted whole. Anticipated endings help to give our actions moral meaning. That is the paradox of what Blake means when he writes of an "eternity in an hour" or of Caravaggio's Christ eating among us.

Deep in the visions and translations of the seer, Joseph Smith, even many Mormons have missed the implications of the belief that the new earth and new heaven would be this earth, this place here, now.[28] Brigham Young at least understood him: "The earth is very good in and of itself, and has abided a celestial law; consequently, we should not despise it, nor have desire to leave it, but rather desire and strive to obey the same law the earth abides.... We are for the kingdom of God, and are not going to the moon, nor to any other planet pertaining to this solar system.... This earth is the home he has prepared for us." The theology of such a restoration promises that the very stuff of our mortal lives will become the stuff of our heavenly existence. This has to mean something more than obliterating our mistakes. It seeks to make strengths out of our weaknesses. There is no room in such a theology for nihilistic anticipation and hope for the coming destruction of the earth. This is a philosophy of hope, hope that mundane, physical life, when properly cared for, might become the stuff of eternity.

This is what Joseph perhaps had in mind in his 1843 revelation: "That same sociality which exists among us here will exist among us there, only it will be coupled with eternal glory, which glory we do not now enjoy."[29] God and his angels are not outside of space and time but in a particular space at a particular moment. They contemplate the past, present, and future because they stand on a globe like a sea of glass and fire; heaven is an earth that has become a great seer stone, which means that nothing, no one person, brother, sister, son or daughter, no animal or stone, is lost. A cosmic move is in store for this earth, too, which God will inhabit after it will similarly be made "like unto crystal."[30]

Somewhere along the way as Amy and I drove the family down Provo Canyon after snowshoeing, we slipped inside of the canopy of inverted and dirty air. The mountains around us lost their clarity and the density of the air ahead was palpable, visible. The inside of our van was still steaming from everyone's sweat, and there was the sound of proud accomplishment in the way the children were laughing. I caught glimpses of new housing developments cropping up like weeds where orchards once abounded. Upon their incomplete wooden frames hung the drooping snow. I have seen the green-filtered images of real estate porn, air-brushed pictures of white stucco homes with giddy children playing on deep green carpets of pleasure, the billboards promising heaven on earth. "Eight children. All daughters. 120 pairs of shoes. HUGE walk-in closets." Sounds like Nirvana, to some perhaps. But if Christianity teaches that we shouldn't pretend to know when or how nature's end is coming, we also can't afford to build false Edens.

The more extreme and sometimes more vocal folks—doomsday environmentalists and militant millennialists—seem to be offering the same package of despair and the same refusal to try to live up to the challenge of having to act with incomplete knowledge. Their tenets include a bottomless nostalgia for a world we cannot recover, a fundamental rejection of the gifts of life, and a paranoid distrust of the vast majority of humanity, and neither group seems to have cornered the market yet on these symptoms of hopelessness. Intended or not, the implication of their arguments can become the same: stop acting in the interest of the whole of humanity and get yourself your own slice of paradise before someone else takes it away.

An unsettled feeling surfaced like the vestiges of a suppressed but still-raging inner battle. A battle of what exactly? A battle, perhaps, between the intensity of pleasure I experience in this place, its remarkable beauty and quality of life, and the nagging feeling that it won't last, that we have already done too much damage. I am undeniably happy to live here, but there is always a part of me that feels for those who never have been. I still remember John's words about never feeling fully accepted. Was that his neurosis or our failure?

I thought, too, of how this place has irrevocably shaped my relationships: my oldest brother who left Connecticut and came to college at the University of Utah just at the onset of deep, clinical mental illness and who is now buried in Salt Lake City; my other brother, who shares my love for Utah's landscapes but does not share my religion; my parents, who were more comfortable in church in the diversity of Connecticut and Miami than here in Utah where they have retired; Amy, who sometimes struggles to understand my emotional intensity and keeps searching for her own. And perhaps most importantly, our children who seem so well adjusted and so happy compared to me when I was their age that I can scarcely believe their happiness is real. I think, too, of my grandfather's first vacation on the river, his banking success in New York, his big house and live-in nannies on Long Island, such a far cry from his brick-mason father; and James Stratton's triumphant peach orchards shortly after the eviction of the Indians from Utah Valley.

Sometimes it feels as if even the beauty of this place will never be enough to draw me out of this inner world of my mind where I am haunted by these paradoxes. Worse still, although this place remains beautiful, its occasional ugliness is often enough to destroy my inner life altogether. My joys seemed to wither at the palpable sight of the substitute paradisiacal world I could see from our van, this world we have built for ourselves and this civilization that values and delineates unique lives but not life collectively, which is to say no life at all.

It didn't take the early Mormon settlers more than a few years before they fell into a spiritual stupor. A wave of repentance swept across the region, inspired by the preaching of church leaders, which led thousands to be rebaptized in a show of recommitment. Like successful marriages, rituals of renewal are needed to come close again to that original moment of rediscovered innocence, or else the complexity of life will destroy the union. I decided it was time for a visit to the temple again. The temple provided for the early Saints the forum for a ritualized restoration of the very foundational moments of the Earth's creation, and it is still my chance for renewal. Something about the growing ease and familiarity of a place or a relationship fosters a complacency that you must struggle against through re-creations of the primordial. As I looked at Amy while she drove and listened to the children in the back, I thought that if I am not careful, the very things and people I love can become virtually unknowable.

Not all auguries renew moral strength. The reading of signs in the heavens or in the entrails of rodents and birds was an old science of escaping the necessity of faith and moral judgment in order to minimize the risks of living, much like psychics, horoscopes, or life insurance plans today. We want to know which battles to fight, whom to trust, how to proceed with hope in the moral murkiness of a politically, culturally, and socially complex world. Like Oedipus, what we would most like to read are signs that ensure both our staying power and our innocence, but if his fate is any indication, the desire for innocence must not outweigh the willingness to accept accountability for judgment and choice. True auguries point to the promises you can trust in but they also outline your responsibilities. Returning again to Blake's "Auguries of Innocence," I am reminded that I must start by uncaging nature. His couplets do not urge upon me merely an agenda of returning to natural purity and rarity, but an ethics of accountability:

> A dog starved at his master's gate
> Predicts the ruin of the state
> . . . .
> Kill not the moth nor the butterfly
> For the Last Judgement draweth nigh.

I never know if I should feel elation or despair when I look upon these mountains rising above the crowded and scarred valley floor with such staggering beauty. Blake's poem would suggest that a recovery of innocence is achieved by learning to balance and commingle despair and hope:

> Joy and woe are woven fine,
> A clothing for the soul divine,
> Under every grief and pine
> Runs a joy with silken twine.

This is the singular meaning of a weeping and triumphant Savior, a God in the flesh. He isn't the promise of delivery from our sorrows but rather of joy in and through them. Maybe in the age of global environmental degradation, we have fallen out of our humanistic trance and we can't look at the works of our own hands any longer in categorical admiration. This growing distaste for our mistakes, however, is no reason to disparage ourselves. We never should have wanted auguries of human innocence in the first place.

Our discovery of the magnitude of our mistakes is part of our journey from ambivalence to acceptance regarding our own irrevocable humanity. Love that does not separate humanity from the creation is love that focuses on the one person, not the ninety-nine, and that notices the sparrow's fall. This is the only love capable of accepting that our actions, no matter how well intended, may always require contrition and restoration.

Despite the dirty slush splashing up from the side of the van and the dull winter grayness that had settled over the valley, my mind returned to the Middle Provo. The first time I was able to witness the beginnings of the restoration work was with John. I was more experienced by that time and in little need of his help, but I still appreciated his occasional coaching. It was never stifling, especially since his gift was generous praise. I didn't know much about the restoration at the time. All I knew was that John had been telling me about the blue-ribbon waters of that stretch of the river and was eager to show me around. As we wandered among the stone-covered riverbanks of the Provo, I felt that perpetually adolescent excitement in turning a bend and fishing another new stretch of the river. It was late in the fall and the cottonwoods had lost almost all of their brilliant yellow leaves, but enough remained in the slanted light and the hard autumn air to provide a canopy of brilliance. The sky was unpredictable all day, posturing as winter with sudden drops of temperature and then suddenly permitting the warm breath of the sun on our backs.

We fished below Jordanelle, taking turns on holes, congratulating each other on our successes and admiring the beauty of the river. Underdressed as usual, I was shivering from the sudden gusts of wind in the shadows of the cold, dark water. At one point, after having caught a brown trout and releasing it at my side, I found my line curling around my legs in the water. My reeling in was sloppy, since I opted to strip the line in by bare hand instead of using the crank on my reel. I didn't want John to see the mess I was in. Fighting an impulse to feel impatient with the tangle I created for myself and frustrated that it had begun to rain lightly, I turned downstream to see where we had fished.

Small diamond sparkles of rain dropped from the sky like threaded beads in the angling light; the yellows of the cottonwoods stood in proximate contrast to the dark woods to the south enshrouded in clouds. As the raindrops hit a bed of large, worn river rock, lying on the north bank like loaves of bread, the stones turned a brilliant pink as if polished into great glass er-ratics. I have never seen the faces of the dead and only in dreams or in my mind have I thought I heard their voices, but I believe in the simultaneity of place I have learned since a child: this planet is my home away from home, my desired future heavenly home, and the way station for the dead await-ing the day of transfiguration.[31] Turns out this planet is more crowded than most know. Something in the opening of the pores, the chill of the bones in mountain water, makes me believe in the nearness of the long absent, ring-ing in the heart-thrumming of my own veins.

This strange transmutation of time, this restoration of breath and palpi-tation to the still stone, I had hoped it all might last. I could hear John up-stream saying something about the fish, but the rush of water and wind mingled all sounds as one. I called to him to point out the river we had just passed through. After I gathered my line in, I turned again to soak in the brittle mood behind me, but it was gone. The quickening mountain air had changed again and the blushing stones had rolled back into a flushing span of indistinction. I stepped out of the river to gather some warmth from the stones and watched while John continued casting patiently upstream. I be-gan to compose a fragment of a poem in my mind:

> hoping perhaps to rewind us
> since memory of light starkly
> upbraids the course of time behind us.

John is no longer here and yet that moment, like a singular shard of bro-ken crystal, remains fixed in my memory. I could see that moment through my window pane and through the snow as my family and I made our way home. And I could hear John's voice mingling with the sound of the wa-ter. The senses are what help to maintain that clarity against the erosions of time, but I suppose it stays with me too because it was that day that John an-nounced with only the most cryptic of explanations that he would be leav-ing for Madison and I began to understand that there were things in John's life he hadn't yet forgiven himself for. I am not sure how many more times we fished before he left, but it seems that it is my last, purest memory of him in the water. He still can't bring himself to step foot in this state or in the Provo again.

If the general rule of nature is its opacity, religion and science beg us to dream otherwise. The temptation is to want to resolve this tension prematurely, which is why I need the patience of metaphor. Like but unlike, nature offers glimpses, promises, of a future fulfillment and reasons for hope, but in this free and forbearing universe I can see what has been engineered, distorted, beautified, bought and sold and no one yet struck dumb by avenging angels who have come to warn of the coming burning. But action with impunity is the illusion of those fools who are offended by the strangeness of the physical mystery. The great poet Pablo Neruda's atheism led him at the end of his life to stare at shells and stones. The closer he looked at the flotsam and jetsam of the sea and the broken material of geology, however, the more he found himself staring into the abysses of eternity and the more his existentialist certainties began to resemble the uncertainty of religious faith:

> to be that which I love, the naked
> presence of the sun on the boulder,
> and that which grows and grows without knowing
> that it cannot stop growing.[32]

Which is another way of saying that to see nature is to look at eternity through a glass darkly. Both mirror and window, it is the physical border of our imagination and the beginning intimations of the infinite. To capture its time-bound glimpses of the timeless in images or words is the abiding of faith, hope, and most importantly, charity…the holding forth, the forbearance. Great art, like great religion, is born out of and seeks to encompass contradiction without recourse to facile reconciliations. To attempt to rewind and defy time is the stated desire to go back always again to the beginning, to trace our human steps, which are also missteps, in the sand. It wouldn't hurt to remember that just because we are facing a global environmental crisis does not mean that we are the first generation of humanity to learn that nature is a promise that teaches us to repent before it is too late. The key is not to be the last.

The twentieth century has gone down in history for a number of ignominious as well as heroic events, but certainly one of its more troubling legacies is its treatment of rivers. As agriculture gave way to industry and massive development of cities, water was victim to an increasingly private and individualistic conceptualization of property. Consequently, rivers suffered greater transformation than in the previous ten thousand years. They

were straightened, diked, and dammed, and where I live water was trans-
ported from less populous areas and fed into the Provo, all to provide more
space for homes, more safety from floods to homeowners, and reservoirs to
ensure the perpetuity of modernization. And as Donald Worster reminds
us, the Mormons played no small role in this harnessing of water's wild and
unpredictable ways, seeing dams and dikes as the way of the Lord.[33] Several
small hydroelectric dams were built on the Provo early in the century, and
then two major dams were built, one in the 1940s and the other in the
1990s.

Within a century of the arrival of the white man, 95 percent of the native
species in the river and of Utah Lake went extinct, this despite the fact that
it had been the meat of the native fish of the river and lake that provided for
humans for thousands of years and saved the lives of the pioneers in those
early, hunger-ridden years of settlement. But this is only the most overt and
measurable of consequences. Aquatic species worldwide are going extinct at
much faster rates than terrestrials. When the fish go, that means the invertebrates, zooplankton, plants, and whole swaths of life go, too.

Rivers are unruly by nature, of course, especially when they are subject to
the ebb and flow of snowpack in mountain wilderness and when they drop
quickly and sometimes with crushing violence. In the case of the Provo,
what was once a meandering, braided series of cuts and turns that increased
in variety, biodiversity, and breadth as the river fell from high elevations
and spread across each flatland with increasing strength, is now what my
colleague and local restoration ecologist, Mark Belk, described to me as a
"moving bathtub," a straight shot of water with decreasing biodiversity.

In the middle of the century, the Army Corps of Engineers did their level best to teach the river to behave with a series of dikes that riprapped it like
some intransigent adolescent who, accustomed to slouching at the dinner
table, is forced to wear a back brace. This was done perhaps not out of any
overt malice but in profound ignorance of what a river is and what it does.
We now know its health must be measured in terms of the entire watershed
over the course of its dynamically changing shape through time, upstream
and downstream, from the surface to the subsurface, and by its relation to
the riparian communities it spawns alongside.

A river is water, yes, but it is also soil, plant, and animal life—a watershed.
Seeing it requires something more than merely historical or aesthetic lenses.
It requires the poet's eye. Zooplankton, invertebrates, fish, mammals, vege-
tation, fowl, all respond to and even depend on a river's unpredictable and

uneven flow, its fluctuations in temperature, and its moods of violent overflow, as well as its vulnerability to drought. So, too, the invisible and larger supply of groundwater beneath our feet. Variety in contour is the rule of
water left to run its own course as it spills over rocks, carries dead wood and
plant life, turns back and braids itself around slight elevations. Its life, in other words, depends on chance, even chaos. This enhances the differences in
temperatures, velocity, and volume of flow that provide habitats for a broad
diversity of life.

But tolerating a river's unpredictability is like tolerating the bald facts of
mortality itself. Consider the two meanings of Isaiah's recompenses: God's
gift of grace of a blossoming desert—the earth as home, as paradise—and
God's vengeance on a wicked world—the earth as exile, as wilderness. It
would seem necessary to learn tolerance for the fact that we are never far
from either one. We need an imagination of deep time, but try selling the
merits of deep time to the homeowner on a floodplain or to the politician
running for election on a platform of economic progress.

It was only thirty years ago that some Utahns entertained the proposi-
tion that the Provo River could deliver its water more effectively if it were
piped underground, which is sort of like deciding to forsake food in order to
get your daily nutrition intravenously or with pills. It took the work of Robert Redford and Sam Rushforth, an ecologist at BYU at the time, and others
to convince people of the shortsightedness of the proposal, not to mention
its aesthetic impoverishment. But this new practice of environmental repentance, the deep art of ecological restoration, is more than preservation; it re-
shapes rivers to their complex serpentine forms, allows life to go about its
business of promoting habitat diversity, and mitigates against the effects of
climate change. A way of saying, no, not yet, not here. Mark Belk, for one,
believes it is not merely his scientific duty but his Mormon stewardship to
be, as he wryly puts it, "out to save the world, one trash fish at a time."

Human developments have also placed limits on the progress of such efforts, but ecological restoration at least signals a penitent response to Malachi's threats. Repentance begins with recognition of sin but ends when
self-loathing is overcome by love. If every species is a living creative response to a particular environment, protecting species is protecting the
integrity of a system as it moves through evolutionary time. Ecological restoration, unlike the work on the Sistine Chapel, is not a scraping away of
time's effects on the surface of a static work of beauty; it is instead a stepping into the flow of time and watching the diversity of life our restitutions

spawn. It is a fundamental recognition of ongoing creation, something un-imaginable within a theology of an ex nihilo creation.

Creationists, in their shallow temporal reckoning, cry foul since a seem-ing snap of the fingers is enough to explain the young and static world around us. Not for Joseph Smith whose understanding of the creation as organized matter accrues in potency with increasing understanding of the emergence of a world of complexity, extravagance, and beauty in deep time: "The pure principles of element are principles which can never be de-stroyed; they may be organized and re-organized, but not destroyed. They had no beginning and can have no end."[34]

The audacity of the prophet Joseph is his claim to have restored an orig-inal form of Christianity, and that would have to include Christianity's original ecological understanding. Was there an ecological apostasy? Are we perhaps just beginning to understand the ecological principles he re-stored? If the creation bears witness to a creator, it would seem that even the eternity of God and his works are inherently temporal. Spiritual work this is, this patient assent to what is. A working back along the path that first led us away from this ticking earth. Healing the earth, yes. But a restoration of our-selves, too.

In the reclamation politics of the Colorado River and the struggle for state autonomy, Utah politicians worked to arrange what became known as the Central Utah Project (CUP), a means to assure ample water supplies for the Wasatch Front and the state's many agricultural industries. After si-phoning water from the Strawberry Valley, farmers in Heber Valley had re-duced the middle stretch of the Provo between Jordanelle and Deer Creek to little more than a canal. But on the hillside of Wasatch State Park, what Amy and I witnessed was a winding stretch of water through a wide swath of vegetated landscape that looked more like the riparian community the river once fostered. Federal mitigation funds for CUP provide a tithe on the costs of human engineering of water sources in Utah to help restore the river to its snakelike form and the riparian vegetation that once provided home to ani-mal life.

The only reason ecologists were able to determine our effects of distur-bance was because of a homeowner along the river who, when approached by the Army Corps of Engineers, refused their services. He was emphatical-ly determined to leave his stretch of the river untouched, even if it made him vulnerable to floods. With these government funds they were able to com-pare the diversity of life in this native, serpentine stretch with the rest of the river and begin buying up surrounding property to create a corridor wide enough to mimic the ecological integrity they found there.

As one walks along the riverbank now one sees shapes formed by the turning river, banks of planted native vegetation of willows, cottonwoods, and cattails, bogs artificially created to the side of many of the steeper turns, and uneven dikes built up to look like carved floodplains of old, backwaters and small streams breaking free of the river and joining up downriver. All signs show that wildlife is returning. I have crossed meadows of high grass while black field mice scurried underfoot and an osprey looked on, perched in his nest atop a dead cottonwood. I have witnessed a snake holding a small fish in his mouth at the riverbank, waiting for us to pass before he emerged out of the water and slithered over the rocks into the brush.

Smithson's *Spiral Jetty* is a fixed endpoint that obtains its visual effect by marking the last sign of a watershed's dynamism: the rising and falling of the Salt Lake. This earth art of the river, on the other hand, aims not for visual but for ecological effect. It seeks to restore the integrity of the watershed itself, to place human labor within an autonomous system of life. It is re-creation. The river will never be the same, of course, and something of the newness of the cuts in the soil and the hints of human hands in the not-yet-thickened vegetation, like transplanted hair follicles on the bald pate, tells you that this is a performance, a moving if incomplete gesture of penitence. Like much modern art, it leaves enough evidence that it is a pretense, a staged and cagey re-creation of the world as Adam might have first known it, an as-if Eden complete with offstage scaffolding still visible from the theater seats. But at least it requires an abdication of the narrower concept of property, that a river is just so many acre-feet. As Brigham Young taught: "[T]here shall be no private ownership of the streams that come out of the canyons, nor the timber that grows on the hills. These belong to the people: all the people." Donald Worster argues that this abdication of property was just a clever ploy to allow Mormon control over water in the kingdom of Deseret, but if that is the case, why do these words chastise us with their utter common sense?

The environmental history of Utah is no different than many areas of the New World in at least one respect: one has to dig far back into history to recover a knowledge of what was native before the arrival of the Europeans. Leathersides, Redsides, Mountain Suckers, the long-nosed dace—these are among the native species no fly-fisherman will ever care about, but the browns and brookies create predation problems for these bottom dwellers. Mark Belk tells me he thinks the river could be designed in such a way to make it possible for native and nonnative species to get along, but we may never have the patience to test the long-term effects of proposed changes. The browns are like so many Mormons in Utah Valley, nonnatives who thrive in a transplanted New World to the point where native elements and diversity of cultural life are squelched. Fisheries keep plopping more sport fish into Utah waters, which isn't the worst of all possible worlds, but it can create what some ecologists call the "Frankenstein effect." Predation results, diversity shrinks, and the health of watersheds declines.

The shape of the river may be the key to a moderated respect for native life forms as well as those, like so many of us humans here, who have been transplanted from other climes. Not enough, some anarchists are saying. Blow up the dams, they say. Destroy the Death Star of civilization, which from time immemorial has been ravaging the land in the interest of human survival. Something there is in the anarchistic impulse that says to the heart: too few have felt this bold for too long and the result is the wheel of damage we keep reinventing. And as long as we lack the political will to seek the path of repentance, it is tempting to assume this kind of opposition.

But we are not a poisonous, invasive species, worse than the tamarisk trees first introduced as windbreakers that now drink voraciously and choke virtually every major riverbank throughout the Colorado Plateau. Of course, neither are we Midas, turning everything we touch to gold. We will not solve our problems by believing we need to pull up the disease-spreading roots of humanity or by insisting stupidly that our current path of destruction is both inevitable and virtuous.

It is a suicidal impulse to wish to sweep people and history aside, to act as if there is nothing worth salvaging from the transformation of land forms, vegetation, and wildlife that has resulted from the Old World's crossing, nothing worthy of admiration in the people who lived that history, who of course are, among others, *us* in our contemporary environmental wisdom. There is no guarantee or enough time in one human generation to know that our best efforts at restoration will make sufficient difference. There is no guarantee that efforts to stem the effects of global climate change will be enough or in time, but to wait until we can act with certitude and with absolute impunity is the similarly suicidal impulse of the adolescent sinner, trusting blindly in his inherent innocence and immortality.

Which is only to say that the good news is nothing new: what we need is faith, hope, and charity. Paul's trinity of values is a fire kept warm by the caretakers of civilization, the poets, prophets, artists. These are they who always seem to find reasons why worn-out trappings can be recycled, renewed, and restored to avoid their abusive results. These are not the Pharisees of civilization, the dogmatists of tradition, who think of civilization as a rock, but those who understand it as a river that connects us to a vast host of neighbors. We have too often mistaken repentance for loud human self-loathing. Already hating ourselves, we make ourselves vulnerable to the pimps who hijack and sell our oldest values to the highest bidder and to fear mongers who suggest reasons to distrust everyone but ourselves. We don't need less humanity. We need it more than ever.

Provo holds one of the largest Fourth of July celebrations in the country, filling a stadium of sixty thousand to listen to conservative talk show hosts emcee a parade of nationalistic fervor. Homeland. Vaterland. Patria. A long history of converting all of nature into property and leaving no space for the indigenous, the aliens, strangers, and foreigners. At a recent political caucus in Provo, one delegate said with a straight face that Satan was bringing illegals to our country. Anti-immigration fervor is at a fever pitch. Among local politicians there is talk of overturning the so-called "anchor baby" clause of the Fourteenth Amendment that grants citizenship to anyone born on U.S. soil. Which tells me that love of land can pull you out of time and seize you with the illusions of rootedness in place, an unchanging and fixed past, and the existence of unambiguous lines of territory. rivers as borders.

But what if what you thought you loved was fluid, elusive, complex beyond any reckoning, connecting you to the headwaters of the past and to the outflows of the future, to what lies beneath you, around you, and beyond your vision, placing you in time's flow? What if you must confess that you are perpetually engaged in a process of becoming placed, that love makes you vulnerable, that it is an affliction? Is not this a chastening love of the mystery of finding yourself on this earth, in this place, in this body, at this moment of time? It makes you as strange and as strangely welcome to the scene as anyone else. rivers as home waters.

Eight

🌿

YOU READ ABOUT THESE GUYS EVERY YEAR IN THE PAPER WHO MEET THEIR end in the snow-packed mountains in Utah. And they are almost always guys—snowboarders, thrill-seeking skiers, snowmobilers, snowshoers, some experienced, some not. Avalanches are what get them, usually. Maybe they were unwitting victims of an imprudent passage below a steep drop of snow-covered talus, or maybe their passage high on a slope instigated the collapse. Maybe it was failure to consult the weather before heading out or maybe it was an expected change in the weather. Family members often console themselves that at least they died doing what they loved most.

Then follows the agonizing search for the body, several days of uncertainty that can stretch into months, but once the snow finally begins to melt, they might be able to count on a glove or a hat appearing on the surface of the spring snow. It is hard to imagine the violence of such a death, how hard your heart would knock against your ribs as you made one last desperate but doomed effort to stay out of harm's way. And then, before the crushing and indifferently cold stillness of the snow's blue-black interior, the white roaring onrush of ice, rocks, tree branches, and the faint hope that maybe you could ride it like a wave.

The analogy almost works. It is water after all, just frozen temporarily by the high winds and cold winter temperatures, and, like the sea, its peaceful rocking is a ruse for its indifferent violence. But perhaps the difference is that snow doesn't fall with the reliability of the ocean's gentle lapping on the shore. The fact is that for most of the ten winters I have lived here, the snowfall has been impotent and runoff negligible. The mountains stand all winter long with hiked up skirts, their immodesty offending the skiers no doubt and compromising the slogan "The Greatest Snow on Earth," to say nothing of the mountains themselves, ashamed to be already baked to a light brown in the early days of spring long after most of the skiers have flown back home. Then bracing themselves for the long hot summer and hoping the wildfires won't punish them for their indecent exposure.

Strange that living in this community, one scarcely hears talk of a climate problem, let alone one we have had a hand in precipitating. Sure, the skiers complain and the farmers grow anxious, but household taps turn on and backyard sprinklers whistle with the same inevitability as before. More highways are under reconstruction for more lanes, and op-eds, syndicated columnists, and vacuous radio talk show hosts broadcast their slanderous doubts about what scientists now know is beyond reasonable doubt, that we are making the world warmer. Strange, too, since the millennium hangs thick in the air for a community of "latter-day saints" for whom the end is not a matter of chance but of anticipation.

Where does apathy come from? From belief in an apocalypse? Does an apocalypse necessarily imply that endings are foreordained? "It must needs be that offences come; but woe to that man by whom the offence cometh!"[35] What did Jesus mean? Read gently and humbly, and prophecy can be a kind of leaning into the future, a way of being alive to possibility, that makes fear habitable. "No man knoweth, neither the angels in heaven, nor shall they know until he comes."[36] So read the revelations of Joseph Smith. If the pervasive and entrenched refusal to accept our human role in environmental degradation is any indication, there is no shortage of those who are pretty sure they know more than the angels. Perhaps this is because they don't have the stamina hope demands of us. They cede instead to an eagerness to accept the signs of nature's dying as God's will, as if we would roll out the welcoming fanfare for the grim reapers of this blue ball.

How could anyone confuse fatalism with love? Maybe the earth is going to die. But why not stay the hands at its throat? Doesn't the nearness of an end only make the interim sweeter, more precious, and urge more determination to not go gently into that good night? It might take twenty consecutive years of drought to accept that we live in an arid climate that cannot sustain us, but why is only one winter behaving as it should, like this one, enough to make indifference seem justified?

This winter we have stood through the long, colorless months surrounded by white-robed, stone-faced priests holding their silence, at least at a distance. Once up on a mountain in the winter, the silence proves illusory. There is the groaning of wind in the creaking trees and the imminent threat of rumbling rows between snow and gravity. Snowshoeing down the backside of "Y" Mountain one winter with friends, I remember the long strides we took in the deep powder as we descended like a shot down a small dip carved by a frozen brooklet and hearing in the distance the thunderous roll of snow crashing down the nearby face of Cascade Mountain. Alert to danger, one is always leaning into the silence, usually to identify something deserving of fear.

Let me die like my grandfather, at his desk with a pencil in his hand, silently slipping away into rest while working on a sentence. That's the way to go. But who gets to choose, really? Maybe that is the impulse of these men, to have the chance not so much to choose their death in a kind of suicide by snow but to choose a life that is calculated to make death slightly less capricious. Perhaps we are strangely attracted to some way of living that makes dying seem less arbitrary, as if we could try to anticipate and thus appear to choose what will choose us. Which suggests that the thrill seekers killed in the mountains are not exceptions but the rule of every car driver blissfully covering ground he believes he never paves, dividing and polluting air he believes he never breathes, absorbing and giving off heat he believes he never feels. As if it is the right of every American consumer to be protected by obliviousness to the damage we do.

When friends proposed hiking Mount Nebo in the dead of winter and in the dead of night, I didn't hesitate to sign on. I have a standing invitation to do Mount Timpanogos in the winter, too, and that would be truer to my reconnaissance of the Provo River watershed, but so far I can't bring myself to accept the heightened risks posed by its even more imposing angles. Despite my rather normal and healthy fear of dying in a state of physical suffering or trauma, I know that coming to know my neighborhood can never be without some physical risk. What most interested me was the chance to know more directly where my waters are cradled and secreted in the high dawn of snow and rock. I eased my fears with the thought that I would be guided by experienced mountaineers, but over the coming days waves of panic seized me in the still moments of half-sleep at night.

Ever since my brother's death, I live with a perception that the world as I know it can suddenly and cataclysmically disappear or with rapacious violence change beyond recognition, and this is without seeking danger. Sometimes, in quiet moments, an irrational terror of what might come consumes me, almost as if I can hear the rumbling of a far-off surf, or a tremor in the ground, that will bear us all away. So I wondered if my immediate acceptance of the invitation wasn't a maudlin desire to put an end to an unidentified anxiety, acquiesce finally, and jump into the abyss. While I must allow for the possibility that I am motivated by this dark desire, there is something truly nihilistic about living in denial of death's proximity. My mad desire for sensation, for experience in the outdoors, might easily become escapism, but it more often feels like a way of querying the meaning of Kenny's suicide. The recompense for that one singular loss has been a widening circle of kinship with people and places.

We planned our departure for midnight on a Friday. That night my wife and I went out to dinner with friends, and I could scarcely focus on the conversation and, when asked about the impending hike, tried to change the subject. I was feeling the kind of fear I used to feel before walking on stage in a high school play, or the kind of anticipation I felt before calling a girl I liked. I knew I would not or could not change my mind but I also knew that the drumming of my heart would not abate until it was over.

Standing like an anchor on the southern end of a 180-degree arc of ridges along the eastern edge of Utah Valley, Nebo is the highest mountain along the Wasatch Front, standing at just under twelve thousand feet. It sits almost centrally in the state's geography and provides a particularly good view of the transitional geography between the Colorado Plateau—the high land of mountains, canyons, and rivers—and the Great Basin—the bowl-like desert plain that fails to carry mountain water to the Pacific Ocean. It is, in other words, an ideal site for understanding the competing forces of aridity and of rainfall and for thinking through the duality of the Lord's recompenses.

In the early years of Mormon exploration and settlement, Nebo was an important emblem of the "everlasting hills" that promised refuge for the Mormons from the world, what Jared Farmer calls the "biblicist mountain tradition within Mormonism." It was well known, having appeared on old maps, and was climbed by the Mormon poet William W. Phelps in 1849 and later by the likes of Thomas Moran and John Muir. Farmer demonstrates that Timpanogos, although shorter in elevation, won out as the preeminent mountain in the valley over the course of Mormonism's Americanization in the twentieth century and its transformation from an agricultural to a more industrial and finally more suburbanized community.

As the community transitioned from direct dependence on the whims of the watershed to our modern methods of mechanized hydraulics, there was a move from direct and sometimes violent interactions with Indians to a more secular and typically American sense of place in which the indigenous presence quickly receded. If the waters of Utah Lake were the source of conflict, they were also the site of an unrealized cross-cultural collabora-tion. Nebo's lesser status in the valley today, in other words, is a symbolic challenge to the modern Mormon sense of place, devoted as it is to remem-bering a history that is suitable to what we seem to want to forget.

Timpanogos feeds the Provo while Nebo's runoff feeds the Spanish Fork River where it eventually mingles with the Provo in Utah Lake. Nebo's sum-mit is a favorite summertime destination for ambitious Boy Scout troops be-cause of the strenuous trail that ascends on the east side of the mountain, but its wide body angling to a more narrow and evenly serrated head stands at a lonely remove from most of the population of the valley, enough so that to the eyes it appears a modest peak. The arc plays on the mind, much like one's own stories, giving the false impression that every self is at the center of a stony kingdom.

Mountains might look largest to the one who stands close, but once you get smitten by the spirit of reconnaissance and decide to climb it, its size hides behind the more immediate surface you are ascending. You still feel at the center of the maelstrom of stone, since what is nearest makes the most immediate claim on your senses, but you begin to learn to anticipate what it hides. Even at the conclusion of a hike to a summit, it is hard to imagine that anything could be higher, even if you know the maps say otherwise. "Firm as the mountains around us, stalwart and brave we stand." Hymns of praise to the mountains are familiar to any Mormon ear, but from our puny point of view, they are the most changeable, mercurial, elusive, and difficult to grasp in size and contour.

I am accompanied by six friends: Dan, a tall, lanky mechanical engineer, forty-something father of five, who grew up in Ephraim and spent his col-lege years, as he tells it, hiking every peak in the West he could get to; Wade, a convert from Alaska, former professional football player in Europe turned political scientist and father of three; and Mark, a soft-spoken painter in his fifties recently moved from New York City, with bushy eyebrows and an im-pressive ability to rock climb with his college-age sons. And there is Taylor, who wasn't used to being displaced as the oldest of the group. A father of three, nearing fifty and proudly wearing his flowing, white mane of hair, he seems born to be on a mountain and always enjoys outhiking the young and fit. Vance is the kind of guy you want on a trek like this because he carries extra equipment and is strong enough to haul one of us out if he has to. A patient, gentle, and financially successful father of eight in his late thirties, his hiking pace is more like what most of us would consider jogging. And

George, half-English, half-Czech, contemplating an uncertain future after his recent graduation from college.

Not exactly a cross-section of American diversity, we arrive in two minivans at close to one in the morning on a dirt road on the western foot of the mountain. As we park, dress in the cold dark, and pack our snowshoes, we quickly find the single-digit temperature eating at our bones. I am the slowest to be ready to head out because of a loose buckle on my backpack and so find myself heading up the path in the dark trailing the group by a tenth of a mile or so. Lunging forward with long strides, I hope to get some feeling into my hands and to stop my body from shaking from the cold. I am not encouraged. I have done enough of this kind of winter activity to know that I am vulnerable to the cold, that I chill and shake easily, and that I need to guard my inner warmth with care.

The trail heads upward to the center of a tilted hollow formed by the mountainside that precipitously drops to the valley floor. Willow Creek runs alongside us as we climb. By the time we have arrived at the beginning of the ridge we will follow directly to the north, we can see the immediate range of the mountain fanning out in all directions, almost three hundred degrees. The weather does not call for snowfall, but the air is bitter cold and the winds are expected to present some problems, especially as we rise in elevation. The moon has not yet risen to its full height, but we catch glimpses of its glow over the easternmost ridge where it will soon appear.

The conversations among us are steady, warm, and full of laughter, about parenting, marriage, our life in the church, and occasionally about work or politics. George is relatively quiet since he has less in common with the rest of us, but he and I catch moments at the back of the group to talk about his desire to discover more of Utah's landscapes and his questions about his uncertain future. His eighteen-month-old son is with his in-laws, and he speaks proudly of his development as a toddler, but there is a layer of anguish right under the surface. We have spent enough time together for me to know something of the degree of pain he is in, but it is still hard to imagine. I remember visiting him and his wife, Summer, as their new married student ward bishop when she was undergoing treatment for early indications of Hodgkin's disease, which she was told was 90 percent curable.[37]

A native of a small southern Utah town square in the middle of the downwinder belt where the radiation of nuclear testing in Nevada has left no small legacy of pain, she was especially hopeful because it was the same cancer her grandmother from the same town had already survived. She had lost her hair and was wearing a bandana, lying limply on the couch while George fetched her whatever she needed. Wedding pictures on the side table displayed extraordinarily beautiful blond hair, flowing in wavy curls around her shoulders. They both cut a profile of almost embarrassing good looks, but there was nothing in their demeanor but genuine warmth, humility, and eager hope to be over this soon. The cancer abated, she became unexpectedly pregnant, and then, after the baby was born, a tumor the size of a grapefruit was found in her chest.

I ask about how things have been most recently, and although articulate, his words come slowly and are measured.

"I can't explain it," he says. "I do a lot of reminiscing at night, looking at photos, reading journals, anything to be nearer to her, you know. I want some experience of reassurance that she is with me, and although I know she is, I just can't feel it. All I can feel is the fact that I am entirely alone. I don't think I've told you about the journal she left behind. I've been reading it."

"What has that been like?"

"Well, you can guess. It's been very emotional. I revisit her first impressions of me, of her expectations about getting married, about the illness. She loved me with such forgiveness. I've had to read it in parts because it's too much to take in at once, as you might imagine."

I can't really. And I confess as much and tell him, however awkwardly, that I admire his ability to work through this.

"No one and nothing can prepare you for this. You would do it, because you would have no choice."

I remind him that lots of people don't rise to accept the choices fate has assigned them, that this takes a certain quality of faith and inner strength. The moon has risen over the crest of the mountain to the east, bringing an ethereal ambience to this snow-covered ring of slopes, exposing to the eye naked patches of rock, evergreen stands and brambles of scrub oak, separated by the glowing skin of snow. Reflections from a hidden sun bouncing off the moon, bouncing again off the white snow, it seems as if the air itself is glowing. Everyone has turned off his headlamp. Still thinking like a bishop even though I completed my term several months earlier, I cite the revelation to Joseph Smith that speaks of Christ in the light of the moon and the stars.

We pause and look around us. This is the kind of light that is ubiquitous since it is as if it comes from all angles at once, no shadows, no blind spots. The paradox is that it is a light diminished by so many distant reflections. "I know, I know," he says, almost with a tone of melancholy. Then after a pause, "I've started writing poetry, you know. And I think I want to be a teacher. That much seems clear."

It is a delicate subject still, but I tell him I am confident he will love someone again.

"That's not the point," he says. "Loving someone will never bring her back, and besides, I know now that love is a risk. It means I have to accept the possibility of this pain all over again. Maybe someday, but I'm not ready for that yet."

Maybe when we are young, it feels as if love happens to us. It is only in the wake of loss and the pain that love causes that we come to terms with the fact that love is a choice and a measure of our suffering. For that reason loving in the wake of affliction is also a profound expression of faith.

The verses continue in my mind. "The earth rolls upon her wings, and the sun giveth his light by day, and the moon giveth her light by night, and the stars also giveth their light, as they roll upon their wings in their glory, in the midst of the power of God.... All these are kingdoms and any man who hath seen any or the least of these hath seen God moving in his majesty and power.... The light shineth in the darkness and the darkness comprehendeth it not, nevertheless the day shall come when you shall comprehend even God, being quickened in him and by him."[38]

Our voices have lowered because we don't want others to hear us. There is a sadness to the look of the still mountain, as if it is softly breathing in an exhausted sleep. "There hath pass'd away a glory from the earth."[39] I guess this means that no matter how much Wordsworth took in, he couldn't shake the feeling that beauty only signified that something was already lost, or that it soon would be perhaps. And yet he remonstrated himself for this:

> O, evil day, if I were sullen
> While earth herself is adorning.

If passing beauty teaches the reasons for sorrow, it still causes unstoppable elation.

I had read this poem to Summer in the hospital a few months before she died, when the doctors thought she might pass away any day. She was racked with anger and fear, and this had caused George and her parents considerable sorrow. She wasn't afraid to die in any existential sense, but leaving her young husband and their little boy behind caused her ravaged body to shake from the tears. A few desperate attempts at experimental treatments provided them a few months of respite and quickened strength. I remember talking to George on the phone during those weeks, and it was like talking to an adolescent in love; their peace was finally proportionate to their despair. Then came the precipitous decline. A figure in white appeared at the foot of her bed to beckon her, and although she recognized him as her grandfather, she asked him to leave the room, that she would come in due time but that he was spoiling her last moments with her family. It was like her to negotiate between the two worlds like that. She died two days later.

Snaking our way along a ridgeline is certainly safer than climbing ravines, but it means we have to pass through brambles and over rocky crags, and eventually it means we have no choice but to ascend the most precipitous climbs directly. We are low enough in elevation that the snow has undergone a kind of annealing, melting and freezing again to the point of sealing itself in a hard, barklike crust. It isn't snowshoeing time, nor will it be for some time yet, because the angle is far too steep and the snow too hard, but the conditions occasion slipping feet and tire the ankles from the cutting back and forth. Our ice axes come in handy, but they aren't a guarantee of safety because beneath the crusty surface the snow crumbles easily, like hardened and aged salt in an idle shaker.

Once we have risen the first thousand feet or so (we will have to rise a total of seven thousand), we begin to see the costs of a slide to the bottom. The ridgeline breaks at frightening angles from where we are pacing ourselves, and at a few rests for food and water, we begin to feel as if we are floating in the air. The moon has taken center stage with no competition from the clouds, giving off rings of reflected light as its beams pierce the atmosphere. Despite the moonlight, we cannot discern any sign of the ground. It is as if we are on islands of rock in the sky. Our only two choices are a dangerous descent down the way we came or the wall of snow straight ahead.

It is close to 4:30 a.m. No one is talking because the adrenaline has worn off and the hours of labor in the long night have finally caught up to us. And of course the stakes are now higher. The temperature is bitter cold, which isn't a problem as long as our bodies continue the work of ascending, but it begins to dawn on me that I am one twisted ankle away from disaster. We occasionally stop for a rest, a drink or a bite, usually at a place that shows signs of where elk have been bedding at these unwarranted heights, chased as they have been over the last century away from the valley floor. Within minutes I begin to shiver.

A constricting and suffocating fear wraps itself around my throat. I keep telling myself that the sun will rise, that the task of moving my feet upward is not complicated, and that I will eventually arrive, but I don't seem to be able to control the precipitous downward pull of emotion in this shapeless, timeless black. The moon has finally disappeared and, even though my eyes have long since adjusted to the dark, I search in vain for shifting shadows around me. I could almost say out loud "I am dying" and believe myself. It is as if I have forgotten what sun feels or looks like, and without previous experience of the terrain I don't even have a mental image of the future. What an idiot I was to try something like this. How stupid and pointless it would be to die this way. Say what they might at my funeral, I know I was the one who chose not to be holding my wife in a warm bed, deeply dreaming.

How strange it is that the end feels so foreboding, I think. Like most teenagers I lived life with an oblivious and irresponsible sense that life's pleasures were eternal. But the illusions shattered when my brother died, and I have spent my adult life assenting to Wordsworth's dictum that "our birth is but a sleep and forgetting." The mind says—and nature only confirms—that, yes, all things die, but it is when you face death's abyss that you realize how superficially you have contemplated endings, how cheaply you have treated life, and in the growing awareness of having taken thoughtless risks, it seems the height of absurdity that fatality was ever thought to be congruous with inevitability. The soul needs contemplation of an end in order to reach for something far deeper that says no, not yet, not ever. I begin to wonder if this isn't simply cowardice, if I am incapable of accepting or risking death on any terms, or if my fear is only proportionate to the superfluous nature of what I am doing.

It is as if I have walked into the waking reality of my deep dreams, dreaming with my eyes open, and finding myself in a nightmare of my choosing, which is a lot like how sin feels. I start searching my mind for analogies, for reasons why I can imagine that this experience is more transcendental than it feels. I do think to pray silently to myself, asking for strength, protection, and feelings of hope, but the only feeling that comes to me is that I must keep walking. In the dark moonless black, I keep thinking that all I want is the real thing, not the reflection, and nothing else will do. It feels as if I will either go mad or die if sunlight doesn't strike my retinas soon.

I assume that these feelings have to do with my vulnerability to depression and need for natural light in the winter time, but I notice there is very little conversation among us and the few words spoken by others are muttered in more plaintive tones. The incline has only grown more unforgiving, and it is taking everything we have to keep moving. It appears that we are about five hundred feet below another ridgeline that will turn us northeast to the peak, but it is hard to say for sure. We have been at this long enough now to distrust all appearances, to anticipate that reaching an end involves a longer battle than our eyes can reveal this close to the mountain. In the distance we can see the lights of the Currant Creek power plant, one the most recent plants built to meet the electricity demands of the booming population below. Infrequent lights of white and red indicate the occasional passing car on I-15. The distance is staggering, about an entire mile of elevation below us, but instead of inspiring courage and feelings of accomplishment, it only reminds us how far we are from any respite.

I start to lose the feelings of panic but not because it has been replaced by hope or new courage. Instead, it is as if I have simply acquiesced to nature's law that all things die, that I am, after all, destined to die at some point and that if it were now or later, the end would be the same. This isn't exactly cause for elation but it does feel like what peace might be, and in a strange way I feel more determined to persist. If I survive to see the day, I know it will be a gift, not something I have believed I have a right to.

I keep checking to see if the sky is reflecting the dawn against the east shadow of the mountain. I think I finally notice a contrast. With each passing minute, the sky becomes noticeably lighter, almost pinkish, and I feel a change in my entire inner being. Even though the sun will not crest over the mountain for some time yet, its reflection is already scattering shadows on the lightening surface of the gray mountain. This is elate light, indirect and auspicious, presaging a sharpening of the senses. The only foreboding comes from the winds that pick up as we approach a line of tall pines above us. Leaning out against the air at vertiginous angles, their bent trunks provide protection and rest for breakfast.

We drop our packs and begin to wolf down peanut butter and jelly sandwiches, a much preferable fare to the Powerbars, jerky, and nuts we have been nibbling at for hours. Congratulations are offered and a growing euphoria begins to spread. Before long, we are gabbing away, joking about our old bodies, about this pitiful effort to hold off old age. I look at George

who smiles back at me. I think of these lines I read from the Mexican poet
Homero Aridjis:

> He who is afraid to die feels his time stop
> and watching the dawn does not know
> if his own sun is setting
> then in the festival of light
> signs appear for him alone.

It is no doubt my own fear that makes me want to believe that the sun
rose for me alone, but the winds don't allow for such comfort. We pack up,
put on our snowshoes and parkas to fend off the wind, and begin our ascent
to the east in what quickly has become deep powder. At this elevation, after
such intense climbing, breathing grows especially heavy, but it feels good to
be using different muscles and to have less stress on the ankles, good enough
to convince me that with proper caution, I will be strong enough to finish
the hike.

Before long we leave the trees behind us, switchback our way through a
field of jutting boulders on a steep incline that drops precipitously to our
left, and are now on a narrow ridge heading straight toward our destination.
From where we stand, the world is entirely white, interrupted only by occasional rocky teeth that jut into the air. The wind is strong and the danger of
deceptive cornices has us on high alert. The ridgeline is irregular, at times
intensely curled, and white and sparkling in what is by now intense morning sunlight. Just to punctuate its wave-like appearance, Taylor poses like a
surfer at a safe distance from the edge of a cornice.

The world is sharp in relief, pale blue angled lines of shadows cutting
across the diamond-like sparkles of undisturbed snow. Many of the sun's reflections on the white snow seem nearly as bright as the sun itself. I find myself angling my eyes away from their intensity, following the lines of shadows
with my head down. Directly to the north is an enormous, cavernous cut in
the mountain where avalanches clearly make their living. There is scarcely
any sign of vegetation in a long, steep drop between the ridge we are on and
a similar fin of mountain wedging its way in a northwest direction.

The most troublesome spot is the narrow sliver of a saddle that separates
our ridge from the beginning ascent on the peak itself. The crossing requires
no more than a steady straight walk over a ridge of snow just wide enough

for one's snowshoes. On the left, for about fifty feet or so, a misstep takes you down an intimidating expanse of sheer white dropping at close to a seventy-five-degree angle. On the right, just as steep, the angle of white disappears into a mist of morning clouds. As I cross, I try to stare only at my shoes, but curiosity gets the best of me and I glance down both sides. I feel shots of vertiginous fear pass through the marrow of my bones, but I notice that having identified the proper object of fear has heightened my joy in the midst of uncertainty and inspired grateful elation for the chance of a rare, unrepeatable experience.

I find myself whooping childishly and full of annealing affection for my companions as I begin the ascent up a bald face of snow, deep and steep enough to require frequent switchbacks, each of us taking turns as trailblazer in the seemingly bottomless powder. Wade, who was worried about how prepared he was for this climb, leans on his poles every thirty steps or so, grunting at himself, "Come on, Wade! Come on!" I opt to walk behind him to keep him focused on shorter-term objectives. It was several hours ago now that he had thought of turning around, so clearly the only thing driving his engine at this point is will power.

As we draw nearer to the top, we can look down to another saddle cutting across to the south to a lower point on the mountain. The snow gleams and turns like the surface of the sea, looking far more benign than it really is. I am utterly exhausted, but the bright sunshine reflecting off the surface of the snow, the sharp angles of snow and rock, the deep blue shadows, and the staggering vistas in all directions create a world worth suffering for. Besides, with something to compare to my despair in the early morning dark, I feel that no matter what happens at this point, I have escaped the jaws of death. The fact that going back down is the most dangerous part seems irrelevant.

The summit arrives rather unceremoniously, the pitch of the mountain simply leveling gradually until there is no white wall before our eyes. It is almost eleven a.m., over nine hours since we began. We are greeted by high streaks of clouds against the pale blue winter sky and white-capped mountains that dot the landscape in all directions. We are far above the thin line of particulate inversion that blankets the valley, and the predominance of clean mountains, like upside-down chalices awkwardly catching water on points of jagged rock, makes the sea of houses in Utah Valley stretch out in a faint and seemingly insignificant mirage. The basin below has to wait to receive its water after this season of precarious gathering, a kind of forbearance for the fact that all things eventually come down.

The wind blows fiercely, and we zip up and cover our heads for protection. Taylor, proud of his heritage, pulls out his Welsh flag for a photograph. It is something to contemplate why transfiguration always occurs on mountains. Moses had his own that led to a vision of creation. Of course, Moses's own gravesite was never marked, leaving a lingering rumor that he was translated on a moutain, after pleading with the Lord for more time on earth. No doubt he wanted to see his promised land up close, because after years of anguish he was indifferent to death but not to the glories of the creation.

On the descent, the powder is like a playground, allowing long strides in the snowshoes and short sensations of surfing on the surface of the snow. As I watch us prance down the mountain, giggling and whooping like adolescents, I wonder if it is some kind of religious gene that brought us to conquer this mountain like our ancestors, just to prove that we still have rights to this land over others. The conquering impulse communicates a deep drive to accept the illusion of freedom to claim a land as God-given, to cherish lost treasures as our own. Reconnaissance feels like a kind of freedom, knowledge of the land as the right to claim it as promised and as protection against the violence of any number of Babylons.

I do like the way this mountain feels like freedom, but it is a freedom that teaches the strangeness of finding myself here, now. Babylon is intolerant of difference, human and more-than-human, and territory is its consequence, a man-made kingdom. Its monuments, technology, pride of the eyes, all a raging despair at finding ourselves on this peculiar ball of fire. On a visit to Utah Valley, long before I married and settled here, I dreamed one night in a fit of religious fervor that I was taken up in the twinkling of an eye. I floated up above the valley floor in a blue-black night sky, with the mountains receding below and stars surrounding me like balls of fiery love. And then it occurred to me that my life had just ended, that I would never marry or have children, that this and all other lands I had come to love were no longer under my feet. I remember feeling a confusion of sorrow and elation. When I awoke and arose, it was as if I had forgotten everything and could see the world for the first time, and I knew that despite the diminishments of time, life was imperishably good.

When we cross back over the saddle, I think how strange it would seem to our ancestors to see us ascending mountains just for the experience and yet so unfamiliar with the raw strength they learned from this land. How strange, too, to our descendents if we would have enjoyed these pleasures without due measures taken to preserve what is left of what we sing are the "everlasting hills."

It is a full three hours of descending, so it is easy to lose one's concentration, to become somewhat indifferent and physically exhausted and bored by the monotony of the pitch and pull of gravity. After awkwardly glissading over hard and icy snow that gives way to a more slippery and softer turf, I find myself walking drunkenly through a field of boulders, with occasional mud patches and slush, and my feet go out from under me, my poles sprawl, and I land awkwardly on my right hand. Using a handful of snow to wipe the mud off my fingers, I examine my middle finger, sure that it is broken. These accidents feel like the few moments before sleep when you aren't sure what is real or what matters. It is too easy to give in to these temptations, but my throbbing finger keeps me alert enough to make it to the trail that took us up past Willow Creek. Now the snow is melting everywhere, water trickles in all directions, the air is warm, and I start to feel a glow of warmth in the flushed blood vessels all over my skin.

I open the car door almost in disbelief that the long journey is over. In the moments before everyone but me, the designated driver, has fallen asleep, someone asks what Mount Nebo is named after. A few mumbled responses, and then the clarification: it was the mountain Moses climbed to for his one and only glance at the promised land he would never inhabit before he died. "I have caused thee to see it with thine eyes, but thou shalt not go over thither," Moses was told, surely one of the more strange cruelties in all scripture. The great Moses, still strong ("his eye was not dim, nor his natural force abated"), left to be taken up by the Lord, somewhere in the mountains or the plains, no one really knows.[40]

Brigham Young, the American Moses, had ample opportunity to survey the promised land of his people, but that does not settle the wonder the land inspires. What is it that makes promised lands so elusive, carved out of the geography of nations with some degree of violence, and never without persistent controversy over their precious borders, real or imagined? What glory is it that Wordsworth claimed has passed away from the earth? Has it passed away despite or because of our best efforts to capture it in our houses, our cities, and our claims for a homeland? There is a secret buried in Paul's curious comment about Moses, Abraham, and the other patriarchs who were denied their chance to live in the cities they sought to build: "They all died in faith, not having received the promises, but having seem them afar off, and were persuaded of them, and embraced them, and confessed that they were strangers and pilgrims on the earth."[41] It is not ingratitude for the pleasures of family, friends, and community that this place affords to confess that I am likewise persuaded.

Nine

THE YEARS HAVE PASSED, AND FAMILIARITY HAS BROUGHT ME ITS PLEA-
sures but also its disappointments. With increased knowledge of this place, its
history, and its complex vulnerability, it is hard to fight off rising anger at our
unsustainable ways and the feeling of seemingly inevitable decline. We do not
appear to have been on track to build any kind of promised land but have instead been eager to lay waste to what we have been given. It's hard, too, not
to notice the ways in which the overwhelming religious homogeneity of this
community makes us lazy and resistant to hard self-questioning. The only alternative to anger seems to be to acquiesce to a numb apathy. I remember that
first year of exploration with John, and already it seems as if I am seeing those
scenes of a rediscovered bliss from behind some screen.

I need to go fishing. It's March, winter has lasted long enough, and I have
grown tired of spring's indecision. Snowshoeing or cross-country skiing into
the mountains sustains me in the long winter months, especially when I am
lucky enough to catch a day after a storm, blue-ball skies capping a white
world interrupted only by the green pines that never seem bothered by the
weather. But living in the mountains also means that winter will fight a more
prolonged battle before it loosens its hold. Just a hint or two of its weakening power and you start looking for something that isn't there yet, some
other world of green mountain grasses, budding wildflowers, and lime-
green canopies of aspen leaves shimmering in balmy breezes. Recompenses
for your longsuffering.

It has occurred to me the longer I live here how mysteriously essential
mountain waters have become. I almost worry that it seems unnatural somehow to be so dependent on their animate life. They are my manna, the stones
on my tongue, the glass into which I look darkly to contemplate my being.
They are nothing more than the means by which I have learned to confront
my memories, define my humanity, and negotiate the terms of my mortal
place in this world. Nothing more, and nothing less.

I don't blame the winter, of course, for my not fishing. I can always decide to withstand the cold, to fish with numb feet, and to awkwardly tie on

my flies with leaden stupor as the cold invades my forearms and wrists. Such suffering has usually paid off, too. Like the sunrise that first year I fished with John. We drove up Provo Canyon in the dark just after five in the morning. By the time we reached the upper section of the river below Deer Creek Dam, the sky was only just beginning to show a hint of reflected light from the still-distant sun.

John was euphoric, as always, hoping to name a hole in honor of our trek that morning. We sought fish by casting streamers and wooly buggers heavily onto the banks and stripping them in with intermittent jerks. I was new to the technique, but he gave his usual careful instruction about how to pull the line frequently enough so that the streamer bobbed and jolted underwater like a minnow. The contrast between air temperature, well below freezing, and the warmer moving water created a permanent mist hovering over the river, as if it were simmering just below the boiling point. An impression belied by the shocking contact my hands made with water when I caught my first fish, just as the sky was turning pink. "Sunrise Hole" was all I could come up with. But John seemed pleased.

Or the bright winter day, just after a snow and only a mile farther down from the dam, when the deep blue of the sky startled the eyes against the brilliance of the white-dressed mountains. An eagle crossed above our heads with a trout wriggling in its talons, in open mockery of our inefficient methods. Before we had given any thought to what to say, we both yelled to the skies above us just to acknowledge what we had seen. It was then that I finally understood what Walt Whitman meant by a "barbaric yawp."

It was not far from that spot that I caught my largest fish on the Provo, in February. It was a twenty-inch brown that took a size 22 Griffiths gnat with sudden violence across the current that separated us. That's a fly the size of a small pebble with a hook fortunate enough to have wedged between the tight sinews of the fish's mouth. John was coaching me on my cast, standing just off to my side, and I had managed to get my arm, rod, and line in perfect synchronicity to his instructions to land the fly softly on the edge of a curving riffle that ran parallel to an "S" bend on the bank. The take was hard— the fish dove and then jutted into the air, almost three feet above the water, it seemed. In my mind's eye I can still see my rod tip raised high, my arm above my shoulder, and the line taut above the water shimmering in the gray winter light, the fish dancing in midair. And John yawping some more.

I tried writing poems in those days because of the torment of my fish dreams. One night I floated along a deep stream lined by red canyon walls.

I balanced myself along the limestone shores, red sand flaking in my wet palms, while older men stood on the shores holding their rods in wonder at this novice who appeared to have fallen and ruined the waters. I offered apologies, but then a rumbling commotion below me bounced me like a buoy. Looking beneath my dangling feet, I could see the curving dorsal of what appeared to be a giant lurching eel. I frantically pointed below in hopes of vindication from the men (wizened poets perhaps, symbols of staid tradition) but all I did was make it inevitable that we would all have to imagine what could have been. I pulled myself out downstream sheepishly and awoke haunted.

I would have hoped that memories of those days on the river would bring comfort this late in the winter, but the sunken feeling I have about my failure to create new memories overwhelms the pleasure old ones provide. Memories, even poems about them, are not enough to sustain oneself in prolonged seasons of sun deprivation or nature-deficit disorder. The vitality and continuity of sensation provide the fuel that fires our awareness of the distinctions of the human condition and of our tenuous place in the physical universe. But experiencing beauty often comes at greater physical cost than we can afford.

That alone doesn't explain why it would seem I have grown tired of beauty, however. It is, of course, inadvisable to fish alone in the winter, and I have fallen enough in cold water to know the violence with which such cold seizes the body. Lack of winter fishing is one of the prices I have paid for John's departure, a kind of penance for my failure to keep him from his demons, just as an unsutured wound never finishes the work of healing. The truth is that I have always depended on social networks and the initiative of friends to provide me the experiences in the outdoors that keep me aware and alive. Since he left, no one seems interested in five a.m. drives up the dark hollow of the canyon. I have tried to imitate his passion for experience, his skills of adoption, but over time, left alone without sufficient social motivation, my natural inclination is to revel in the known and to seek impossible satisfaction in monotony.

I cannot deny, of course, that my discovery of excursions in the cold has helped me to see its extraordinary beauty. In the snow, I remind myself I am witnessing rivers in embryo, that this deprivation is really just a storing up for the bounty, but as much sensation as it affords, the stillness of winter conceals. I like what Dillard says: "Live water heals memories." Like most people, I suppose, I do my best to accommodate myself to the unpredictable length of winter, but once the world hints at spring's renewal, I grow dizzy with anticipation of the recompense of a world that conforms to my dreams.

But spring is an unfaithful lover. She's impotent and indecisive in putting the cold away once and for all; her rebirths are slow, intermittent, and feeble. Which in a land so vulnerable to drought should be endured with greater patience, I know. Snowpack is the land's gold currency. Eliot thought April to be the cruelest month, but had he lived in Utah, he would have made a stronger case for March.

Better to suffer through the dark cold unprovoked by hints of spring thaw in the air, one starts to think. SAD, isn't it? This is one of the most bitter acronyms around, invented by some clinician with a sick sense of irony. Sometime in my thirties I began to recognize my weakening ability to get through March. One schizophrenic uncle and Kenny's suicide at the young age of twenty-two are enough to keep me on guard. After all, it was here in a Utah winter where he suffered his breakdown after arriving from Connecticut for his first semester of college, and it was here we buried him five years later beneath the indifferent gaze of the Wasatch Mountains, on Christmas Eve. I had tried during that first year of living in Utah to recall those events to John, but even with such a sympathetic and inquisitive audience, I kept many of the details of my memories only vaguely defined. It gave me the illusions of telling the truth and the comfort of friendship, all without risking the pain of resurrected memories. I think I have approached too many of my most important relationships with this guardedness. Why, I am not sure. Maybe I will never find the perfect audience to help absorb them, but to revisit them, to dust them off and sort them out, would be an act of faith. And maybe I am afraid I don't have that faith.

Strange that now, all these years later, precise and fragmented details float idly about me. Like illegitimate children, they threaten to divide the patrimony I have created over time, persisting in their appeal for a name, for recognition. It seems only fair that after so many encounters with the losses of others, I must learn to reckon with my own. Best get on with the business of getting acquainted with these lost scions, I suppose.

When I moved to Utah, Kenny's gravestone was one of the first visits I made. I had only seen it intermittently since that winter so many years ago. This time it lay beneath the neatly trimmed bluegrass, which spread out in all directions, with cleanly designed surrounding neighborhoods of graves.

As I have tried to visit the gravesite every year since, the jagged stillness of the mountains has provided the only solace. The rectitude of the etched stone always seems to trigger the weeping, a sorrow about a past that is sealed away, about a life that we were never able to share. My wife and children he could have loved. Loves he might have had.

I am old enough now to have been his father. I was eighteen then, and he almost twenty-three. Because of his emotional struggles and my adolescence, we hardly knew each other. But I was proud of his sinewy and forceful strength, his dark, thick hair and good looks, his gentleness, and his extraordinary intellectual passion. He read Maugham as a teenager and was possessed of a dark and somber passion for serious music—Schubert quartets and Brahms symphonies—and when he spoke, his eyes darted nervously. Every so often I will have a student in my office or I will meet a young man at church and a light of recognition turns on inside me. Bright and articulate men, possessed of deep-seated perceptions of the inner world of life, and yet reclusively shy and darkly self-destructive.

I only have one letter from him, something for my birthday with a hand-drawn cake with candles and advice about the value of having focus.

He lies not full fathom five, as Ariel put it, subject to the strange chemistry of nature's resurrections, but sealed off within a coffin where his bones can quietly decay in complete solitude. No communion with worms, no bones soldering into coral, not even daisy fodder.

We passed on the stairs and I asked him for some typewriter ribbon. He was moments away from putting a bullet in his head and yet he told me where the ribbon was. It was only later, of course, when we tried to piece together the final hours, that I realized this was my last chance to see him alive. It was then, in my mind's eye, that I could see the anguish on his face. The image lies there still behind the curtain of my eyes, as if one of only a few things I have ever truly seen. And yet it feels like a dream. Maybe the anxiety of the impressionists was justified. They felt that they didn't see so much with their eyes as they did with their minds and they did so belatedly, anachronistically. A patchwork impression of rough brush strokes, their masterpieces nothing more than what they could cobble together in the streaming of the world.

There are sounds, too. The sound of my mother's voice emanating from the corner of the family room where she lay collapsed and immobile. "That poor boy!" she wailed over and over again. I remember hearing my brother Bill moaning somewhere, maybe in my room where he had been helping me with something, while our father dealt with the police. I can see myself sitting on the couch upstairs in the living room, looking through the window at his limp body lying on the grass outside. There wasn't enough light to see all of his definitions and what certainly would have been a red pool of blood on our Connecticut lawn, a stain our neighbors cleaned from the grass while we were burying him in Utah. I could see his body draped in the heavy tan coat he was wearing on the stairs.

Some police entered and asked me questions. I stared back at them blankly.

I must have moved because my father now stood in the basement by the bookshelf, talking with someone about the hospital. I could see a large blood stain on the leg of his pants from kneeling beside his son's body. To my left, in the dark, my brother Bill held my mother on the couch to help slow her unstoppable flow of pain. I was conscious of my pants, too—the ugly gray dress pants I was wearing when I returned from choir rehearsal. I thought them ugly, and when we prepared to go to the hospital, I changed into my jeans, as if in complete denial of what had transpired.

And I recall touch. My bishop held my knee wordlessly with a quivering hand at the hospital. Kenny lay in a bed with a heavily bandaged head, like a large round turban. His eyes were covered, and only enough of his face was visible to see how swollen his entire head was—what little could be seen was virtually beyond recognition. An artificial respirator moved his chest up and down, like a plastic chest used in CPR classes. We prayed around his bed, and the bishop asked that the Lord's will be done. Dad was told he would be "worse than a vegetable" if he survived, and after what he had witnessed on the lawn, he knew they were right. His body died two days later.

For weeks afterward I had fearful dreams that left me trembling on my pillow. I can still remember them vividly, more vividly than the nightmare of what I experienced in my waking moments. Dreams of walking on a sidewalk happily with friends when suddenly one of them fell and hit his head, spilling his brains out on the uneven cement. Laughter turned to utter horror. Someone at school pounded on the window of the cafeteria from the courtyard, pleading to be let in when suddenly his head burst open and blood and brains sprayed against the window. To this day I find myself perpetually renegotiating the inner spaces of my mind to accommodate the persistence of my fears of impending cataclysm, as if all appearances are to be mistrusted, as if all promises of stasis and stability are lies, as if beauty will never last. I never know what it might be that will rapaciously change the face of the world. Most of the time I keep myself above the downward pull of an almost addictive urge to be paranoid about joy because the fear causes me to cling to the transient and endangered beauty of the physical world with the desperation of a young child who does not want his father to leave.

I can see now that this is why this land's beauty haunts me, why I am drawn toward it, and even why I hunger so intensely for home. The finality of death is what makes history the eulogy it is: something happened, uniquely in its time and place, and no matter how I choose to remember it, it remains real and irrevocable, stagnant in eddies of stasis and oblivion. It offers itself as a line that defies me to cross it, even these many years later. I must learn, it seems, the art not only to live with the knowledge of impending death but also with irrevocable loss. The merciful gift of this pain is that it teaches one not to sacrifice any chances for whatever beauty is still left or might yet come.

I was going to go fishing but I found that I was wearing a pair of river sandals that strangely had a buckle between them that bound my feet and inhibited my movement. I simply unbuckled them and felt freed to fish. My sandals gave me sufficient support in the cold current because the bed was soft and firm, not rocky and mossy as the Provo usually is. I picked my spot on the opposite bank just at the edge of an eddy where a riffle snaked its way below some stones. The water was clear but I could discern moving shadows beneath the flickering reflections. A fish struck, but as I pulled it toward me, it appeared to be nothing but a blob of green moss.

Disappointed with what appeared to be a monstrous snag, I began to reel it quickly in. As it crossed the current, however, I could see that it was indeed a fish that had merely taken me into weeds. It started to shed its moss, revealing an athletic shimmer of flesh. It made its way artfully behind a small island in the middle of the stream. This forced me to cross downstream of the spit of land while keeping my rod high. He tore loose from the island and jetted downstream. I sensed that at any moment the line might break, something I have learned from too many mistakes not to allow. Losing a fish that you have come close enough to see is worse than never getting a strike. It takes a learned patience to let him fight against your impetuous desire to handle the palpitating life beneath the stillness. Just in time I released some pressure so that his refusal to surface, not my greed, would wear him out.

After a slow pull upstream, keeping my elbows low and close to my chest, the fish finally drifted with the current at my side. I lifted him in my two hands, and before my eyes was a species I had never seen before, more beautiful and rare than even the native Bonneville cutthroats I have occasionally pulled from the upper reaches of the Provo, with a stunning white coloration on its skin. It gasped heavily in my hands. I looked around to signal to others what I had found, but I saw that I was alone.

Returning my gaze to my hands, I saw that I held a beautiful, dry, clean baby boy with a frosting of white hair and penetrating blue eyes. His skin was like silk and I held him out in front of me to take in the sensation of his heft. Like Thomas, I touched and prodded and finally clutched him in a desperate embrace. I held him out again to get another look, unable to assimilate his beauty.

It was a dream, of course, one I had just recently, that left me shaking when I awoke. Was it Kenny? Possibly, since he is on my mind, but the baby had light blond fuzz on his head, something closer to what my only son, Sam, looked like when he was born. The odd sensation was that despite what felt like an immediate bond, I knew I had no idea who he was. He was a totally new human being, as if the very fact of an individual existence were miracle enough—no metaphor for someone else but someone never before seen and more beautiful than my eyes had witnessed, the very body of inexplicable hope. He shone and radiated a newness and innocence that was tangible, fleshy. Some son of a god, perhaps, but no angel with wings.

For a long time, when I tried to remember Kenny's death, it was the fact that in my memory he was always about to die but still alive that was the most difficult to bear. Shortly after his death I had dreams in which he would appear to us suddenly in the living room in his tan jacket, his hair tossed as if he had just arisen from the grass. He was not bloody but it was as if the trauma of his death had been the result of an illusion, that it was some kind of cruel joke that had been played on us all. He never spoke in these dreams but looked at us wordlessly. This pushed me to the very edge of fear, and in the morning I found myself unable to ascertain the limits of my own body or the reality of the bed upon which I had slept. Touching my feet to the ground and pulling myself out of bed with the help of my desk would begin the process of living and believing in the physical world's apparent permanence, but the phantoms of my fear followed me throughout each day, unsettling my feeling of belonging to this world.

Only weeks after Kenny's death, Bill had returned to college. Bill had agonized about the decision to return, but it seemed to be the best thing to do. Once there, he cried alone most nights and struggled to find the right openings with friends to talk about it. I was alone with my parents. We spent evenings in the kitchen talking and remembering everything together. Almost nightly my parents and I recounted every detail of the final days, of Kenny's many talents, his ambitions. This was healing pain, but years later my parents confessed that they cried every night for a year as they held each other in the dark, an intensity of sorrow from which they tried to protect Bill and me. I am not sure they succeeded, nor should have wanted to.

I lived in the basement bedroom of our house. My window faced the backyard where Kenny had lain in his own blood, and every sound of the furnace, every creak of the boards throughout the house, every indication that the solid world could move and make sound, terrified me. Change had become intolerably cruel and horrible; it wore the mask of terror. I was a young boy all over again, afraid of dark rooms before I could reach the light switch and afraid to be alone. It seemed that only a well-lit static and dumb world would do, a world in which the outline of things was certain. Such a state is impossible to maintain, of course, but for a time death had me in its grip, had me thinking that nothing else was true of human beings than that they died, that they disappeared from among the living, and that was the end.

One night as I strained over papers and college applications at the desk beside my bed, I became uncontrollably frantic with fear from recurring memories. A loud crack. Bill saying, "What was that?!" Shrugging my shoulders nonchalantly. Seconds more. Footsteps pounding down the stairs and entering my room. Dad's voice announcing with terror, "Kenny shot himself!" I found myself on the ground, praying as well as I knew how, begging for peace. After I climbed into bed and lay in the dark, I froze with sudden terror at the impression that Kenny had indeed entered the room in the dark and was facing me. I had to make something move, so my lips expressed something of my love for him. I don't remember everything I tried to say in this imagined dialogue, but I remember a distinct warmth surrounding the top of my head, as if a light were pouring its heat into my skull. And these words: *I am happier than you can understand. I love you.* For a brief moment it was as if I could feel his joy. I repeated these last words out loud and seemed to startle myself with the hollow ring of my own voice within the walls of my room. It was only after this experience that I understood Lehi's curious phrase: "I have dreamed a dream, or in other words, I have seen a vision."[42] Sometimes I am tempted to tell the story as if it were a dream and at other times as a vision, and neither approach seems any less truthful, or any closer to the truth.

The nightmares never returned.

This March morning as I recall these things, springtime is struggling to assert itself. Winter will not give up the fight. I see green grass and daffodils frosted with wet snow, leafless tree limbs hanging expectantly with buds wise enough to hold their tongues until the parent seasons have ceased their bickering. This will be a fecund spring, however, precisely because of the prolonged struggle for reconciliation. An arid land like this needs our tolerance for the ambiguity of seasons, which is to say it needs our spiritual fortitude to tolerate the contradictions of being who we are.

One March, winter ceded its authority with such cowardice—all of us walked in the sunlight, giddy but foolish for having prematurely embraced the promises of warm sunshine. This is the same emotion that has some people welcoming the warming trends of climate change and that sends us all running headlong from the struggles of the physical conditions of life. The result was a short spring, a brief dash of green before the declension into dry grasses on the mountainsides of the Great Basin bench. It was a disaster for the mountain snowpack, 70 percent of which was lost to sudden evaporation and absorption into the earth, bequeathing to us a long hot summer of wildfires. Our reservoirs showed no gains for all the talk of drought's end after an extremely wet November and December. Late in the fishing season that next fall the rivers were so low, I could scarcely find holes deep enough for my ankles.

But this year the spring skies are drizzling, as they have been for several days, occasionally turning into a kind of spitting wet snow, and the tree branches outside my window reflect the subtle shades of brown and gray of entrenched winter. Truth is, if we don't get many more winters holding out like this, we may find ourselves calling February the cruelest month. Farmers will get their longer growing season but without the irrigation water. Despite positive gains this year, the soothsayers aren't making any promises. Do I have the courage to thank God for this prolonged confusion?

Two weeks before his death, my parents had come home one day and Kenny confessed with innocent dismay, "You know, Dad, the strangest thing happened today. I had this urge to kill myself. I went into the bathroom and filled the tub with water. I cut myself just once...and it snapped me out of it." Dad pressed him to go to the hospital with him immediately, but Kenny was adamant that it was an aberration. "I would never do that, Dad," he had said.

Ever his own scientist, he mentioned a possible connection to his visit to the doctor only the day before. His doctor was trying to determine what environmental agents were provoking his depressed condition and had placed under his tongue a drop of Maltox, a chemical used in pesticides for peaches and apples that has since been banned in some commercial forms. Kenny had lost control and shaken incoherently in response. They both agreed to ask the doctor to cease with such experiments.

On the next Sunday Dad asked me to come home early from church to be with Kenny. I thought this strange since I was the younger brother, but he explained that sometimes when people get as depressed as he was, they try to take their own life. This was incomprehensible to me. I found my imagination drifting to what it would be like to receive the pity of my friends, and of girls in particular, for having lost a brother in such a tragic fashion. It wasn't as if I didn't wonder and worry about how Kenny was feeling, but it was beyond me how or why he might do such a thing.

He was already planning it not long after the first attempt. On a Monday he had another visit to the doctor and inexplicably received another drop of Maltox. Did he ask for it? Did he not try to protest? On Tuesday he went target shooting with a friend, something he had never done before. They went again on Wednesday and this time he took a gun home with him without telling his friend. The friend called that night and asked for Kenny. Dad went to get him unsuspecting of the content of the conversation. The friend asked if he had taken it, and Kenny replied, "Yeah, I did. I just wanted to clean it. I'll get it back to you tomorrow." He had obviously neglected to mention the bullet in his pocket that he would use the next day.

And then there were the drafts of letters, showing careful if irrational forethought, found in the pocket of his jacket and on his desk. There were six of them in total, all without a date and all directed at either "Dear friends" or "My dear family." They express love and gratitude and apologies for the pain that he may have caused, but they insist that the agony he was in could no longer be endured or controlled. Some phrases jump out at me now as I look over them. "It was the environment that slayed me and not myself." And the perplexing contradiction: "I have no control over this urge, but it is absolutely necessary." His expressions of love still shake me: "I rest in peace and watch upon you with love." In one brief essay he wrote about his medical condition, he explains: "My physical and mental agony is unbearable. At every turn I'm exposed to some new offender. My immune system can't handle the load. There is a defect intrinsic. Oh, and I've seen such beauty, and now it seems so far away. And all the sensitive and gentle creatures which I thought I could help and hold, pass distant, as in a novel, unreachable now, characters in a movie which once I thought I was a part of. I can't defeat reality with feeling." He describes the onset of the illness as acute, a result of perhaps one night, after which, "everything in my body felt chemically 'altered';...what do I know, right? I know one thing very well, and that is that what happened to me was something completely beyond normal experience and stands out more clearly in my mind than any other experience in my life, painful and pleasurable. It was as if someone had turned off the tap of life on me."

When I think of the intentional and outrageous damage done to the earth and the crime of so many mistreated bodies, when I think of our headlong whoring of God's green earth and our aesthetic impoverishment, it seems the height of absurdity that a young man, who once saw the world inhabited by "sensitive and gentle creatures" and with no blood on his hands, found himself incapacitated by his own physical existence, victim perhaps of the way toxic materials insidiously find their way through our skin, our lungs and mucous membranes, or our mouths, or perhaps victim of his own marvelous biology. Once made enemy to the physical world, the only thing real to him was what managed to stir in the receding eddies of his mind.

Which isn't to say that the rest of us are any less vulnerable to the illusions of the imagination, but there is something in a sustained dialogue between dream and experience, spirit and body, heaven and earth, that allows for ongoing and mutual transformation. This interchange is the stuff of life and the bedrock of all art and religion. I think it is true what my father presciently said at Kenny's funeral years before the breakthroughs in mental illness treatment, that he was killed by a disease as real as cancer and every bit as indiscriminate. What else can explain his sudden awareness that he stood behind a glass, unable to feel the ecstasies of beauty?

But the question remains: was his final act a symptom of his illness or the last gasp of freedom? The impulse to despair gives a clue to that something in him that contradicted the claims of biology, that refused to be taken even by his own toxic body, something that despaired because of the physical beauty he could see but no longer *feel*. It doesn't minimize the tragedy or acquiesce to what never should have happened to say that it is a far greater disease to fail to see beauty at all, or to be indifferent to its destruction. Nor to say that this open wound in my life has compensated me with an awareness and hunger for the healing beauty of living waters. And the hunger has given me community, friends, and relationships. To be indifferent to place feels like the worst kind of acquiescence, the greatest dishonor to what he suffered. Insufficient vessels we are, not built to withstand the daily tremors beauty offers, but at least we can avoid the dangers of justification by confessing our weakness from time to time.

Hadn't I seen his hands in his pocket as he walked down the stairs to the backyard? There was nothing particularly unusual about that fact, but his hands must have felt the cold and sleek metal of the handgun, holding it as the ticket out of his misery. How long had he felt that metal in his hand before he brought it out of his pocket as he sat on the lawn? How long did he wait before he lifted it to his temple and pulled the trigger? Was there deep fear of the icy waters he would shortly drown in or did he simply take a few final moments to contemplate the night sky, to feel the dormant grass below him, to hear the soft sounds of the trees one more time before he opened the door to exit the physical world that had become his nightmare?

That very spot on the grass where he died had been my place of meditation, for smoking cigarettes clandestinely under the stars. The grass there slopes slightly downhill facing a gully filled with tall, leafless trees. It was a good place to be alone beneath the stars and in the company of the chorus of the woods. Funny that now, after all those years of playing in those woods, I have no idea what kind of trees they were. The edge of the grass at the bottom of the slope is marked by the dark ground of the woods, deep, soft soil covered with paper-thin layers of decaying leaves.

Although the lawn presumably marks the edge of the man-made world, it never felt that way. Eastern grass has the look of maturity and nativity. Because it is afflicted by the occasional brown patch, rocks, and the uneven terrain of aged surfaces and protruding roots of old trees, the grass looks more like the fur of an animal hide than the green and groomed carpets of western sod that are typically overfertilized and overfed by imported mountain water through elaborate sprinkler systems, the plant equivalent of industrial chicken. I knew my lawn almost as well as I knew the surface of my own hands, having spent every summer since I was twelve taking turns with my dad mowing it and countless hours lounging on it in the moonlight. But I hadn't seen what had surely shattered my father's capacity to absorb the event that night. "I can't put into words what I saw," he once told me years later. And then, in reverent tones and with shocking precision, he did.

That March a high and deep green patch of grass announced itself prematurely, before spring had properly arrived. My father initially couldn't bring himself to mow down the tuft. After I spent the summer out west in Idaho, I came home before leaving for college that fall. I remember mowing the late summer lawn and found myself looking for the place where he had lain. I stopped where I thought it must have been, and in an act of what felt like perverse curiosity, I ran my hands over the grass, wondering why over the summer months regeneration had already dispersed and concealed where his blood had soaked the soil. The touch of the indifferent leaves of grass—Whitman's "beautiful uncut hair of graves"—made me shudder.

I knew I was soon leaving this place, and I had long since given up on my adolescent transgressions in the night. Perhaps for this reason and because I had spent the summer in the high dry air of the West, I felt myself more detached from the surface of the ground and unmoved by the resurrection of little lives in my yard, things like the moss growing up the side of the tree trunk to the left of this spot of earth, the strange shapes of fungus growths in the grass after a recent rain, the deepening green moss on the stones that protruded from the grass like so many broken bones.

A few weeks later I departed for the West once more, never again to witness the way an eastern spring restores the garden of the world. Strange how, despite my apparent indifference at the time, I find myself in the West as hungry as ever for the way the eastern spring transfigures the world into one great green and tremulous body. But I am learning patience with the unpredictable ways of such grace. Out here, it might rain or more likely it might not, but either way you know Stegner was right: you've got to get over the color green.

I feel a heavy exhaustion as if even my head is too heavy to hold. I glance again through my bedroom window at the Asian branches of our Catalpa tree. It is warm enough to make fishing tolerably comfortable and cold enough that spring runoff wouldn't muddy the waters. Camilla enters the room and, as is her wont, silently throws her young arms around me from behind, shaking me from my stupor. Wordlessly I stroke her hands across my chest. When the weather is better in a few more weeks, I finally tell her, I will take her to the children's pond at Vivian Park up in the canyon where she caught her first fish last year. "I would like that," she says.

The word on the river for fly-fishermen is that in the confusion of seasons the pale morning duns are hatching now and that fish are feeding on the surface of the olive water. My heartbeat increases at the familiar thought of standing in the cold current watching dimples pierce the surface of water pockets, of motion below the stillness, and I decide impulsively to see the beauty myself that afternoon. I don't know much about the science of fishing, no more than your average amateur anyway, so I rely as much on my own imagination and on grace itself to satisfy my fish lust. I suppose with more knowledge I might catch more fish, but I don't mind humbling reminders that the world has never been of my own making. Besides, it is the transient feel of water I crave anyway and the angling at its passing. It is fair to say that I prefer fishing on the edge of uncertainty, because on the best days when my drift is just right and the fish are compliant it seems that, like Caravaggio's bewildered men, I can no longer tell what the difference is between revelation and desire. Lord knows I could use some of that confusion.

Spring

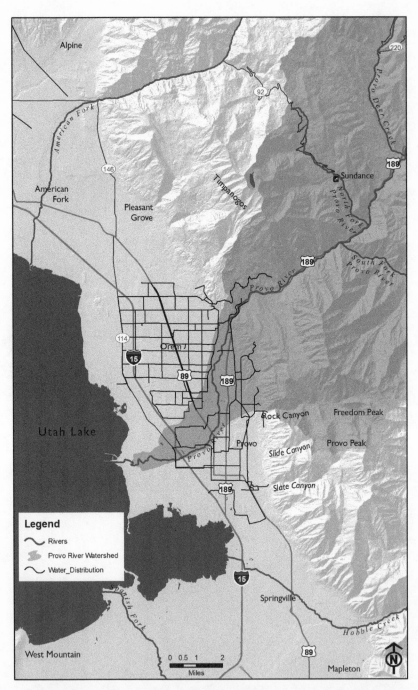

THE LOWER PROVO RIVER, PROVO CANYON, AND UTAH LAKE

Ten

*

"ARE YOU READY?" THE QUESTION WAS REALLY AN ANNOUNCEMENT THAT she was ready. Amy and I had opted for a loop behind "Y" Mountain up Rock Canyon, just two minutes from our home, and down Slate Canyon, a route which would require parking a car at Slate Canyon, a ten-minute drive to the south, and then returning to Rock Canyon for a hike of some four hours and three thousand feet elevation change. It was a slightly overcast day, the snows had largely melted, and there were signs of rain in the early morning, but by late morning the clouds cleared. Getting away from the house and the children has always been a complicated matter, but as they have grown older and as our marriage approaches its third decade, we know how much we need this.

After parking the two cars, we began the ascent up into the mouth of Rock Canyon just beneath the towering presence of Squaw Peak, a prow-like rock that angles into the high air and stands at some 7,500 feet above sea level, straight above the mouth of the canyon. It was from a day in February 1849 that it got its name. In the midst of a battle between the Mormons and the Timpanogots on the banks of the Provo River, an Indian woman committed suicide here in the mouth of the canyon. The familiar story of spilled blood, like Cain and Abel, with which civilizations begin. I began to tell the story to Amy as we entered the canyon. The canyon's two mountainsides slash downward to a narrow opening that expands skyward, exposing tessellated rows of teeth, a gaping maw of some monstrous being with a cannibal appetite, enough to devour any past.

They say virtually no corner of the British Isles is not already man-made, no hillside, no embankment, no irregularity in the surface of fields that is without a human, hand-made explanation. Castles. Roman walls. Celtic ruins. Stonehenge. And mounds of unexcavated ruins from thousands of years ago still remain unexplored, unknown. Remnants of the more recent past, which to a British Islander begins about 1,500 years ago, facilitate the claims of continuity between the present and the past, between people and the land—broken stone walls, hedge lines, rows of trees squaring up green meadows. Out here our monuments to the human past include a pioneer trek, reenacted every year, and Anasazi rock art that stares back at us illegibly. Perhaps it is at least some comfort to know that the English really have no idea how to interpret Stonehenge.

Think on this. The contours of these mountains shout down puny human claims upon them. It is more than a New World consolation to acknowledge that it might be a dangerous thing, then, to live with the illusions of history's claims. Dangerous because what happens when the world no longer surprises, when it becomes ordinary, mundane? What was it the peasant poet John Clare wrote? "Its every trifle makes it dear." Better to descend into his madness lest I find myself preferring the feel and sheen of chrome to the unruly edge of a hot stone, a golden calf to goldenrod.

Passing beneath the burning rocks, Amy and I heard our voices echo faintly, as if the crags were inhabited by chattering beings. I had stopped my narrative about nineteenth-century bloodshed, and now Amy was talking about the kids. Eliza's social network. Is it wide enough? Should she continue to take dance and piano lessons? I tried not to let my inner obsessions drown out her preoccupations, but I found myself nodding and hmming knowingly in that way that somehow does the job of appearing to listen. I know better by now than to try to expect her to laugh and cry in simultaneous sympathy with my every passion, but I felt that familiar vertigo swelling inside my temple. Can I accept my own irrevocable solitude? Can't I expect more? After a while, the climbing made talking altogether too difficult. The silence only pushed my thinking deeper, seeking allegories from old stories.

An old prophet in Jerusalem had a dream. A boy prophet in America had a dream of an old prophet in Jerusalem having a dream. The old prophet's dream was enough to make a family leave the Old World for a New World wilderness, sailing east. The young boy's dream of the old man's dream was enough to make thousands more pull up roots and move west to a New World wilderness. There were those who believed the dream of the old man, those who believed the dream of the boy of the dreaming old man, and those who believed these two to be nothing more than dreamers. The dream of unity splits the same family into different hemispheres, different worlds. Two dreams faced each other across the same river and the streaming shadows of their forms standing proud and resolute, bound by the chains of blood and memory that held them, stretched and split and confused in the tossed and trembling waters.

And then, arising from the waters, these words: "For it must needs be, that there is an opposition in all things. If not so, my first-born in the wilderness, righteousness could not be brought to pass, neither wickedness, neither holiness nor misery, neither good nor bad. Wherefore, all things must needs be compound in one; wherefore if it should be one body it must needs remain as dead, having no life neither death, nor corruption, nor incorruption, nor misery, neither sense nor insensibility."[43]

This is the devil's doctrine, William Blake's devil, that is.[44] Because, as Blake explains, a body isn't spiritually alive until it has suffered the contradictions of life. Only through feeling, seeing, smelling, touching, hearing a corruptible world can we begin to perceive the lineaments of the incorruptible. "Death is the mother of all beauty," echoed Wallace Stevens, which is more profound than saying that suffering is necessary. That there would be such an intimate and deep connection between oppositions that nevertheless continue to face off, unless the whole cosmos were to fall apart and God would cease being God—that is something else altogether.

Wasn't it what Robert Frost and all poets yearned for, to drink from waters "beyond confusion," to wrap the world in the arms of love, to pour its broken pieces into a holy chalice that promised some ritual healing, some restoration of what has been lost? Is this not the gesture of religion? Is this not what the Book of Mormon, from which these lines come, is intended to offer? A narrative that constitutes the world anew, knowable, whole, bathed in God's sweet breath? And yet, here Lehi is saying that such a narrative, if it were to complete the work of restoration one final time, would become a dead, floating body, beyond sense and sensibility.

Like the best of a poet's metaphors, the narrative impels but doesn't complete the task, since it still seems to break up and pair off in new oppositions and contradictions that only settle quietly and unspeakably in the soul. When I first opened the holy book in earnest just months before my brother died, I felt the intimation of some final restoration of all the broken pieces of the main, and my own soul healing. I didn't know enough to understand how much more imagination would be required of me to continue to imagine what a whole world might look like. Nor do I now. Maybe having a New World holy book doesn't allow an escape from opposition or the need for imagination, but at least it teaches the shape of hope: The earth as spiritual home and humankind as a family of long-lost siblings.

My eyes were drawn again to where echoes crackled from the lines of flaming rough stone that licked the sky, and it occurred to me that the voices we had heard weren't ours, nor the ghosts of the past, but those of the men reportedly stealing stone from the canyon. Not too long ago, an old nineteenth-century deed of mining rights to this rock was purchased by a man intent on taking his plunder, and immediately he began hauling stones down from the jagged walls. Apparently they don't have enough rocks in Las Vegas, because folks there have been paying upwards of a half million dollars to these men to line their deep green lawns with this red stone. Although protected by some paper deed, their actions were what Book of Mormon prophets call priestcraft, selling what is sacred for a price. His asking price to cease this mining is $15 million. A local community group has garnered resources to try and stop him. The fight continues and the fate of this ancient beauty is still unknown.

But that, too, was my imagination.

As much as I stared into the jagged teeth for signs of a human story I might recognize, I couldn't help feeling their silent and indifferent stare. I don't know whether it is the fatigue of the British landscape after all those centuries that would have signaled the fall of the last great resistance to the unrelenting human story or whether it is the arrogance of British historians who fail to see that geology might have something more to say than a few brief millennia of human footprints. Heaven knows that both are possible. Looking at Squaw Peak every morning from my window and seeing daily reminders in this borderland wilderness, I can't imagine taking such liberties.

Some millions of years ago a plate of deep earth rose, broke unevenly like bread, and left a gap wide and steep enough for spring water and runoff to pour down into the Provo River and the Utah Lake. Thousands of years of human suffering later and now its modest waters are largely piped out to feed the taps in houses along the mountainside to the south, including my own. Lifeblood. The very cells of my body renewed by a story more ancient than human language. My feet turned on the unforgivingly irregular earth, demanding conformity from my heels, ankles, knees, and back. Wind passed across waist-deep weeds while castellated heads of stone refused to nod.

The eponymous peak is much higher than the Indian woman could have climbed, but when I stare at its prow sticking into the sky proudly, I find myself searching the multiple and jagged edges of rock for a possible location. There was a small riverside fort, built from timber cut in Provo Canyon and floated down the river, closer to the lake. The Mormon settlers sent down from Salt Lake only two years after the pioneers arrived in Utah were living a fragile existence in this fort among a band of Utes, who were rightly beginning to suspect that this was no temporary settlement. Before the white men had been allowed to enter the valley, the Mormon interpreter, one Dimick Huntington, was asked to raise his hand and swear they had no intention of driving the Utes out of the valley. There had already been some skirmishes over stolen cattle and tensions were simmering. To avoid conflict with the Indians, Brigham Young had been hesitant to settle the area, but a rag-tag group of Mormons had pressed him for the opportunity.

It all started with an elderly Indian, nicknamed Old Bishop because the settlers thought he looked like an older brother of the Mormon bishop at the fort, Newell Whitney. Jerome Zabriskie, Richard Ivie, and Rufus Stoddard went hunting down toward the lake. It's a bit unfair to mention their names, since they don't matter, of course, but I am intrigued that I have seen the surnames in the phone book. As they walked, they stumbled upon Old Bishop who backed away like a startled fox behind the brush by the river. His eyes flashed and snapped nervously in that way of his, the bend of his hooked nose his unmistakable identifier.

"Whoa, take it easy, Old Bishop. Where you goin'?" And then, "Hey! That's my shirt. I knew it were stolen. Now give it back!" Ivie barked.

Old Bishop spoke broken English: "I pay. Shirt mine!" he said defiantly.

"The hell you did!" At that Ivie lunged for him, helped by his companions, and began to strip the shirt from the old man's back. His tight, sinewy strength was harder to contend with than they had thought. He slipped away and within a flash had drawn his bow and arrow, aimed right at Ivie's throat.

An instant flash of light, a blast, and simmering smoke. Ivie turned around and saw Stoddard lowering the gun. Old Bishop lay in a crumpled heap, blood pouring from his forehead and a hole out the back of the head where his brains began to trickle into the soil.

That, at least, is what the survivors eventually confessed. Maybe the anger of the struggle got the best of them and one of them smashed his head against a rock. Maybe he was so old that he slipped and snapped his neck. Maybe he did draw the bow and arrow, but they knew he was too old to be taken seriously. Maybe.

"My God, what have you done?! Now what are we supposed to do?" Zabriskie lost control of his emotions first and found himself screaming in panic.

Trouble in Paradise, to be sure. Cain killing Abel? No apparent deal with the devil. The devil had long since learned not to make his intentions so public. It was rage, fear, and hatred, all bottled up into one violent throw of a fist, a stone perhaps, a gun, or a knife. But of course there was land at stake, survival, and feelings mixed up with perceptions of God's favoritism. Is it too romantic to call it a fratricide? My holy book would say so, would say that Cain and Abel and their weeping parents were somewhere mourning yet another lost opportunity for a grafting of Old and New Worlds. It would say that this land is no rupture but a restored piece of the great cosmic puzzle of God's strange geographical imagination. Indians as lost tribes, Christ and his covenants crossing the seas, the unity of the world fractured by Columbus as the beginning of some great dizzying restoration. Maybe so, but it seems that in the meantime, we have to live in a state of unfinished healing.

There was a knife, we know, because after a few minutes of panic, and rifling through ideas for ways to get rid of the body, they decided on the brilliant notion of disemboweling him, filling his ribs with stones, and tossing him into one of the slow-moving bends of the river, where they hoped he would remain and decay into the stuff of lake water. A biodegradable forgiveness. But insidious collaboration with nature is risky business since erosion and decomposition can just as easily expose human crime. Hands pushing stones against the bloody ribs, digging with makeshift stones to bury the entrails, and sewing with sticks like stitches through the old man's abdominal skin. Bad seamsters, those Mormon men—it wasn't more than a few days before he floated to the top and was found by his people bloated and wrapped around a dead tree jutting out from the next bend of the river.

The accomplices remained silent, swearing to each other in hushed tones behind a grove of trees, leaving their people vulnerable to increased aggression that appeared unwarranted. The Timpanogots demanded an explanation and threatened violence. It wasn't the only incident, of course. For hundreds of years this valley had been theirs, its game to hunt and its fish to catch. They had already learned enough of the ways of white men that things were not likely to change for the better. And the Mormons? They had experienced years of persecution, moving to yet another wilderness, the sound of their children crying in the dark night for fear, for food, for some respite from the suffering of life on the frontier. Hadn't Brother Brigham said that they were brothers, lost tribes that they stole because they were hungry and ignorant? But maybe this band of Indians was too far gone to worry about. Maybe peace was for places like down there in Mexico, where they got a load of treasures, ruins of temples, signs of that old Zarahemla where Christ healed white and dark alike. These ones are more like the cannibal Indians Moroni and them had to hide from, the ones who were so dangerous that God said go ahead, now, bury them plates in the earth where no one no matter how wicked can get 'em.[45]

In any case, tired of battling the repeated thefts of food and property and either unaware of Old Bishop's murder or unwilling to expose themselves to criticism, the leaders at the fort appealed to Brigham Young, describing an inexplicable increase of Ute aggression. Unaware of the original sin, Brother Brigham sensed that without direct action the Mormons would lose the respect he needed from the Utes to be able to settle the area permanently. "Peace or extermination" were his orders.

Maybe Old Bishop wasn't the *casus belli* after all. Maybe he was the excuse the more bloodthirsty among them wanted. And there were such men on both sides, Old Elk for one, and Hickman, a man with war-crazed eyes. Battle was forestalled on a number of occasions due to calmer heads prevailing. But knowing the Indians would have a harder time hiding in the mountains during the deep snows of winter, Brigham Young sent down troops to demand peace or to suffer war. One group of Indians appealed for peace and was granted amnesty.

The troops arrived and approached the Ute village on the bank of the river. They found felled cottonwoods stacked up and packed with snow surrounding a steep bank of the river carved in times of flood but now dry. Small holes through the snow had been made for obvious purposes. The chief came out and seemed inclined to agree to peace. Was it Old Elk inside the fort who talked him out of it? The Indians opened fire. Hot balls and whirring arrows thudded into the snow with the sound of a muffle. A whole day passed.

Like a great many of these conflicts, it is poorly documented from the point of view of the defeated. One young Mormon boy, aged seventeen, foolishly disregarded the advice of his companion to keep his head behind a tree. Maybe it was the cold and his teenage impatience, but he stuck it out and earned a ball in the neck, killing him instantly. How many Indians were killed? There is no tally. Thirty years later an eyewitness described finding a Ute woman after the battle with her legs torn off from the cannon the Mormons fired into the encampment.

The survivors were chased into Rock Canyon, including Old Elk, who had sworn that no white man would occupy Utah Valley. The Mormons followed their bloody tracks in the snow, until they cornered them in the canyon. Hiking straight east up the canyon, one eventually reaches an opening, most precariously situated for winter avalanches beneath the steep mountains in all directions. Another steep climb over a second mountain ridge and one arrives at the source of a south fork of the Provo River. From there, hiking north following the descent of the water, one can reach Provo Canyon. Maybe they hoped they could escape up and over the mountain. Or maybe they sought the protection of the gods in this temple. But the deep snow prevented further flight and the Mormons waited patiently at the mouth.

A Mormon sniper climbed the northern face of the canyon, which is especially well suited for hideouts, until he could see a small camp nestled into a ledge below him. He began firing. A young woman scrambled up the rocks with frenzied tears. He pulled up his rifle because he recognized her as Old Elk's wife. Her movement stopped at the edge of one stone and then she flew outward like an eagle before her head tipped forward in the air and her body slapped and twisted against the rocks below like a rag doll. When the men finally arrived at the Indian holdout, they found the frozen body of Old Elk. William Hickman, the one with the crazed eyes, sliced off the warrior's head at the spine of the neck and brought it back to the fort to hang, tongue wagging and bloody. He remembered hearing that Jim Bridger would pay a hundred dollars for such a relic.

The violence got worse before it got better. An army had arrived from Salt Lake in order to chase the Utes out for good. A battle took place on West Mountain to the south of Utah Lake. Twenty or so Indians who refused to surrender and give up their arms were shot at close range or chased out onto the ice-covered lake, slipping and sliding in their own blood. Their bodies were left in a bloody, unburied pile on the mountain.

These weren't the stories I had hoped to find to root myself here. And they aren't the ones we use, of course, because there are many—no less truthful—of acts of sacrifice, gentleness, and modest communal living. An episode like this, standing baldly and virtually unknown at the very foundation of a contemporary community of some half a million people in the valley, a surprisingly high percentage of whom directly descend from the early pioneers, leaves a pit in the belly, an empty echo in the chest.

Within the momentum of time, the story seems like nothing more than a brief flash of light on the river's surface. The water has long since absorbed the blood from the riverbanks, long since recycled the stuff of the past into its deep cycles of regeneration. Why not follow Walt Whitman's advice and let the sweet peace of nature's strange chemistry become the flag of our disposition?[46] I wonder if it is that simple because, if the metaphor holds, there are also old milk jugs, soda bottles, bike wheels, shopping carts and car parts I have seen through the blurred translucence of the river lying on its bed, thrown carelessly into the water and staring blankly back at me. Some sins don't recycle so quickly. It's simple really. The ugliness won't go away until someone steps in the water and pulls the garbage out.

I could hear my own and Amy's breathing growing heavier as the grade increased. We passed a water treatment structure and a small pipe dripping fresh spring water. We were still several weeks away from the heat of summer, but not knowing the exact nature of the climb that lay ahead, we took a drink. As Amy leaned over the water, I heard a rustle in the bushes behind us and just a hint of watery vowels spoken farther up the trail. As we ascended, we found the source of the murmuring we had heard. Since most of the water is piped down underground, only in the late spring can you anticipate the creek bed will fill with white torrents of runoff. But that is only if it has been a cold and wet winter and this was a dry year, making spring hikes like this possible without snowshoes.

"Maybe we should wait a little longer before watering the lawn this year," I said.

"We should be waiting longer in any case," Amy rejoined.

"Right, right," I said.

The landscape turned a deep green when we forked off to the south up several steep slopes. Wildflowers on the verge of blooming, aspen trembling in full splendor, new grasses groping to touch any part of us they could. We could see infant ferns like green nautiluses, posing questions on the sloping earth, hear the sound of the mountain water, and smell the bracken and the tender wisps of wild mint caught in the occasional breeze. In the leaves of spring trees, the early signs of wildflowers, the ripe red roots of willows, color, too, enters stage left like an impatient and ill-timed act.

Evidence of spring was short-lived, however, because the higher we climbed the farther back in the season we went. We found ourselves on a neglected trail that wound through naked, leafless willows.

"Coming down this in the snow sure would beat climbing this, wouldn't it?"

"Hmmm. This isn't so bad."

"I can feel hot spots on the back of my heels. Maybe those socks were too thick."

She made a noise of recognition. "This is a workout for the back, don't you think?"

"How do you hike so fast?" I asked after a few minutes.

"This beats carrying Sam. Or groceries. And walking up and down stairs all day."

We reached an open meadow, Upper Bear Flats, where we rested on some logs placed around an abandoned fire pit.

While I chattered on about the beauty of the spot, expressing my regret that I didn't bring a camera, Amy leaned forward and rested her head in her hand, elbow on her knee. She wasn't in a chatty mood, which wasn't unusual for her, and it seemed as if something was bothering her, but I had to accept the fact that I was unlikely to know what it was. Of course, I am not so naïve that it hasn't occurred to me that this may be her way of dealing with the disappointments I cause. After all, this is what happens in committed relationships: you learn to accept the disappointments, and if you are lucky, you might find a way to love them. If not, they can intensify with time, so you are going to have to find room for lots of forbearance.

With her head rotated at a slight angle, she gazed at the distances around us. Finally still after so much climbing, I noticed how cold the air was at this elevation, as if we had gone back a full month or six weeks into the late winter. The beauty of the place felt lonely. The high clouds protected us from the direct sun, but a gray light was diffused everywhere. We could see a fire road heading west up a mountain slope. To the north, Cascade Mountain, with its sunken ship ridgelines angling skyward and the triumphant face of Timpanogos. Amy squinted slightly, revealing her crows' feet. I hadn't remembered seeing them before. I reached across to pull some loose strands of her hair behind her ears.

Something strange there is about familiarity—beauty and surprise always scurrying away and with the wear of living pretending to grow more dim. And then unexpectedly it stands boldly before you, making believe that you were always looking but just never seeing. As if seeing beauty were a form of remembering what you always knew, as if looking too hard will make you blind. I know this much: I've got to stick around if I want to catch it.

Behind Amy, leafless aspen poked into the air in crooked lines, like in a Dutch landscape painting.

"Let's keep going," she said after several minutes. She rose and started walking south. I sat for a few moments, feeling temporarily wounded by her abruptness and alone with my too-busy thoughts. We have always had this emotional difference separating us, and since I only know one marriage, I am never sure if it is just our idiosyncrasy or if I am experiencing something more fundamental that separates everyone, what C. S. Lewis called the "wound of individuality." And in a relationship like ours, full of long days of hard work and service, focus on children and community, with enough compensatory moments of fulfillment and profound joy to keep us on our chosen path, I wonder what difference it would make to know. She has always implicitly made me feel chastised for my overexercised imagination and my intense self-reflection. This was the attraction she offered, so it was a dialectic I wanted, but in my more selfish moments, it feels like an injustice.

As she disappeared among the grove of aspen to the south, I stood to catch up to her. After a quarter mile of walking, I was alone on the slope of dark soil amid leopard-spotted aspen trunks with boiling black knots, each branch holding bright green buds like candles, some starting to poke out leafy fingers with feathery lightness. To the west I could see where another trail dropped toward Slide Canyon, probably my most frequently used trail, which provided an unparalleled view of Utah Lake. Amy and I took Eliza and a group of her friends to the top of "Y" Mountain there a few years ago. They were a boisterous, lusty group of gangly boys and long-legged girls, bounding up the mountain with aplomb. Like her father, Eliza doesn't think of hiking as her favorite activity and isn't overly zealous about seeking adventure, but give her a companion and beautiful scenery and she will be happy, almost giddy. I have suspected for a long time that as she advances in her teens, she is learning just how much she loves the world. And I have worried, too, about the heartache this might portend.

I finally joined Amy at a clearing at the end of the grove where she stood with hands on her hips. She was looking down on what cannot properly be called a valley, since it was more like a steep bowl, a vertiginous vortex of talus, aspen, and pine, billowy spots of wild, green grasses, and the edges of Slate Canyon down to the right where it seemed all of the immensity of this body of rock was drunkenly sliding, all the world wanting to be a perfect sphere. My eyes darted from one end of the mountain edges to the other. To the east lay Provo and Lightning peaks. To the south the talus ended at the edge of a falling slope of pines, many of them bent by the weight of winter snow and the pull of gravity, broken up by occasional streaks of white, where the spring sun had not yet melted patches of snow.

It was Rilke who advised young poets about the wisdom of guarding the solitude of those we love. And then he promised: "Once it is recognized that even among the closest people there remain infinite distances, a wonderful coexistence can develop once they succeed in loving the vastness between them that affords them the possibility of seeing each other in their full gestalt before a vast sky!" Young and poetic by disposition, I remember thinking this was hard doctrine, and even now I am not sure I am always willing to accept it.

Amy squeezed my hand and then headed down the winding path of loose stone and slippery dry soil of the exposed south face. She was in a mood to be alone, and who was I to stop her. I watched her as her body grew smaller in a matter of seconds. As she dissipated in front of me, I thought of my friend George, who after losing his wife was learning to love again, and I thought, too, of the beauty around me that felt lost almost in the moment I was seeing it. I knew I would always need courage to choose to love Amy and this place, again and again. And in one breathy moment, it felt as if my whole body leaned out toward her, toward the air below, and that I might dissolve in the wind, that we were nothing, absolutely nothing, and that I was loved wholly, unchangeably.

Every lover comes to understand that deep affection is precarious, that it is an affliction. It demands patience in disappointment and abdication of the will to possess, but its recompenses are those brief moments when an unclaimable and indifferent beauty offers itself as a gift, somehow uniquely mine but always free. The senses enlarge the soul, and ardor tempts the soul to climb the skies above, but if I keep a watchful eye on things, both living and inanimate, the budding wild weeds, the contour of stone, the familiarity of a path, the welcome sight of a deep ravine, I have a private tryst, a stolen childhood kept inside, away from the world's clamorous weeping. There is time enough for sorrow, too much perhaps, but healing is the pain that comes of gratitude for the kindness of a broken world's still stammering beauty. Healing and annealing, too, is the long view of committed devotion.

I started my descent. I had to move slowly because of the trail's unevenness and my need to continue staring at Amy's lithe movements glide across the stones until she disappeared into the pine grove below. When I finally caught up to her, she was radiant, buoyant, and her now chattering voice was warm and welcoming. The trail turned west and headed down Slate Canyon, the direction in which all of the rocks and the water were pointing. The canyon offered dense vegetation, startling crags standing erect along the ridges like so many enormous shark teeth, and an unobstructed view of the south end of Utah Lake and West Mountain.

A pipe followed our descent, sometimes near, sometimes across the ravine, now buried, now exposed and cradled over difficult ridges with scaffolding, whirring with hasty water on its way to the homes below. Around one bend, we climbed over thirty yards of granular snow that sometime in the winter had crashed down from the slope to our left. The mound had the appearance of peppermint ice cream, mixed with pine branches and other plants the snow had torn and crushed on its way down.

Amy was reminded of our scare last spring when we got up early in the morning for the biggest hike of the year: Timpanogos. It was an aborted maiden hike for our three girls on a trail that is practically a religious pilgrimage in Utah Valley. In fact, back in the early decades of the twentieth century when my grandparents were in college, a BYU professor of physical education initiated an annual hike that reached at one point as many as ten thousand hikers in one day. These were the heady days of a Mormon claim on this valley, what with the Indians gone to the reservations and few immigrants from other cultures or religions arriving. And they were days that required recreation as a form of adaptation to a more modern and less rural way of life. The new fixation on Mount Timpanogos as the valley's crown jewel was facilitated by an entirely fictionalized and annually reenacted Indian legend of a leaping lover, as if people had grown numb to the challenges of the true story of Squaw Peak. Jared Farmer suggests that two important costs of making Timpanogos a landmark of the Mormon homeland were that the local population grew more ignorant of Native American history and began to neglect the Provo River watershed and Utah Lake, sites that had earlier meant so much to Mormon survival. Homeland, instead of home waters. Property without ecology or history.

My girls were willing to get up early to make it to the top, but the stream below Emerald Lake proved too difficult to traverse safely with small children. On our way back down, a loud crack sounded from the cirque above us and a boulder the size of a small refrigerator came bouncing and bearing down directly at us. Walking in the rear, I yelled, "Run!" and so startled Camilla in front of me that she ran into a rock and fell, cutting her knee. I picked her up and ran with her crying in my arms to where the others stood, just in time to look back and see the boulder pass the trail where we had stood. As we continued our way down, I walked in the back of the group trying to use humor and mathematical probability to reassure them that we wouldn't be experiencing anything like that again anytime soon. No one was very reassured, but once we were well out of danger, the girls finally rekindled their usual chatter. It was at that point that I took stock of my trembling hands.

Prior to the modern hydraulic age, humans went where the water was, and explorers came here in the hope that the Great Basin would provide a waterway to the Pacific and enough commercial traffic and cultural exchange to build civilization in the West. The Great Salt Lake was a great geographical disappointment to a young country growing accustomed to believing that almost anything was possible. The lake's stagnant waters were the vault, the stopping point of all the melted snows that dallied on the tops of the mountains in the late winter and that seemed to offer the prospect of a homeland.

John Frémont thought he might find that fabled river passage to the Pacific, the Rio Buenaventura. He had seen a copy of Humboldt's map, drawn from the work of one of Escalante's companions, Bernardo Miera y Pacheco, that suggested such a passage. But it was not to be.[47] His own map of this interior drainage found its way to Nauvoo, Illinois, after the death of Joseph Smith in 1844 and pointed the way for the Mormons to escape Babylon. In their agony, water's drainage into the New World's Dead Sea did not presage insularity but a promised land, freedom from interventions of government, persecution, and compromises to their plan to build the kingdom of God on the earth.

In 1850, with a promised land identified, the reconnaissance begins in earnest to identify just what has been promised. Parley Pratt and fifty men walked from Salt Lake City to St. George over the course of three months. The journey today would take four to five hours in a car on I-15, driving eighty miles an hour on a straight and undisturbed line of concrete and passing one small settlement after another, all of which emerged in the wake of this expedition's findings. In search of habitable lands and still hoping to find a river passage to the Pacific in the south, they crossed the mountains several times in one of the wettest winters on record, encountering up to eight feet of snow, for example, in Spanish Fork Canyon.

In the family history file my mother sent me, I remember reading an eighteen-page anecdotal life story of John Lowry Jr., my paternal grandmother's grandfather. He was in his early twenties when Parley Pratt called for volunteers. Despite evidence that no Mediterranean was theirs and that the Great Salt Lake would indeed have to suffice as their Dead Sea, the enclosed nature of this geography was celebrated rather than bemoaned. No ports and geographical protection meant the prospect of a New World Zion even if it also condemned the place to perpetual marginalization within the broader narrative of U.S. history. Back in Salt Lake City in a public celebration of the findings of the expedition, the stout and prodigiously strong Pratt stood on a raised bed of a wagon in front of thousands of eager settlers:

> I have read of the sunny climes of Italy, I have trod Europe's shores and the heart of the fertile & productive countries in France, but neither the soil, the elements nor the air, the light of heaven, are free, but here is free soil, free speech, free labor, free Saints. Consider the difference between the situation of the Saints in the Great Basin and the rest of the world where the Air, Earth, and Water are not free but here all are free. We have our history in ruins right here in the stones of these mountains. There are those who have gone on to California in search of gold, but here we have plentiful mines, mountains, and streams, the best defence, the best rocks, the best women, and the most beautiful children.

A roar went up from the crowd and gunshots pierced the air. The passionate Welshman Dan Jones, who had only recently returned from a mission in Wales that saw thousands of converts, spoke of abandoned homelands:

> My good brothers and sisters. It is good and right that we remember this day our brothers and sisters in Wales and in other lands who are still groaning under the weight of tyranny, whose mountains and rivers are not their own. The treasures of their own labor are not their

own. They await the great day of promise when they can work to build the city prepared for the return of the Savior. Here we have gathered from among the nations, and here our hearts should ache to bring this New World to those still toiling away over there.[48]

These are the kinds of celebrations that still echo in the words of LDS hymns, songs of praise for Deseret, for the "everlasting hills," and for the chance to build on promised land. And as these celebrations indicate, it wasn't the hard and bitter desert, either, that blossomed and transformed under the hand of righteous men and women, as the legend would later tell. The land was already Eden and offered radical freedom, and its arms stretched out to all who came to replace the Indians who had been here for hundreds, even thousands, of years.

When the return to Salt Lake proves to be more difficult than the journey out, and desperate for food and supplies, my ancestor John Lowry and the two older men decide to part company with Pratt at Filmore and cross the mountains on snowshoes back to Manti, which they expect is a mere two days away. He has already lost a toe to frostbite, but with makeshift snow-shoes from oxbows and rawhide strings, they climb over several steep in-clines of snow along the Wasatch Front, not too many miles south from where I live. The three men reach the Sevier River and one of his compan-ions, a Mr. Hamilton, says, "John, you try crossing the river first; you have no family to take care of." (Not yet, anyway, Mr. Hamilton. What about all of us waiting to be his posterity?)

John stands wordlessly for a few moments staring back at his two elders and then he begins to unbutton his jacket and layers of shirts until his bare, pink chest pimples in the open air. He wipes the snow off of a fallen tree, sits down on the trunk, and pulls off his boots. Perching himself awkwardly on top of the tongues of his boots, he unbuckles his pants, then bends over and drops them to his ankles. His companions huddle close and watch. A brisk wind picks up and rips through their clothes, which at this point are not much warmer than the air itself. John rolls his clothes up in a blanket, straps the bundle to his snowshoes, and lifts the shoes over his right shoul-der. Without hesitation or a flinch of his muscles, he steps calmly toward the river and walks in up to his thighs. Swinging his lifted elbows in the air, he moves his steps forward over the sandy bottom until he reaches the other shore.

His feet beyond feeling now, he takes advantage of the numbness to press the snow down for a clearance where he can dress. While his companions follow his lead, he gathers willow branches to make a carpet on the snow and begins to build a small fire. Dressed again on the other side, Hamilton complains of growing snow blindness from the intense winds, and that night while John keeps vigil, he moans incessantly. In the morning, Hamilton announces: "I can't go on." It is the third day of the journey and they are still uncertain of exactly where they are. The ration of biscuits is growing smaller.

Was it family pride, or was John really the hero he seems? The narrative, written by a descendent, uses the telltale adjectives: "But father, brave, strong, and courageous, insisted on him getting up. He finally got him onto his feet, tied his snow shoes on, rolled his blankets with his own, and they started very slowly at first, then after a while he could walk a little faster."

Another night on the banks of the Sevier, John reports not sleeping for the third night in a row. Occasional moans from fitful sleep break the silence of the night while the stars pierce holes in the black night. What thoughts run through his mind? He is young, in his early twenties. He already has his eye on a young woman, Sarah Brown, still in her teens, and he has ambitions to help settle Manti for his posterity. He would marry a second time in a polygamous arrangement and eventually father fifteen children. He would spend the next six decades living and working in Manti, helping to build the temple, and burying many members of his family. He would tell stories of his childhood crossing to Utah from Nauvoo, his memories of the dead bodies of Joseph and Hyrum Smith being carried through the city in 1844, and until the end of his life would manifest an extraordinary gift for healing and for visions. I am pained to realize that my grandmother was in her teens when he died in 1915, and yet I have no recollection of her telling me anything about him.

Early in the expedition in January 1850, Pratt's fifty men ventured deep into a canyon draped in large billows of snow. As they listened to the gurgling of a mountain spring several hundred feet below the ridge they traversed, they could see a daunting peak rising in the distance. Pratt turned to the men. "To look at those mountains it could be said that no white man could do it or be rash enough to undertake it or have an enterprising spirit enough to attempt it. The Mormons are the boys for such expeditions. They fear neither canyon, mountain snow storms, gulleys or rivers, because they know they are led by the mighty God of Jacob." That night as they neared the summit, Pratt turned, as he often did, to poetry and began searching for a melody around the campfire:

> O come, come away, the mountains still exploring
> Turn every crook search every nook, O come, come away.
> The secret treasures of the hills
> The rivers, lakes, and murmuring rills
> Are ours boys by Heaven's will, So come, come away.
> We'll search mid the glens where the cataracts are roaring
> The mountains steep, the caverns deep, O come, come away.[49]

The next morning the men stood in silent astonishment before a series of petroglyphs along one slate of stone that bent inward from the edge, protecting its surface from the snow. Perhaps not the kind of treasures Pratt meant but treasures nevertheless. The nearby Virgin River's name notwithstanding, this primitive narrative was enough of a hint that this was not an Edenic world but one with a deep history and inhabited by increasingly suspicious, hungry, and somewhat desperate Indians who were dying of disease seemingly without reason, who fought their own courageous battles with the fierce winter that was upon them, and who struggled to regain their patterns of subsistence after the disruptive arrival of the Mormons. This is what Pratt meant by "our history in ruins," a promised land by adoption.

His exuberance wasn't the first or last time white men would presume the innocence of claiming proprietary and virile rights over a feminized landscape, lying passively in wait, but his enthusiasm is understandable given their already long saga of suffering. And hadn't he said the water and the air, the very earth were free? Maybe all he meant was that resources were without price from a prior owner, but what if he had intimated something much more profound? I wonder if there is an economy that respects the fundamental freedom of the earth and that acknowledges possession as a provisional fiction.

In our modern pursuit of the promises of paradise and the secret treasures of the mountains, we don't rely on blood-and-sweat reconnaissance any longer. We rely on experts and technology to search for fossil fuels, natural gas, and oil shale so that we can live practically anywhere. And we are running roughshod over the same reminders that we are only temporary tenants. The difference is that now those reminders have become mere irritants. Nine Mile Canyon in central eastern Utah, poorly named because it is over forty miles long, still contains one of the largest and most remarkable museums of Native American rock art anywhere in the West.

Of course there are hundreds of other such wonders throughout the threatened wilderness of southern Utah, but I couldn't resist the chance to take a group of students there a few years ago on a brittle, cold, and clear winter day. I have taken students to some of the greatest museums in the world in Europe, but unlike the crowded halls of the Louvre or the National Gallery in London where you are shoulder to shoulder with fellow admirers, here you are alone in a raw and chastening landscape. Here cliffs hold thousand-year-old granaries, and eyries for large raptors, and a dizzying array of artistic depictions of an earlier life: hunting scenes, a man leading another figure on an animal beneath the moon, spirals and circles repeating unknown symmetries, herds of sheep, deer, and elk with fantastical antlers, large sinuous snakes, dotted configurations of some unknown accounting, figures of strange and impenetrable meaning shaped like vases with arms and fingers moving outward like underwater sea creatures or deities in a trance, and then the final irony: a panel of a rust-colored, fat-bodied deer with modern black lettering spray-painted across its body: "This Is Private Property: No Tresspassing." They didn't even have the decency to use proper spelling.

A natural gas refinery operates near the dirt road that traverses the length of the canyon and its large trucks roll by, several an hour, rumbling the ground and stirring the air into a permanent haze of dust. Concerned citizens spoke about the danger posed to the art by this hunger for fossil fuels. My local paper dismissed the concerns about the art and opined, without irony: "For all anybody knows they could be the doodlings of children, the scribblings of a banished criminal or the first draft of a bad screenplay that, for lack of technology, was never produced."[50] The statement is so obtuse as to hardly deserve comment. It would be one thing to argue that economics must outweigh the demands of beauty, but this statement raises the disturbing prospect of an eye that sees no mystery, only ugliness. It would be yet another to point out that we whites can no longer assume the right to adopt indigenous history as "our" ruins, but it seems we have gone far beyond such impatience: in our obsession with property, we have no hunger for memory at all. How did we come to such unabashed nihilism? We could stand to learn something from the silent astonishment those images express, astonishment at the strangeness of finding ourselves on this earth.

What is it exactly that transforms titillating desire for the land and its treasures into committed devotion to making a home? If sexual desire can avoid becoming pornographic, it would have something to do with the work and service that must follow passion, a kind of renouncement of possession. John no doubt was roused by Pratt's calls to Mormon male vim, but his was no short-lived fantasy that the world would conform itself to his will. Despite his decades of devotion to Manti, the Lord told him in a dream to sell everything and move to Springville in his late seventies. His suffering was akin to losing a son. He wrote: "My wife and I united in prayer, and with tears streaming down my face I poured out my whole soul to God, and asked if we might not be permitted to remain here until our life's work was completed." The impression to move never abated, however, and he spent the remaining decade of his life developing a canning company in Springville to store for church welfare the fruits of the expanding orchards of Utah Valley that James Stratton and others had begun a few decades earlier.

It hardly seems possible that this is the same man accused of having instigated the Black Hawk War of 1865–1872. Lowry's in-depth experience working with the Utes made him a useful translator and mediator, but when one of his own cattle was stolen, he acted on his own behalf. The word he got was that the Utes were blaming the Mormons for their dying children, fading away in fits of fever and shakes, and so they threatened to kill the Mormons and eat "Mormon beef" when the winter was over. But the spring was slow in coming, and when Lowry found a carcass of one of his oxen, he approached the Utes and demanded an explanation. Payment was offered and on the next day when they agreed to meet and settle the matter, one Ute continually interrupted Lowry's account of the theft with threats to the Mormons and their cattle.

"Look out, he is getting his arrows!" someone yelled. Lowry acted quickly and pulled the man off of his horse and wrestled him to the ground. The next day a Mormon was killed, and war was on. Lowry wrote in his own account: "I had fully exposed what they intended to do....I have always taken the position that that talk with the Indians 'showed their hand.' I believe they started hostilities sooner than they would have done had not the incident above mentioned occurred. But the trouble would have come just the same."

Was there evidence that the Utes had decided upon aggressive and violent intentions toward the Mormons before the incident? Was this an act to expose those intentions, as Lowry claimed? Or was this a rash act of an inebriated man, as some reports suggest, disgracing an Indian warrior by dragging him from his horse by the hair and beating him? I don't pretend to know how to balance the scales of justice, but I do know that ancestry has taught me that one can't read history innocently.

Aggression between Mormons and Indians persisted for several years even after an official truce, and federal troops refused to help for many years mostly because of the ambiguous political entity the Mormon kingdom represented. Despite evidence that Mormons were generally more willing to collaborate peacefully with the Indians than other settlements in the West, one cannot reconnoiter the past and expect to find a story of blanched white innocence. These were real men and women acting in the dark region of the past, unable to reach forward in time to touch our faces. Whose faces am I unable to touch, even now, when the future seems so foreshortened by my stubborn will?

"Father, brave, strong, and courageous," did you, too, shake your head in disgust with your pettiness, the superficiality of your life? Or were you always that stalwart man, almost made of stone yourself, forever acting on principle and never confusing your intentions? Always living a life of purpose, acting on behalf of a future I could happily inherit? One could have worse intentions than you did, in any case.

All I wanted was to understand my relationship to a watershed, but in my own efforts at reconnaissance I have touched the evidence of the earth's forbearance for our strange pilgrimage in this land. This brings some restoration of sense since such an objective, mixed though it may be with Mormon male middle-class midlife vanity, doesn't preclude the ways in which the mountain stirs me from strange and varied slumbers of the body. Intimations are the best we can hope for. Annie Dillard wanted to tell Moses, "Just a glimpse, Moses: a cliff in the rock here, a mountaintop there, and the rest is denial and longing. You have to stalk everything. Everything scatters and gathers; everything comes and goes like fish under a bridge."

Ah, recreation and its euphorias. A pornography of physical beauty? Perhaps. Especially if we refuse to take account of the long-term impact of our choices on a fragile land and in a fragile cultural landscape still awaiting its New World promise. Especially if our hearts never turn to the children. Especially if freedom means believing that we never have to pay any cost.

As the trail widened out at the mouth, Amy and I could see the lines of concrete roads stretching out across the valley in every direction and feel the warmer air on our faces. The sound of cars hummed. A gray light of particulates held the valley in a proto-smog. Green patches of parks and softball fields stood out in the midst of the mosaic of suburban life. We could make out the pioneer-era Tabernacle and the old BYU Academy now converted into a public library.

We crossed makeshift roads used by four-wheelers and motorcycles for private recreation at the canyon mouth. The visible evidence of the scarring created by so many private fantasies of dirt bikes is not exactly private since the trails can be seen from across the valley. There are still plenty of folks defying the ethics required by public land in their pursuit of their own private pleasures. On weekends, you can sometimes identify headlights of jeeps illegally climbing along the steep Bonneville Trail to the north. Graffiti can be seen on some of the larger rock faces. The first time I walked up this canyon, I was nearly killed by two motorcyclists racing downhill in full body suits around the gate where you could barely make out the sign, riddled with rusty bullet holes, that prohibits vehicles of any kind.

Pick your poison because before this became a dirt bike wasteland it was wasted by mining and brick masonry. The old mine shafts can be seen dotting the sides of the mountains, like open wounds. Construction on homes sprouting along the bench beneath the canyon has occasionally been delayed because in digging foundations they have often found large truck tires, mining equipment, and even an entire truck once, conveniently buried as garbage when the mines were shut down some fifty years ago. When I think of the angel Moroni's warning to Joseph Smith about the hearts of the fathers, it is hard to imagine that we were in the hearts of these particular forebears.

By the end of the long descent from that grove of trees above Upper Bear Flats, our thighs felt wobbly and shaky. The conversation had died down, in part to stay focused on the placement of our feet and out of fatigue, but I suspect it was something more. Strange how a hike opens up the conversation only to teach you in the end that you don't need it, that you can trust silence. I found myself grateful that Amy is so utterly her own, so idiosyncratic and resistant to being steered. It makes the feeling of unity such a surprising and breathtaking gift.

In my explorations of the watershed here closer to home, here where wildness is still proximate but every day threatened more by our growing indifference, I want to say with Wordsworth that the world is too much with us. And yet in the hinterlands of the watershed where I feel that much closer to a system of life that still has integrity, I want to believe heaven is near.

I suppose there are at least two temptations: to hike as a way of escaping time altogether, to feel myself oblivious and tethered to no one but the ageless wind; or to the degree that the world of man encroaches, pollutes, or otherwise disturbs my private paradise, to join the American tradition of honey-and-locust anarchists and stand on the mountaintop, beat my breast, and lament the day white men first entered this valley. Something in me refuses these choices, but not because I believe we don't deserve a good tongue lashing from a loin-clothed prophet, but because I have to admit this much: there is still enough beauty in the world to fuel the human fire of imagination. Scarce beauty is a gift, not a right. It merits love, not lamentation; love enough to make recreation a re-creation, a way of becoming unfamiliar again with the world, of working to blur the horizon line between heaven and earth.

Eleven

*

WINTER HAS BEEN DEFEATED, NO QUESTION. IT IS A GLORIOUS SPRING DAY today, and I can't resist the temptation to get in a run early this morning before the kids' Saturday soccer games. I pick a stretch of the Provo River Trail that winds along the banks through the city. I pass under concrete bridges and across streets to keep pace with the water, which flows in a controlled and only slightly meandering line. The water is higher than usual but not by much. Before the Deer Creek Dam was built in the 1940s and before the grid of middle-class homes began to spread across the valley, the water regularly breached the banks, depositing the sediments brought from the mountains, providing fertile spawning ground for fish, and renewing and enriching the soils of riparian life. Even before the dam was built, small dams appeared on the river in the late nineteenth century. Although a law was passed in the 1890s requiring fishways to allow spawning to continue, few people complied. The assault continued in waves: increasing use of fertilizers that drained back into the river, sugar beet and other industries, saw and steel mills, all dumping their waste, and who knows how many tons of human sewage that impotent laws could not stop from being dumped into the river until the 1950s. The dredging of the river, levees built to protect budding neighborhoods from floodwaters, water depletion from years of agricultural development, and the gradual stripping away of the riparian vegetation that was once the world it made—all brought the Provo into submission. It got so severe that in the wake of droughts in the 1960s the river dried up entirely in the valley, leaving a graveyard of fish rotting in the sun.

I would have to go back many decades to a time when the river at this time of year would be a mad, muddy and spumy force of the mountains, arguing vehemently for the space it needs to expand its vascular waterways in the springtime. Constrained now by the construction of a modern city and by two major dams above, it is a well-behaved mix of olive and bronze rolling along in a straight shot, making occasional turns presumably only because some development project—the large used car store, the supermarket and its broad stretch of parking lot, underpasses below major roads—pretends to lay prior claim to the terrain. There is vegetation along its banks but only modest and slim lines of green, which when seen from the nearby mountains, they appear as slim lines of green cutting through residential neighborhoods, passing a golf course, and slipping beneath roads and the highway.

There are signs along the way of still-existent irrigation canals leaving the river. I catch glimpses of metal, wood, and plastic pieces of assorted things—doors, shopping carts, milk cartons—that have found homes along its banks and in tangled jams in its waters. I slow down when the trail and the river lean to the right and a large parking lot slouches to my left. Because the banks here are high and I am a short distance upriver from where Fort Utah had been, I stop running to look over what is the likely scene of the Battle of the Provo.

I had been in this precise spot one early spring with a group of boys from church to do a river cleanup. It turned out to be an ideal place for a project, something to get their noses out of Game Boys and their hands off of joysticks because the trees, willows, and bushes flanking the trail silently withstood the indignity of hanging plastic bags, grocery receipts plastered against the tree bark, packaging for food, toys, and electronic equipment lying at their feet. This was not some dumpsite, just the accumulation of detritus brought downwind from the parking lot by happenstance.

The boys began their work like a herd of sheep let loose in a field, wandering in circles, doing anything but the work at hand. I and the other leader did our best yelping to keep them huddled and focused. As the morning wore on and their bodies warmed to the labor, they found a satisfactory rhythm and could see that their contribution was making a difference. It was a small victory for civilization.

That was at least three years ago, and now it looks like it could stand another visit. The morning light is faint but contrasts are starting to deepen, bathing the empty parking lot in a gray light. The crowds will come soon enough, pushing their carts full of cereal boxes, cartons of milk, and canned vegetables, but for now the air hangs still and silent. The Mormons had pushed fur-covered sleds for shields as they fired upon the Indians hiding beneath the steep banks behind me. Bullets whistled and thudded in the riverbanks and blood soaked the snow, which slid into the churning winter waters. The wails of mourning mothers pierced the air.

The asphalt wags its indifference while the brick edges of the distant hospital and the billboards sharpen in relief. A rusty and dented bronze station wagon pulls into the lot in front of the supermarket. An elderly Hispanic woman emerges from the passenger side and walks toward the grocery store with a slight sideways tilt—perhaps a creaky hip. She is joined by the driver who looks perhaps to be her daughter. My mind sorts through an index file of possible stories looking for a match. The old woman has to shop with her daughter because she does not know a word of English, doesn't understand American foods, has only recently arrived from Mexico, has no health insurance, is illegal, or can't negotiate the complex world of over-the-counter medications. As their shapes move toward the entrance, I tell myself that I could have loved them if I had known them. And then it occurs to me that Walt Whitman would never have survived our cynical century. How does one spend this affection on strangers and foreigners?[51]

I continue my run beneath a dark concrete tunnel under Freedom Boulevard where Independence Day parades have made their journey for decades. I don't see it coming. I am shin deep in brackish water, because I discover on the other side of the underpass that a sprinkler head is broken and water is streaming into the underpass. As I emerge onto the other side, a large brown patch of business lawn at an auto dealership spreads before me, neglected by the broken sprinkler. It's feast or famine because elsewhere the grass is deep green, long, and waterlogged. I recently read that some business parks in Utah use up to one hundred inches of water a year, enough to grow rice. To my right on the west side of the street I can see a long line of brilliantly colored new Dodge trucks, a vehicle of choice for businesses that demand it, but also for those who merely crave the powerful feeling of riding high. Someone, in some marketing seminar for car salesmen, has been promoting the idea that this green grass, like Muzak, comforts and seduces customers into spending their own "green." They conveniently forgot to advertise the part about what an automobile portends for the good green earth.

My soggy shoes squeak and sputter as I slip through another narrow tunnel surrounded by a chain-link fence on both sides where a neighborhood of trailer homes has spawned. After passing through a grassy park of picnic tables where last year a Hispanic toddler wandered away from the family table and fell into the river, I run into an open and totally undeveloped and unwanted stretch of land a hundred yards or so before the trail passes under Interstate 15. The sound of tires streaming above me drowns out all other sounds.

On the left of the trail, a large stone slab stands surrounded by high dry grass and sagebrush with a brief text describing the location of Fort Utah, its layout, and the most significant dates and names related to its establishment. It appears to have been desecrated several times, since the text is hard to read in places where sandblasting has smoothed the surface. Some vulgar comments remain inscribed in red above the stone-carved words that make brief mention of how relations between the Indians and the Mormons deteriorated shortly after the fort's foundation. I guess they wanted to be as faithful as possible to the historical location of the fort, even if it meant few would ever see it. Of course, I don't know what I was expecting. I had my worries about a divided past, but this seems downright unremarkable.

Or maybe it already protests too much. Maybe a marker of willows would suffice, or better still, a stretch of river restored to its ancient shape. But that is assuming people would know what a willow hides or what artifice lies behind the natural appearances of things. And that is assuming a river cares, that a river could hold its shape. History is useful, mostly so that it can be forgotten by those careful enough to have remembered it.

The past is certainly not commemorated by the way of life in the valley, which is the worst kind of oblivion, an ignorance weed-killed and fertilized by indifference. With the exception of the occasional endangered pioneer home, the old grid of streets at the center of town, and the unusual number of church spires pointing skyward throughout the basin floor, there is little in our architecture, the design of the increasingly fewer places we share, or in the way we spend our leisure time and money that is any different from the rest of America. Given its sometimes rather unremarkable appearance, I have often wondered what home it was I thought I was returning to when I moved to Utah. The strange thing is, this is no Vermont where loners drift into voluntary solitude but a community with a deep and shared history. Ironically, this hasn't translated into a predominant ethos that celebrates public land. Instead, the political culture here bemoans the fact that so many staggeringly beautiful acres of democratically accessible land should be considered for wilderness protection.

Not far from the banks of the river, one finds crabbed stretches of manmade rivulets pouring over backhoed river rock by a strip mall and everywhere a shocking intolerance for open space. And yet what Edward Hoagland calls the "tidy climates in gated selfishness" appear in backyards, all part of the race to own and enjoy one's private slice of paradise. It's not as if my home culture here is short on public life or public will—it has both in spades. Perhaps because America offers respite from the burdens of community, we are coaxed, cajoled, tempted. Apprehensive, not yet accustomed to the bright sun of modern capitalism, our Mormon grandparents crawled out of obscurity to explore the pleasures of the American Dream and now we find ourselves storm-raked, unable to stay the hand of a cultural mudslide. It is not their fault, of course, since by now we have had enough chances to know better. After all, didn't He promise that we wouldn't be tempted beyond our capacity to resist?

And the small patches of orchards and their local summer sales of peaches, apples, and cherries, can they outlast my children? There is one small patch of a dozen acres or so near the mental health hospital up the hill from the city cemetery, surrounded by high walls of concrete. You can smell the apples from a mile away. Rumor has it that some of the fruit trees in our backyards along my lane may have come from old orchards. In my case, I doubt it, because my apricot, apple, and pear trees seem only as old as my house. They were the previous owner's way of commemorating the orchards of the past, for which I remain grateful. That my house lies on what was deemed arable land is evident, however, in the gully in my backyard where the Timpanogos canal runs, cut out of the river at the canyon's mouth three generations ago to feed the land downhill to the west. Now it is buried in a pipe, passes silently and without notice beneath the soil, and on an arcane schedule that no one seems to understand or pay any attention to, water is released in the gutter running down an adjoining street, passing family residences whose green, sprinkler-fed lawns have no use for it.

Dozens more such canals run in all directions throughout the valley, but most of them are buried. Aeration holes, gates, and turnkeys provide the occasional reminder of the subterranean water that spreads throughout the valley in a complex of private and public waterways, historical and modern negotiations of water rights. The wooden gates at the edge of the gutter on each property in my neighborhood remain shut, and the water pours in amber light through the concrete gutter, providing only what appears to be a chance for stick races for young boys. One portion of the sidewalk shows signs of cracking, and when the water is running, it bubbles up from under the concrete like some hot spring.

And then there are the Stratton orchards on the Provo Bench, shrinking with each passing year but still a viable provider of fresh local fruit in the valley. It hadn't initially occurred to me that these were the same orchards my ancestor had started, even after I had learned his life story. I guess the ubiquity of familiar names in the valley had lulled me into a historical stupor because I had been eating Stratton peaches for three or fours years before

I realized I had been eating my history. This wasn't exactly cannibalism, or even transubstantiation. It was more like the invited guest who comes to a Mormon meeting and takes the sacrament unwittingly. Without knowledge, intention, or belief, it was meaningless. But his story had been preparing me for the requisite repentance.

Savoring the orange flesh and its blood red interior, I wiped my mouth. "Do you think these peaches come from James Stratton?" I asked Amy naively one day a few years ago in the kitchen.

"No, because those are Allreds," she answered with a grin. But the next time she bought from Stratton's, she asked for me. It was possible after all. I finally got up the nerve to call the orchard one day and asked to speak to the owner, Vern Stratton. Are you descended from James Stratton, I asked. Why yes, he was. Who was this, he wanted to know. We exchanged information about family trees and agreed to meet.

It was on a day like today in the spring. His house was hardly visible from the busy street, a few blocks west of a new strip mall that ate up acreage of the old family orchard and now named apparently without intended irony, "The Orchards." The house was set back behind four or five rows of unusually large and thick peach trees in full pink blossoms. From the driveway where I parked, I walked around to the front. With no front yard or walkway to speak of, I just stepped out of the orchard and up to the door. Behind me speeding cars swished by, even though as I turned to look at the street, I could no longer see their motions through the thick trunks of the trees. At the door I was greeted by a tall, gray-haired man with sun-narrowed eyes, tawny complexion, in pale blue and well-used overalls and a wrinkled white shirt. His wife, in blue jeans, a brown blouse, and brown hair, stood behind him and welcomed me in. It was a one-story, ranch-style home with lots of windows each staring at trees. The pastel-colored walls were covered with black-and-white blown-up pictures of ancestors. We sat down and I started to ask questions.

We talked of James and Eliza, whose story they knew as well as I did. I confess I was disappointed that all they had were the same five pages of life stories I had read. I had hoped for some weather-worn journal, a poetry of memory rich enough for a novel. But Vern's own history and memory ran deep and it was in the more personal account of his life that I was able to feel the fleshiness of the past.

"They cleared the sagebrush up here on the bench, you know. They built rock and adobe homes so they could live year round. Then the following year they decided to try and get water out of the Provo River that was in the river bottoms a little ways away. They surveyed from the mouth of the canyon and followed the grain of the river about a mile down. They brought it up onto the bench, and they cut it back and made a ditch, which you can still see at Center and State Street in Orem where the ditch goes down. They started with alfalfa and grain for the animals, you know, but the next year they decided to start planting peach trees and berry fields."

"What year was that again?"

"I'm not sure," he looked at this wife for an answer. She shuffled some papers.

"That had to be in the 1860s," she finally said.

"Albertson's grocery store is right where the original homestead was," Vern added. "At first it was an adobe home but they went up Spanish Fork Canyon to get those big, red rocks out of the red narrows up there and made a beautiful red rock foundation. We bought that house and fixed it up and lived in it for ten years. I grew tired of so much orchard work there, so I decided to sell. Never had the guy put in writing that he would never tear it down. One of those mistakes, you trust people, you think their word is as good as their bond."

They showed me a picture of James, as an old man, standing in front of the red brick home. He was short, bearded, wearing a wide-brimmed sun hat and surrounded by the family that loved him in his old age.

Why did he go into farming at all, I wanted to know. Vern was younger than my grandfather, closer in fact to my own father in age, but he had clearly clung to a way of life that others had left behind years before him. He was college educated, but with the exception of a few years in the military, a mission in Texas, and graduate school in Washington, he had remained on the land.

"I was in the service, you know, at the time of the Belgian Bulge. When I got back, I said to my Dad, 'Help me find a piece of land. I've seen enough of the world. I've been knocked around. I'll try farming.'" James Stratton had had a similar experience in the Mexican War before turning to the Mormon life and eventually settling here on this same stretch of land. I wondered about what it was about war that would inspire agricultural aspirations. By the sweat of one's brow, perhaps, there was that promise of a new harvest and redemption, like that Winslow Homer painting of a man beating swords into ploughshares after the Civil War. I didn't know him well enough to ask what he meant about being "knocked around" during the war.

Vern had seen a great number of laborers over the years. He and his family could drive their trucks into town and simply pick young men up from the streets who wanted work, until the Dairy Queens and McDonald's started hiring them away. So they turned to prison inmates, and the last year of the war, they used German prisoners. After the war, the pattern was to hire Mexicans through a labor association that went directly to Mexico to provide documentation, and Navajo Indians, until their habit of cooking outside burned down some of their buildings. The entire area was once agricultural, of course, and orchard blossoms filled the valley in the springtime. The Mormon Church still owned some of those orchards until a few years ago as welfare farms, but even they have gone the way of the dinosaur.

Nowadays Mexican laborers, most of them undocumented, huddle around gas stations looking for landscaping jobs. No one knows who got it started, who tells them where to meet, but as they sit waiting early on a Saturday morning, a car drives up and hauls them off, usually to some expansive house that requires extensive lawn care.

"What was the river like in the spring before the dam?" I wanted to know.

"Terrifying. I almost got killed one time. We had climbed up the north side of the river just at the mouth there where that new park is now to investigate some more canal possibilities. I don't remember why, but I had to lean out over the waves of churning muddy water and almost lost my footing. The roar was deafening. I stared at my life passing before my eyes. You just didn't go near it at that time of year if you could at all help it. All these fancy homes now in the River Bottoms. I just had to laugh when they first started building in there. They wouldn't stand a chance in those days. There were always a few deaths every year from someone falling in. Once you were in, you were gone. The water traveled too fast, too deep. But you know that's the energy the canals channeled to the fields. Sometimes we found fish flapping in the rows on the fields where the water was irrigated."

Unruly, muddy, angry. Someone had started the process of taking from it, bit by bit, James Stratton among the very first, and now we had tamed straight lines of water crossing the basin floor like some mosaic pattern of tile. "The wilderness and the solitary place shall be glad for them; and the desert shall rejoice, and blossom as the rose. It shall blossom abundantly.... For in the wilderness shall waters break out, and streams in the desert. And the parched ground shall become a pool, and the thirsty land springs of water."[52] Isaiah's elations expressed a hope for survival that the expansion of American empire would bastardize into a political mantra. It takes a small imagination to believe these words could only describe technology and engineering and not a deeper receptivity that should be the substance of our dreaming, to believe that a desert only blossoms with the aid of our hands and not by the art of seeing.

Out of the window I could see Vern's own trees in full pink blossom. The roots and branches were filled with boles and boils from too many years of pruning.

"Those should have been taken down a long time ago," he said noticing my glance out the window. "I just can't bring myself to do it. They are too old to produce like a younger tree, but I like their appearance, don't you? They aren't as old as I am, but close. I planted them not long after we got married." We both looked out at the mosaic of branch and flower.

I knew, too, that this nostalgia was foolish because it was bottomless. Those primitive canals once meant the latest in modernization, but I knew that to go beyond them was to resent the very presence of these people and this civilization we might still stand a chance of building. Blame the damn Mormons, "the Lord's Beavers," as Worster calls them, who according to one historian "banished themselves" to the wilderness just to see if they could conquer it, and you will have a giddy, nodding audience. No, blame those green, godless environmental bastards. Or the militia men, hungry for revenge against the invasion of so many foreigners and meddlers, willing to drive their ATVs en masse up riverbeds just to prove their point. And then the giddy futurists, like old Mephisto, will tell me to relax, to believe what we make of the world tomorrow is always better than what it has made of us.

But I want out of this caravan of time, this tethered logic. I want myths, and we have them, but can anyone believe them? "And out of the ground made I, the Lord God, to grow every tree, naturally, that is pleasant to the sight of man; and man could behold it. And it became also a living soul. For it was spiritual in the day that I created it; for it remaineth in the sphere in which I, God, created it, yea, even all things which I prepared for the use of man; and man saw that it was good for food."[53] So says Moses. Or Joseph Smith, if you don't believe him. Even some of his defenders have spent more energy learning how to argue for the authenticity of Joseph's revelations than thinking deeply about the implications. Perhaps we are reluctant to be answerable to mystery. You can have your peach but before you eat, again I ask, can you behold those trees aflame with petals turning their dark arms in an unbounded embrace of the sky and believe it?

"I guess it is inevitable they will all be gone someday," Vern announced after a silence. "I understand that. My neighbors are good about letting me do my work, but I know they see me as a dying breed." We kept staring out the window at the knotted muscles of bark and the pink clouds of blossoms.

One of his sons was already planting orchards on the southernmost edge of the valley in Santaquin, one of the remaining spots along the Wasatch Front with ideal climate, irrigation possibilities, and soil for orchards. They could never get them going up the canyon in Heber because of the short growing season, so ranching became the way of life there. Food was grown where the river system was the most diverse and most healthy, but now this is where the land is, the most populated and most damaged. Heber residents got their fruits and vegetables from men like Vern who trucked goods up there on weekends. Recently, Amy and I got wind of a community-supported organic farm in Ogden, about sixty miles away, and signed up. It has been an education in ancient and long-forgotten arts. Amy joked with honest humility to some friends after we started, "I have a vegetable in my fridge, and I don't know what it is." Another son had taken to the greenhouse Vern built to help get an early start on tomato and pepper plants. He experimented with flowers and now sells them as adornments to homes throughout the valley.

Everyone wants their own Eden, I suppose, their piece of land after the war. The only difference now is that, like carefree recreation, few want a relationship to the water and soil that sustain them. For that reason, I would rather have my canals than my faucets and sprinklers. Water and soil now are for creating the illusion of living in a spontaneous garden of grace and bounty but not to be mixed with our blood and sweat. Instead of working for my redemption in the soil of my ancestors, I buy décor for my private garden. Anything to protect myself from ever knowing my own sins in the reflections of the waters. There is nothing to be seen in the transparent streams coming from my taps except the refracted form of shapeless white basins where I wash the invisible germs from my hands every day.

As I continue on past the memorial for Fort Utah, I cross underneath Interstate 15 and its blur of cars and trucks. After a few more miles of housing developments, softball fields, and parks, the land starts to open up. I catch the first glimpse of farmland, with two horses and a small handful of cattle. Over my right shoulder I can see the Wasatch Front towering higher over the land the farther away I get from the bench where I started. Living as I do at the feet of those mountains, their staggering presence suffices for a diurnal experience of awe every time the afternoon light casts its glance against the craggy outline of Rock Canyon and the steep, sloping lines that careen downward from the top of "Y" Mountain which stands at eight thousand feet.

But from this distance, they stand dwarfed by a second ridge of mountains almost four thousand feet higher that lies behind them including Provo Peak, Lightning Peak, and Cascade Mountain, which tips violently in a frozen moment of titanic drama while its striations heave skyward. Timpanogos stands tallest here where the splayed streets of homes shrink to a line of gray and black between the green before me and the green of the mountains. My running is repeatedly interrupted by efforts to absorb the expansive ring of mountains that run a full two hundred degrees from north to southwest.

On the last two miles of the trail I begin running underneath a long line of cottonwoods, like bearded elders, that reach eighty feet in height. The deep cuts of bark are the result of the slow inner force of growth that had thickened and split the trunk outward in all directions. A surface coloring of silver appears on the outermost edges. Cotton floats everywhere about me, and the motion of my body brushes the white traces on the trail like windswept snowfall. Cottonwoods this size are hard to come by in most places in Utah, but they are still too young to have been pre-irrigation. Even the appearance of the river's meandering folds as I approach the lake is not enough to mark its beginnings. This stretch of the river is entirely man-made, after it was moved and dredged to make way for a recreational bay in the lake. Deep, still pools of olive green water simmer along the steep banks in the morning light.

I enter the park on the edge of the lake and find myself in the midst of great swaths of green grass, picnic benches, sprinklers throwing spears of white water everywhere I look, and not a person in sight. Winter is close enough in my memory that I feel especially exultant in the warm sun that has now risen completely above the mountains. The cloud-wrapped tops of the highest peaks are still covered in white. I think of the deep snowpack I have witnessed on top of Mount Nebo in the Uintas, near the cabin, on the backside of Squaw Peak, that ubiquitous white silence that muffles the world above seven thousand feet and muffles the voices of the past. It will continue to dissipate into the ground and into the rivulets that rib every mountain in this valley and its discourse will bleed into a chorus of boiling spume, intoning nothing for no one. By the time it arrives here at the lake, not a single drop of it is unowned, unclaimed, or unused, so it will have long forsaken its cryptic game of wildness and we may have long forgotten the churning renewal of ourselves that it portended.

Genesis. Well, not exactly. It was a second or third beginning, a beginning on the order of a reassembling. It was in response to a drought. Eden was a distant memory. All he wanted was home. He brought his bride to the land of the Philistines. Foreign land but native, too. His father had dug wells in these soils but their enemy had stopped them up so that he could never enjoy his promised land. The son hoped he might tap their source and establish a home in the wilderness. The surface of the soil began to boil and finally a muddy birth surged into the air. This was not the miraculous striking of a rock but the careful scouring of the landscape for evidence of his father's hand. It was a dig, genealogical as much as geological. But the Philistines needed it. Esek: Strife. So he moved on and dug up another. Another came to claim it. Sitnah: Opposition. A third. This time they left him alone. Rehoboth: Wide open places. That was metaphorical, considering the proximity of his neighbors, but that's the way of it in a shared haven. Were they enemies? God had said this could be his land. He had also said that his seed would bless all the families of the earth. So why not neighbors instead of enemies? So Isaac built an altar and made the land holy. And invited his neighbors for a feast, a covenant of peace sworn as the sun rose in the pale morning. Native land but foreign, too.

As I retrace my steps, the familiarity of the parkway trail now melts entirely the pretense of whatever it might mean to be Utahn, to be Mormon, to be home. I am as homeless as ever, but I no longer feel the old anxiety or the lust that this thought once inspired. Something Martin Heidegger once said strikes me: "As soon as man gives thought to his homelessness, it is a misery no longer. Rightly considered and kept well in mind, it is the sole summons that call mortals into their dwelling."

I will always be a "practicing" Mormon. I attend to all of the rituals of the religious life, repent when necessary of my mistakes, give of my time and talents to building Zion. And I do so because it is the best way I know how to increase my chances for renewal. Perhaps I haven't yet arrived at that moment when my left hand no longer knows what my right is doing, when I can truly lose myself in the most self-fulfilling way possible, because in the end acting the part is not enough. Something deeper inside me must cede control, but I keep holding on, as if in fear that I will fall into forbidden chasms and disappear. It is a privilege but also a risk to have been endowed with ancestral memory, to grow up feeling called of God by name, to see my very being intertwined with the lives of an extended family of fellow believers. A risk because I also know enough of the bitterness of exclusion and the pains of my own sins and weaknesses to distrust the ease of such rootedness.

I wonder if it isn't religious belief at all that causes this division, however. Maybe it is insufficient faith in God's power that explains why we prefer the comforts of kinship and narratives of familiarity to the estranging powers of the unfamiliar. To say nothing of the estranging powers of nature, which alone seem to teach me that my truest being is nurtured by the tenuous balance between the laws of ecology and the freedoms of the imagination. Nothing, except service and worship, provides the fullest experience of selfhood like the aesthetic contemplation of the world's beauty that stammers and stuns without the least regard for whether we are paying attention. Because when I have tried to keep my focus and when I have worked to be there at the moment of revelation with clean hands and a pure heart, I have dared to believe that what I feel is the merciful love of God. Like a flickering candle hand-guarded in the winds of winter, it is a light that is easily extinguished. But because it has always proved capable of reigniting, all the repeated rituals of devotion, all the mundane hours of habit, seem a small price to keep possibility alive.

Twelve

On the morning of Amy's fortieth birthday, I surprised her with a blue tandem kayak placed on top of our sofa in the family room. In my excitement I had been telling others about the surprise, and one friend finally chided, "This isn't a Grandpa gift, is it?" When asked for explanation, he said, "Every year my grandpa would give gifts to his wife that he really wanted for himself. One year he bought her a shotgun."

There was no doubt I was going to like a kayak—a lot—but it was Amy who first discovered a love of rowing on the water in college and who ever since sought opportunities to rent canoes or kayaks on lakes. It was a new interest I hoped we could cultivate together. I was not disappointed by her surprise and pleasure when she came down the stairs that morning. We started to make a habit of sneaking out early on Saturday mornings to drive the few miles down to the lake for a ride on its shimmering glass that extends outward in every direction in a broad horizontal line. We were told that a good place to put in was just below the bridge at the entrance to the state park. We like this stretch because it gives us a quarter mile or so of river to enjoy before we enter the lake.

Our first venture was a modest one. We put in and began rowing downriver, chasing ducks and the occasional swan out of our way as we cut across the still waters. The sun, which takes until well into the morning to rise high enough above the eastern mountains to warm our home in the foothills, reached the river's delta just as we were parking our car. At this time of year, when the days become increasingly hot, the first hours of the morning and the late hours of the evenings are the best for any relaxation and recreation. Above us, the towering cottonwoods shook at the occasional breeze, their deep lines of bark torquing at slight and uneven angles skyward. We waved to the occasional biker and walker along the Provo River Trail and passed several pipes dumping used and probably highly phosphorous water back into the thick, slow current.

After almost a century and a half of irrigation and channelization, the webbed network of veins entering this heart of water has been reduced to a single deep cut in the land. The deeper waters here attract anglers, usually with spin rods, as it provides habitat for both river trout and the lake's beefier population of catfish, carp, walleye, and bass. This is the meeting ground of two versions of this valley's human history, one that sought to use and reshape the river for irrigation to support a burgeoning population and the other a radically modified lake habitat that has suffered for serving as the resting point of industrial effluence, phosphorous, and other matters we have preferred not to think about.

It was once a rather attractive lake, as history has it, but today it is often assumed that one would not want to eat the fish or swim in the waters for fear of contamination. It is not an entirely unfounded fear, of course, even though the lake is far healthier these days than the local population realizes. We have yet to rediscover it. The lake has been transformed over the past one hundred years or so of its history, to the point that its current fish population and its murky turbidity would be virtually unrecognizable to the valley's nineteenth-century inhabitants. A shallow lake exposed to high winds, it is understandable why it is vulnerable to turbidity, but the loss of vegetation within its ecosystem has made the problem worse. The most important measure of the lake's historic and unprecedented changes is the desperate life of the June sucker, a species native to no other water in the world, which was listed as endangered in 1986.

The June sucker is not what you would call a trophy fish, but it is a beautiful and vital species that serves as the most important indicator of the health of the balance between this watershed's human and natural histories. A large silver fish with touches of rust color on its belly, on average weighing about three pounds and measuring from one and a half to two feet, its body shows an intricate and regular pattern of small diamond shapes from its crisscrossing lines along its torso. Their life span runs from ten to forty years. It was listed because water development and settlement of the flood plain in the valley had altered the natural flow of the water, disrupted the stability of the lake level, dumped increased sedimentation into the lake, and blocked migration corridors. The changes in water quality have also resulted in higher water temperatures, less oxygen, and greater turbidity.

The first irrigation ditch was dug in 1849 with the founding of Fort Utah; then came the Big Ditch along the Provo Bench where the Strattons lived and homesteaded, to be followed by the first dam built at the point of the Jordan River's outflow, thereafter redefining the lake essentially as a reservoir. Other reservoirs, of course, would follow: in the 1890s in the high

Uintas, Deer Creek—the first of the modern dams in the area—in 1942 after a devastating drought in the 1930s almost dried the river and the lake. Ten miles upstream from Deer Creek, Jordanelle followed in 1996. Today a total of nine dams or diversions dictate the temporality of the river, making it extremely difficult for the sucker to spawn in June, as it is wont to do, in the mouth of the river as it enters the lake.

Combine this with the arrival of nonnative species, the most devastating of which has been carp, which was introduced in the 1880s to provide protein to the growing human population in the valley when the Bonneville cutthroat began to disappear from the lake. Gobbling up surface pondweed and subaqueous vegetation, the carp reproduced like a bad weed and the sedimentation of the shallow lake began to stir after thousands of years of calm, creating the appearance of dirty water. You can still see their scaly dorsals surfacing in the shallows of the lake and watch them jump as your boat nears. There are now two million and counting, and no one has any idea how to reduce their population. For now, millions of pounds of fish are dumped every year in landfills. Some use the carp these days for fertilizer. Consequently, rooted aquatic vegetation is hard to come by, providing little protection to young suckers from aggressive predators such as walleye and bass that voraciously consume sucker larvae and fingerlings.

So we are still in need of much more aggressive restoration. We have hardly begun. Is there any return to the braided complex of currents, temperatures, and riparian vegetation that once sustained thirteen native species in the lake and provided a staple diet for hundreds of years of human habitation? Five-thousand-year-old human remains were found not too long ago across the lake in Goshen Bay. There was a time when the very idea of the Endangered Species Act inspired acts of violence, such as on the morning in 1984 when scientists were holding suckers overnight in cages for breeding and dozens of fish were found clubbed to death by thoughtless criminals. Despite these efforts to revive the sucker population, there is still talk of building a bridge across the lake to support development on the mostly barren western shore. This will only make inversion and air pollution worse, of course.

I have dim hopes for a moratorium on development, especially at the river mouth where the sucker spawn. Where will the funds come from to buy up nearby land to create a corridor large enough for an aggressive restoration of the river's heterogeneous waters, similar to what was done in Heber Valley? This can only happen, of course, along the few remaining miles of the river by the lake where a handful of farms are holding out for a few more years against the increasingly aggressive seductions of developers. Maybe no one is going to move the strip malls, double-laned roads, or residences that now choke the riverbanks upstream, but this small restoration would at least remind us of the hand we have played in the transformation of our garden. Is this too much to hope for?

Amy rows in front. We speak infrequently, enjoying the silky feel of the water, the pleasure of gliding across its surface with agility, and the warming sun. As we enter the channel next to the parking lot of the state park, we can see the fishermen lined up along the jetty, sailboats dotting the lake like white brushstrokes on the horizon, and the occasional water-skier cutting across the top of the water in the distance. As we emerge into the lake, at this low altitude and distance, the mountains gain in towering force and volume in every direction. We stay close to the shore, occasionally taking detours through the bulrushes for fun. Most are still tan from a long winter, and many lie broken on the lake's surfaces from the winter snow. But we can see green stalks emerging with the promise of summer's arrival.

We can hear and see a multitude of birds, some diving in the water, others nesting in the bulrushes. I don't know many names yet, but I want to learn them. Close to the dense groves of bulrushes, they are as noisy as a street corner. I can't escape the feeling from this low vantage point that all the world is blue and wet. Maybe this is because the water is so still, holding itself like a giant mirror reflecting the blue of the sky. If I take my focus off of the distant view, the turbidity of the water beneath my oar mitigates the effect of its reflectivity. I keep thinking of the implied metaphor: working for a cleaner watershed makes for clearer self-understanding.

"When he shall appear we shall be like him, for we shall see him as he is."[54]

So wrote Mormon. To gain that kind of holiness, he says, we need a gift of love that we will never muster from our natural inclinations but, he reassures us, is there for the asking. Weaknesses as unrealized strengths, our humanness as an incomplete image of the divine. Which is to say that our willful bodies are the vessels of the transformation we have been seeking elsewhere and otherwise, always expecting something yet to come, something more than the helplessness with which we started this life. This is no hubris. Deserts don't blossom without a deep reckoning of our own nothingness.

Moses was denied the chance to see his promised land, but according to Joseph Smith's translations, he gained much more. He is eventually privy to a totalizing vision of the long chapters of human history and the much deeper natural history of the cosmos itself. After seeing only a portion of it, he lies on his back exhausted, staring up into the heavens. After several hours, he recovers his natural strength and muses to himself: "Now, for this cause I know that man is nothing, which thing I never had supposed."[55]

While there are those who argue that the Judeo-Christian story seems to have emphasized the uniqueness of humanity at the expense of other living things, Moses's discovery of his nothingness appears to be his unique human privilege, thus proving this as a false dichotomy. Moses is uniquely situated among God's creations to discover his own nothingness in relation to the complexity and beauty of the whole. Awe and wonder are his human privilege, not knowledge or possession. God tells him, face to face, that he is God's son, "for thou art in the world," he says. But this special humanity in the world is defined by what he has the radical humility to witness: the world as revelation, physical life as a gift. What good does it do to deny our centrality if it means we can't access the healing and transformative power of the creation? For that matter, what good does it do to deny our nothingness if it means we are blind to the brutality we have unleashed on the world?

But the ordeal isn't over. Satan appears, tempting Moses to worship him as the god of this world, which only goes to show Satan's central and abiding interest in perverting our relationship to the creation. Moses is not persuaded. "I could not look upon God, except his glory should come upon me, and I were transfigured before him." Seeing you doesn't require or change a thing. All I do is open my eyes and there you are, like some old chair. I am made to see God's glory, he says. Why else would I be His son? Why else would he pull me out of these tired bones in my days of weariness and set me upon the feet of the mountains? Why else would I find such joy in knowing I am nothing? "Get thee hence, Satan; deceive me not. I will not cease to call upon God, I have other things to inquire of him."

And then the reward for this insatiable hunger: "Moses cast his eyes and beheld the earth, yea, even all of it; and there was not a particle of it which he did not behold, discerning it by the spirit of God." The creation unfolds before him, a dream of worlds without number, beauty that never ceases to surprise, and numberless forms conceived behind the eyes of God. Then, light appearing in the heavens, the blue ball of the earth spinning in the blackness, rolling waters cutting through rock, plants and animals shaking off the dusts of still and insensate imagination as if to prove their independence, man and woman standing astonished before the pleasures induced by the dangling branches of a tree, "a living soul." And then God staging a drama of the varieties of life he invented in order to see what they would call the beasts, the plants, the waters, as if naming the world would test the mettle of their divine parentage.

Maybe we got ahead of ourselves and forgot that naming was our privilege, not our right. Maybe we assumed names had the power of procreation to remake the world in our image—an earth Googled, a world delineated and charted—because we grew tired of the responsibility we feel in the face of the unknown. I remember that inescapable feeling when I named my first child, Eliza, that it was by no means a fiat but instead closer to what it feels like to search for a metaphor. My attempts to describe and name my home, too, like the wildflowers I first saw at the headwaters of the Provo, are nothing more than the substance of my dreaming in response to the fact of a tactile and gifted world.

Science tells us a great deal about the workings of that world, of course, and this is not to be disparaged, but science becomes a new religion when it offers the pretense of unambiguous apprehension of a cosmos that we see only for its instrumental value. This is not to say we should ignore the findings of science. Quite the contrary. When science is telling us that air pollution is inextricably linked to public health, to the well-being of pregnant mothers, young children, and the elderly, and that breathing this air for a lifetime is the equivalent of a lifetime addiction to cigarettes, when science tells us that our addiction to fossil fuels is compromising the climate and the oceans, threatening the poor in far-flung places on the earth, and endangering the prospects for a blossoming desert for future generations in the West, we should listen.

So far the response around here has merely been to cry foul, either in the name of a materialistic secularism or in the name of a dogmatic political ideology, both perverted by excessive devotion to narrow self-interest and fear of the moral burdens of uncertainty. This is the reason why we need action guided by the best knowledge we can find but also by the highest principles of accountability to the gift of life. Science alone can't seem to make moral sense of our own nothingness, which is one reason why it is time to begin naming again, morally chastened by an appreciation of what our cartographic imagination has failed to understand.

"We can be ethical only in relation to something we can see, feel, understand, love, or otherwise have faith in."

If Leopold was right, maybe we need water for more than our survival. We need it to recover our humanity.

We have fallen into a silent, rhythmic rowing, scissoring our way across the placid water as we head back to the mouth of the river. I watch a black cormorant drifting aimlessly above me, a harbinger of the coming recompense Isaiah warns us about. We are floating on the surface of what was once Lake Bonneville, a lake of staggering proportions, as large as Lake Michigan today. It stretched across the northwest corner of the state of modern Utah until about fifteen thousand years ago when its waters broke and rushed to the Pacific, giving birth to the valley floors along the Wasatch Front and leaving behind a handful of lakes, like puddles on the pavement after a rain, Utah Lake being the largest of the freshwater bodies. This water would never flow to the Pacific again.

Thoughts are shutting down and the body finds its own rhythm of breathing and moving, its heart drumming, causing me to believe for a moment the illusion that maybe I will never tire. The bulrushes whisper along the side of the kayak as we hug close to their warmth. We enter the mouth and chase down the remaining quarter of a mile of the river until we find ourselves sliding into the sandy riverbank.

As we strap the boat onto the top of the car, we begin to discuss the plans for the day. The most immediate event is that we have Camilla's soccer game to attend and all of the kids will be meeting us there. When we arrive at the edge of Grandview Bench, we walk to the field where bright red and bright green jerseys are warming up on opposing sides of the field. We find our other children gathered by the edge of the field to watch our youngest daughter play. We have forgotten our portable chairs, so we lie on the grass by some friends whose daughter plays on the same team. Eliza cheers audibly for her sister while Paige and she talk soccer. I grab Amy's hand. I greet the parents of the other children with whom Amy has been talking, all neighbors, fellow parents of children at our local elementary school, and many members of my ward. There are strangers, too, but it hardly seems to matter what the dividing line is between the known and the unknown. All in good time.

The sun shines warmly on our backs and I can feel my sweat drying and leaving salt on the skin. While the girls push the ball around the field in herds, Sam is running on the grass pretending to be playing with a ball of his own. Around me parents are yelling encouragement, laughing, and talking with one another. The teams swap momentum back and forth, and there is just enough ability displayed by the girls that it feels like a real competition. The mountains draw up like curtains around this staged rite of suburban living. My heart does not seem to want to still, so I take a few deep breaths and run my left hand over the thick and soft Kentucky bluegrass beneath me. Joy and woe, Blake said, and always something as yet uncaged. My heart continues its pounding.

I have lived here going on twelve years now, which combined with the first seven years of my life here means I have lived in Utah twice as long as any other place in my life. I am reconciled to the fact that I may never feel any more at home than I was when I made it my objective to learn this watershed. So many stolen moments of time in the mountains and on the river, and they are no more precious to me than the human warmth of these faces of my family, my neighbors, and even of so many strangers. No more precious, too, than the manila folder memories I carry forward from my ancestors, the photocopies of photocopies of unknown faces staring blankly back at me.

Truth is, maybe less precious. Loving the watershed felt at first like a return to my origins, a laying claim to a past I had ignored at my peril. It was sweet because it was private, solitary, entirely my own. But then it started to feel like a tryst, an escape from the ugliness of man-made waste. I confess, too, that I sometimes sought escape from the constant sense of responsibility I have felt toward my community. Those burdens are especially acute when they seem to bleed and blend into one another, never allowing for compartmentalization. I spend my days laboring for Zion at the church-owned university, devoting my evenings and weekends to service in my church community, and serving and loving my family. All of this service, of course, has its deep rewards, but there is a tax on the spirit when you hold yourself and others to high ideals only to have to confront the weakness of ordinary lives.

But once I came to understand that no rest for the soul can be found in impatiently escaping—even temporarily—the human community, nature ceased to provide prodigal returns or exotic escapes; it offered instead atoning healing. The familiarity of humanity never leaves us, even on the high ridges of summer's ecstasies or in the depths of winter's muffling stillness.

Maybe there is dignity in accepting that we need nature because we need each other. To pretend otherwise is nothing short of suicide.

I now understand that the watershed is my palliative for the numbing effects of predictability. It startles me into wakefulness, disturbs the easy illusions of selfhood, and challenges and molds the imagination to be something more than idle fantasy, something truer than a worship of a god after my own image. This I know because its pleasures spawn gifts of companionship, community, speech, and the unnamable generosity of will that wants all memory, all people, all living things. So I have been running headlong into this community with every step. I am as convinced as anyone of the dangers of anthropocentrism, but no one will convince me that natural beauty has meaning if it doesn't matter to *us*.

I know that my mania for finding time and means to explore places beyond the scope of my own property or immediate neighborhood is a privilege of class, that there is something inescapably contingent and personal about my moments of transcendence. Besides, someday my body will tire, give out, or maybe the Good Lord will take away my physical capacity in one stroke. Worse still, we may become so indifferent to beauty that we will have allowed its last remains to wash up on the shores. What then?

Recompenses. Beauty requires more than physical access. Since it requires an activity of the mind that makes of experience a literal re-creation, a world of my own making, my memories will have to suffice. If Leopold's observation is to be believed, maybe they are all we ever had: "I know a painting so evanescent that it is seldom viewed at all, except by some wandering deer. It is a river who wields the brush, and it is the same river who, before I can bring my friends to view this work, erases it forever from human view. After that it exists only in my mind's eye."

The experience of the senses is kept alive in the sharing, in the yearning ache of recollection I heard once in my Grandpa's voice as we talked of fishing by the cabin. That is not to say we stand existentially apart from the world we love, but if the world of the mind can retain a margin of its independence, we at least still stand a chance of finding the creativity to act in the interest of different futures. Perhaps this is why Leopold thought that quality of mind was more important than the political questions that consume so much of our energy: "Recreational development is a job not of building roads into lovely country but of building receptivity into the still unlovely human mind."

Perception, the last great clean and renewable resource. Leopold was right, knowing full well, now sixty years ago, the steep loss of biological diversity that our raptures of mechanization were causing. If building receptivity into our unlovely minds enhances our capacity to see beauty, it may be the only means left to apprehend and hang onto the diminished diversity of the world that remains. This may be little recompense for our losses, but since they are indeed *our* losses, it is the substance of our best hope.

When we pull into the driveway after the game, I can hear the familiar sound of piped canyon water running beneath the pavement of our street. While everyone empties out of the car and into the house, I get out and stand looking at the manhole cover in the middle of the sloping lane from which the water's sound emanated. No one is driving or walking by. Everything lies still except for the quail rustling in the neighbor's bush by the sidewalk.

I walk to the edge and then slowly step into the street and stand over the cover. I kneel down and place both my hands on its edges. Small vibrations pass up to my elbows. I press my right ear to the warm metal plate for several seconds. I can see my house and the sycamores standing perpendicular and an ant crawling toward me on the asphalt. Above the milling, metallic roar that reverberates inside my head, I hear a sudden low rumble above me. I shoot my head straight up and quickly sprint to the curb to my right. A car sweeps by. I stand shaking. The guy hadn't even seen the stop sign or me.

"What were you doing, Dad?"

Sam has reemerged from the house to play on his scooter.

"I was listening to the sound of the water under the street." At that age, doing something like listening to a manhole doesn't need much explanation. "Did you see that guy? He almost hit me. Please be careful and avoid the street."

"I know." His skills on the scooter have advanced to the point now where he has begun his circling around the driveway and onto the sidewalk, around the semi-circle of bishop's weed and along the pull-in patch of concrete by the front door. Because it is such an immediate and steep drop on the street, he hasn't been allowed to venture farther on his scooter without adult company. He is good about keeping his turns within the limits we have prescribed, even if I am eager to set him free.

I stand for a few minutes with my hands on my hips, staring at the steep pitch of the street, trying to imagine the water flowing underneath.

"Dad? Where does water come from?" His head is down, but I can tell his mind is at work. How I would like to learn what he sees, how he makes sense of his world. I have given answers to this question before, but it has been a while since he last asked. It comes in a series of questions about the sky, our bodies, God, and animals. I give the best answer I can, about rain, springs, snowfall, and snowmelt, but when I start to explain drought, he interrupts me. He is in full learning mode, looking up, eyes darting and eager to fire questions at me before I can finish each answer. He asks why we need it. This is the first time he has asked, but as soon as I begin my answer, he recalls with gesticulating hands what he already knows. This is nothing to be ashamed of at his young age, of course, since joining the world seems to be a matter of practicing what he has heard. I feel a parental urgency to make sure he hears what is at least minimally necessary. He will eventually realize that it becomes a matter of wrestling with what he doesn't know.

"Oh, I know, I know. The plants, the fish, our bodies. We all need it. Most of me is water, right? So when the water comes out of the rock, you know, it comes out like a volcano, right?"

I explain that it is often more subtle than a volcano, that its story is hard to capture. Water seeps through the edges of stone, leaps out of rocky walls, or surges from beneath the soil, and it grows in size and momentum as it flows downward from the tops of the mountains. Little capillaries of water meet up with others to form small rivulets and streams, which meet others still in naturally formed transepts, until a river takes shape and creates inverted mountains to aid its way down. Down to the sea or directly to the clouds from where it drops on the mountains again.

He has developed a fascination with "real" stories that he asks for at night instead of a book from the library. The more fantastic the stories sound, stories about Utes and pioneers on the Provo River, about my brothers, my parents and grandparents, our ancestors, he wants that reassurance that they are "real." I have a hard time explaining how memory works. For some reason, though, when we talk about the workings of the physical world, he and I never discuss if those stories are real. Why does the stuff of human experience always beg the question of truth? Are we just dreaming our human life, always trying to wake up to the physical reality before us? Or is experience a belated discovery that the toothsome world is what we have always dreamed? He couldn't see then that there's a lot more to say about the subject of water, that it demands more from us than we have been willing to give.

Hopefully you can see this by now. You asked, and that is why I have told you.

The earth is the Lord's, and the fullness thereof;
the world, and they that dwell therein.

For he hath founded it upon the seas,
and established it upon the floods.

Who shall ascend into the hill of the Lord?
or who shall stand in his holy place?

He that hath clean hands, and a pure heart;
who hath not lifted up his soul unto vanity,
nor sworn deceitfully.

Psalm 24:1–4

Acknowledgments

WHAT I HAVE WRITTEN IS ULTIMATELY MY RESPONSIBILITY, BUT MANY friends, colleagues, and family members have been careful and helpful readers of various drafts of this manuscript, providing much-needed criticism and suggestions for improvement. I only wish I could have pleased them all. At the risk of neglecting to mention everyone, I would like to thank Heidi Hart, John Torres, Chip Oscarson, Amy Irvine McHarg, Wade Jacoby, Helen Houghton, Tim Slover, Stephen Trimble, Ashley Sanders, Dian Monson, Steve Peck, Jonathan Galassi, Paul Elie, Kerry Soper, Stan Benfell, Lance Larsen, Ted Lyon, Scott Miller, Laura Hofmann Torres, Melanie Benson Taylor, Christine Edwards, and the anonymous readers at the University of Utah Press. My wife, Amy, read several versions; my brother, Bill, and my parents, Ken and Kate, gave indispensable and courageous feedback. Mark Jackson gave generously of his time to produce the maps. I am indebted to Terry Tempest Williams for an unforgettable hour in which she filled my sails. I would not have begun the book but for the friendship of John Torres, who first planted the idea in my mind and who gave unstinting encouragement. I would not have finished it were it not for Derek Walcott, who read a few pages of a nature journal and saw something in it that deserved the discipline of art. I had the privilege of showing him some of Utah's wonders, and in a roadside café in Beaver, he asked about my brother Kenny and insisted I write about him. That night under pouring rain in Zion National Park, I dreamed about fishing and holding a baby boy in my arms, and the book was born. Over the next two years he provided honest criticisms of subsequent chapters, including occasional deserved chastisement for my fears. I don't know that I deserved his attention or that this is the book he had in mind, but I am deeply in his debt.

I am grateful to my employer, Brigham Young University, my generous dean, John Rosenberg, and chairs Stan Benfell and Mike Call, who have provided valuable research funds and encouragement. I am deeply grateful for the interest and help of Susan Rugh, and thank also her husband, Tom, for the unforgettable trip to the *Spiral Jetty*. Thank you to Vern Stratton for agreeing to meet with me and share his love for the watershed and to Mark Belk for enlightening me on the art of ecological restoration. I have been fortunate to participate in many conversations throughout the state about religion and the environment with the generous sponsorship of the Utah Humanities Council and on behalf of the Southern Utah Wilderness Alliance's effort to stimulate dialogue about faith and stewardship. I have made many lasting and wonderful friendships as a result.

I cannot begin to summarize the contributions of my many wonderful and brilliant students at BYU with whom I have shared countless hours of deep and probing conversations about faith, stewardship, the intersections between the humanities and sciences, and from whom I have gained immeasurable wisdom and insight in our readings of many of the greatest writers of our time. I will treasure our classroom hours, office visits, hikes, and field trips all of my life. No one needs to remind me of the privilege it is to be a teacher, least of all to students like these whose ecstasies of learning and hopeful expectations keep me going in hours of darkness.

I am also unspeakably grateful for the companionship of many friends whose conversations and zeal on hikes, fishing trips, snowshoeing, and other ventures have perpetually renewed me. These have become vital rituals and pilgrimages. There are many to thank but thanks most especially to Amy, of course, and my children, and Kerry, Wade, Chip, Dan, Ted, Matt, Alan, Tom, Vance, Jim, Lance, Stan, Bryan, Gary, George, and, as always, John. Although we have shared many of these experiences together, Amy has been understanding of my need to find solitary time and space to do some of this exploring, thinking, and writing. It is no small thing that not one time did she waiver in her support, even when I wavered in my emotional bearings.

This book is for my children, Eliza, Paige, Camilla, and Sam, my greatest gifts.

Notes

PROLOGUE

1. I borrow the terms Aquarian and Hydraulic ages from Donald Worster's analysis of irrigation in the American West, *Rivers of Empire*. Worster suggests that rivers, once brought under the mechanisms of modern irrigation, are no longer sources of "faith, value, ethics, purpose, and analysis." This is because a canal or dam is no longer an ecosystem but an instrument of convertible value that "destroys traditional religion and value, denigrates all genuine philosophy, recognizes no transcending purpose."

2. These and the previous verses are from Isaiah 34 and 35, prophecies that are important to a Mormon sense of place in the arid West. Isaiah is additionally important to Mormon belief because his verses appear in somewhat redacted form in the Book of Mormon, as cited by the prophet Nephi.

3. Stegner does not, however, account for the experience of millions whose displacement was not the result of the whimsical use of economic freedom but the consequence of colonial or economic oppression. Nor does he explain why millions more, forced by circumstances to remain in place, should not be expected to develop an affection for their location as home. For a somewhat different definition of a New World sense of place, see my book, *New World Poetics*.

CHAPTER 1

4. Contemporary debates rage continually about the definition of wilderness in Utah. "Untrammeled" is the word used by Wallace Stegner in his famous wilderness letter that led to the 1964 Wilderness Act. Local populations in Bureau of Land Management land throughout Utah insist on their right and history of recreating on the land, while environmental regulations seek to limit damaging ATV use. As long as we remember that wilderness is only a *rhetorical* space of difference from civilization and that it bears witness to a common heritage, it will serve the needed purpose of chastening and inspiring us. Denigrating the very idea of wilderness is often an excuse to believe we can ravage the landscape with impunity.

5.   Climate studies consistently identify the Western United States as one of the most vulnerable areas in the country to the devastating effects of increased warming. See John Gertner.

CHAPTER 2

6.   The field of ecotheology was born in response to Lynn White's provocative 1967 essay, "The Historical Roots of Our Ecological Crisis." Since that time, a host of religious scholars have written extensively about the environmental ethics implicit in the beliefs of all the world's major religions. I have provided an overview of some of the major works in this field in the bibliography, including the recent growth of work done on Mormonism. Additionally, we have seen an extraordinary outpouring of institutional effort by many of the world's religious leaders on behalf of better stewardship of the earth, including the Pope, the Dalai Lama, Ecumenical Patriach Bartholomew, Lutherans, Evangelicals, Baptists, Muslims, Hindus, and many others. Suffice it to say that ecotheology, as it is known, is one of the most important ethical developments within religion in recent memory. There are signs of progress in my home state, where I have come to appreciate how deeply Mormons care about environmental stewardship, how willing they are to criticize themselves, and how Mormon beliefs have motivated many to work to stem the tide of environmental degradation. I have also seen how much more sympathetic environmentalists are to the value of religion and Mormonism's deep history in this land. The Southern Utah Wilderness Alliance, a much maligned agency in many small southern Utah towns, has been fostering dialogues about faith and the land in an effort to build bridges and find common ground between science and religion and among the diverse faith and ethnic communities in the state. The first dialogue of this kind I attended was quietly sponsored by the LDS church, in the Joseph Smith Memorial Building in downtown Salt Lake City in 2005. The results of these dialogues have been nothing short of a miracle—once people put politics aside, they gravitate toward the same values to describe the ways in which nature enhances our sense of family, community, individual worth, and the sacred. I have been deeply moved by the religious leaders of different faith communities throughout Utah—Jews, Episcopalians, Muslims, Quakers, Greek Orthodox, and others—who work tirelessly and devotedly on behalf of good stewardship. I have also seen the LDS Church make significant strides in greening their architecture and other designs in downtown Salt Lake City.

7.   The Book of Moses is one of five sections in what is known as The Pearl of Great Price, one of four books of canonical scripture of The Church of Jesus Christ of Latter-day Saints. Joseph Smith worked on this translation of the

Bible from June 1830 to February 1831. This process resulted in what are fragments of translations of the books of Matthew and Genesis. Translations for
Smith were revelations and were in many cases only loosely associated with a
primary text. They came more as visions than as translations. Although similar to the original Genesis account of the creation, the Book of Moses departs
from the Biblical narrative in significant ways. Most important to concep-
tions of earthly stewardship are the following doctrinal concepts: all physical
life is created spiritually before it is created physically, making of all of creation—plants, animals, and human beings— a community of "living souls";
a vision of the creation that includes all the known universe, planets, and
stars; a description of a fortunate fall; and this chiasmic structure to our duality as spiritual and biological beings: "inasmuch as ye were born into the
world by water, and blood, and the spirit, which I have made, and so became
of dust a living soul, even so ye must be born again into the kingdom of heav-
en, of water, and of the Spirit, and be cleansed by blood, even the blood of
mine Only Begotten, that ye might be sanctified from all sin" (Moses 6:59).

8.　In his classic novel, *A River Runs Through It*, Norman Maclean describes a fish
that got away: "Poets talk about 'spots of time,' but it is really fishermen who
experience eternity compressed into a moment. No one can tell what a spot
of time is until suddenly the whole world is a fish and the fish is gone. I shall
remember that son of a bitch forever."

9.　Ralph Waldo Emerson, from his essay "Spiritual Laws."

10.　William Faulkner's novel *Absalom, Absalom!* describes the lasting and haunting effects of the past of slavery on Quentin Compson, a young man facing the beginning of the twentieth century but weighed down by legacies of
memory, to the point that the narrator remarks: "his very body was an empty
hall with sonorous defeated names."

11.　From Rainer Maria Rilke's *Letters to a Young Poet*.

12.　According to Mormon revelations given to Joseph Smith, we lived with God
before this mortal existence, and we chose, with great anticipation and joy,
the chance to inhabit bodies under a veil of forgetfulness, so that we might be
tried by experience to learn to choose the good.

Chapter 3

13.　The lines are from William Wordsworth's poem, "Lines Composed a Few
Miles above Tintern Abbey," one of the most important poems of the Romantic era. Wordsworth compares the experience of playing in the woods
in his youth to his life as an adult, now carrying with him those memories as
well as an awareness of loss in an age of increasing urbanization.

CHAPTER 4

14. I am borrowing here from the title of an important book, *Last Child in the Woods: Saving Our Children from Nature-Deficit Disorder*, by Richard Louv, a book that decries the decreasing recreational opportunities for children in nature and the consequent loss of the therapeutic and formative value of early nature experiences.

15. Service in the church is the norm for Mormons. The Church of Jesus Christ of Latter-day Saints depends on the service of a lay clergy drawn from the general membership of the church. Only men hold the priesthood, which grants holders the authority to preside over the church when called by revelation. Bishops of wards (geographically defined congregations) and stake presidents (usually a larger conglomeration of eight to twelve wards) call members to staff the various organizations of the local church. Usually all active and practicing members of the church, men and women alike, will hold a calling at any given time, which can require service from one to several hours a week. Callings are never permanent, except for a small number of church leaders, known as General Authorities, who are called to serve in their callings full time and until advanced age or death. This is one of the most significant reasons why Mormon life produces a deep sense of community, but it is perhaps also one of the reasons why some Mormons struggle to find time for service outside the church.

16. The words are from Paul in Corinthians 8:2.

17. In a revelation given to Joseph Smith in March 1832, Smith inquired about the meaning of the "sea of glass" in the book of Revelation. The Lord responds: "It is the earth, in its sanctified, immortal, and eternal state" (Doctrine and Covenants 77: 1). In Mormon doctrine, the earth will die and resurrect, along with all physical life, and in its immortal state will be the site of the celestial kingdom, the highest level of glory obtainable by the human family where God and Jesus Christ will reign. The earth, in other words, is heaven, and our corruptible bodies are necessary for eternal life. These doctrines have important environmental implications, not the least of which is that they overturn the Christian tendency to assume that this life on earth and in the body is a mere veil of tears to be suffered through in the hope of a better and different condition after death. Joseph Smith taught that happiness in the next life depends directly on and extends from the quality of life we obtain with the body, in human society, here and now on this earth.

CHAPTER 5

18. The line is from Frost's poem, "Birches," which explores the role of poetry in providing the imagination's release from the weariness of life's burdens but only so that we might return to earth with greater resolve to love it. Rilke's *Duino Elegies* explore the paradox, among other things, that human beings, unlike nature, experience different seasons simultaneously. It is our self-consciousness that divides us from others and from the physical world. The impulses of sex, art, and religion are to seek reunion and to overcome this experience of division. For Rilke, when the spiritual and the physical no longer feel separate is when we come closest to this experience of reunion. When body and spirit are unified, even the angels will envy us. Happiness consists not in rising but in falling, in things departing and dying. Both poets express a notion of the inherent value of this life and the difficulty in truly seeing and feeling that value, and they understand that it is paradoxically through the metaphysical urges of human consciousness that we gain better footing to more deeply appreciate the physical. While religion may have once committed the mistake of looking too longingly past this life, Michel Serres notes that global climate change has necessitated a "diligent religion of the earth," a devotion, in other words, to a "collective ethics in the face of the world's fragility."

19. Moses striking the rock to bring water to the desert is a familiar Biblical image, as is the hot coal that is placed on Isaiah's tongue to cleanse him from iniquity so that he could become God's mouthpiece. The final image of God's finger is drawn from the story of an unnamed Book of Mormon prophet, known simply as the brother of Jared, who comes before the Lord with several stones he hopes can be illuminated by divine power and thus provide light in the darkness for a vessel in which he and his people will cross the ocean. So great is his faith that the Lord's finger and then His body are revealed. These images suggest that revelation is the moment in which an integral relationship between earth and heaven, stone and spirit, is formed. It is worth noting that even Joseph Smith translated the Book of Mormon with the help of a seer stone.

20. Lehi is the first prophet of the Book of Mormon account of an immigrant people who leave Jerusalem at the time of Jeremiah in the Old Testament. In the wilderness, before arriving at the shores of the New World and their promised land, Lehi dreams he partakes of the fruit of a tree which is "desirable to make one happy" and "most sweet, above all that I had ever before tasted." His son, Nephi, later receives a revelation about the meaning of the dream and indicates that the tree is the tree of life and that the taste of the fruit is the sweetness of the love of God.

21.   Many environmental histories of the West suggest that the Mormon desire to make the desert blossom—to irrigate, plant orchards, and improve upon the Great Basin's native beauty—set a pattern of antagonism with the desert. For example, in his fascinating history of the role of irrigation in the creation of empire, Donald Worster calls the Mormons "the Lord's Beavers." Marc Reisner tells the troubling story of the damming of the West and remarks that before they began intensive irrigation, early Mormons "banished themselves" to the desert. Bill McKibben argues that religious values can and should play a role in environmental stewardship but insists that "Mormons have made a great project of subduing nature, erecting some towns in places so barren and dry and steep that only missionary zeal to conquer the wild could be the motivation." In his survey of religious values and environmental stewardship, Max Oelschlaeger mistakenly concludes that the "only denomination that has formally stated its opposition to ecology as part of the church's mission is the Church of Jesus Christ of Latter-day Saints." Mormons did not banish themselves to the desert nor did they arrive with an empty zeal for conquest for its own sake. They arrived in desperation and sorrow. And they were not the inventors of irrigation or even the first to use it in this part of the country. (Historians point to both Spanish and indigenous origins for irrigation in the West.) And Mormons certainly were not the only ones possessed of what became a widespread American ideology to make the desert blossom as a rose. What today appears mistakenly to Oelschlaeger and a host of others to be a church-mandated antagonism toward the environment (there is no such thing) is a widely shared cultural distrust in the federal government throughout the Rocky Mountain West. It is true that Mormons deserve criticism for how they allowed the primordial struggle with the elements for survival to become a triumphalist mantra that what humans make of nature is always better than what nature might make of us. You hear such language often spoken by Utah politicians. However, Mormons deserve more than an unsympathetic gloss on their pioneer experience that erases the history of persecution or that superficially treats their belief. The bottom line is that finding the collective values that will motivate preservation and restoration is more important and effective than any amount of finger pointing.

22.   In Mormon wards, a priesthood ordinance is performed usually within a few months of a birth to give the child a name and a blessing. It involves one priesthood holder, usually the father, holding the baby in his outstretched arms while a circle of other members of the priesthood—family members and friends—extend the right arm under the child and place their left arm on the shoulder of the person next to them. The father offers a prayer, announces the name of the child, and gives a blessing according to inspiration.

23.   After an initial vision in 1820 in which two personages, identified by Joseph
      as God the Father and Jesus Christ, gave him forgiveness for his sins and in-
      structions to join no church, he reported four visitations once a year in the
      years following from an angel named Moroni. The angel told him about gold-
      en plates buried in the ground that contained an authentic record of Christ's
      visit to the ancient Americas. Moroni cited these verses from Malachi each
      time he visited the boy prophet. Elijah himself later appeared to Joseph, re-
      storing the keys of what is known as the sealing power, so that what is bound
      on earth will be bound in heaven. This authority and power provide what is
      known in the Mormon tradition as celestial or eternal marriage, the crowning
      ordinance of Mormon temple ceremonies, by which families are sealed to-
      gether for "time and all eternity." It is also the power by which all saving ordi-
      nances are performed by proxy for the dead, allowing those who have passed
      on the opportunity to accept the saving ordinances of the gospel of Jesus
      Christ. The temple, in other words, is central to Mormon experience and to
      Mormonism's claim to be a universal religion as is the spirit of Elijah, or the
      call to learn one's genealogy.

CHAPTER 6

24.   This is from the same Book of Moses cited earlier (Moses 3:5), describing the
      spiritual creation of the world before it was created physically, implying that
      all matter is animated by spirit.

INTERLUDE

25.   This is from an 1832 revelation to Smith recorded in Doctrine and Covenants
      88:7–13. This sweeping revelation covers extraordinary range, spelling out the
      design of the heavens, the structure of eternal life, the importance of learning,
      and the signs of the last days.

CHAPTER 7

26.   For a thorough overview of the state of native species, hatchery plans, and
      restoration efforts on Utah rivers, visit http://www.mitigationcommission.
      gov/index.html.
27.   In the 1890s John Muir and Gifford Pinchot became friends, working togeth-
      er in their aim to protect many of America's wilderness areas from exploita-
      tion. While Gifford believed in conservation as a means toward effective and
      more utilitarian management of natural resources, Muir tended toward pres-
      ervation of wilderness for its power of spiritual experience and renewal. The

two eventually parted ways and staged a series of public debates on the ethics of protection.

28. Joseph Smith's revelation on April 2, 1843, indicates that the earth will be the site of the Celestial Kingdom. The earth "in its sanctified and immortal state, will be made like unto crystal and will be a Urim and Thummin to the inhabitants thereof." Urim and Thummin, from the Hebrew, mean "Lights and Perfections" and refer to a divine instrument given to humankind to translate and prophesy.

29. Doctrine and Covenants 130:2. The inherent physicality and earth-centered quality of Joseph Smith's heaven is perhaps most dramatically demonstrated by his belief in a God of flesh and bones, that the resurrected Christ who eats with his disciples is in the image of His Father. This implies that only a union of the spirit and the body, as another revelation states, is the highest state of being: "The elements [physical matter] are eternal, and spirit and element, inseparably connected, receive a fulness of joy" (Doctrine and Covenants 93:33).

30. See Doctrine and Covenants 130:9.

31. Joseph Smith also taught that this earth, in its current mortal state, is the way station of the dead, that their spirits live and move among us awaiting the day of the Final Judgment.

32. From *The Poetry of Pablo Neruda*, the poem "Keeping Quiet."

33. See Donald Worster's *Rivers of Empire*. As indicated earlier, I am sympathetic to Worster's aims but not persuaded by his suggestion that there is a necessary relationship between Mormon belief and reclamation.

34. The words of Joseph Smith, from *History of the Church* (6:308–309). Smith's notion of the creation and even of the core intelligence of humanity adamantly rejects the postulates of an ex nihilo creation.

CHAPTER 8

35. From Matthew 18:7. The phrase seems to criticize our difficulty in knowing how to make good use of prophecy. While prophecy teaches what the present portends, it is not an excuse to remain passive and indifferent in the face of tragedy and evil.

36. Echoing the revelations of the New Testament, this revelation comes from Doctrine and Covenants 49:7.

37. The Brigham Young University campus consists of dozens of student wards, divided by single and married status. Leadership for these wards is drawn from neighboring stakes. Bishops of these student wards usually only serve three years, so as not to pull them away for too long from their home wards. These bishops are not infrequently also faculty members at the university, as

was my case, making for some interesting overlap in a professor's concern for the intellectual and spiritual development of students.

38. Verses 45, 47, and 49 in Doctrine and Covenants 88, a section cited earlier.

39. These and subsequent lines are from Wordsworth's "Ode on Intimations of Immortality" which is a poem well known to Mormons because of his suggestion of a premortal existence ("Trailing clouds of Glory do we come/ From God who is our home"), a beloved doctrine in LDS belief.

40. From Deuteronomy 34:4, 7.

41. Hebrews 11:13.

CHAPTER 9

42. Lehi, the prophet of the first book in the Book of Mormon, lives in Jerusalem in 600 B.C. but dreams he must take his family to a promised land to the east. These are the words he speaks to his sons in explanation of their move. Two of his sons, Laman and Lemuel, remain skeptical that their father's dream was revelation and instead call him "visionary" in the pejorative sense. Lehi does not deny he is visionary and insists that were it not so, he would not know what the Lord would have him do.

CHAPTER 10

43. Lehi leaves Jerusalem in 600 B.C. because of visions and dreams that tell him to depart with his family into the wilderness in search of a new home, a promised land. Considered mad by his peers and even two of his sons, he and his family sail east to a land that proves to be the Western hemisphere, keeping records of their genealogy. Joseph Smith, no stranger to accusations of madness, in 1829 translates this ancient record of the Americas, including the content of Lehi's visions and dreams and the record proves reason enough for thousands to leave the British Isles and Scandinavia in the 1840s to come west to Deseret as the ancestors of many in modern-day Utah. These last words are Lehi's instructions to his son in the desert from 2 Nephi 2:11.

44. In William Blake's "Marriage of Heaven and Hell," he uses the voice of the devil to articulate a philosophy of necessary opposition and of the centrality of physical, sensual experience in the working out of our spiritual salvation, a theology he believed was much closer to original Christianity than the more distrustful views of the body predominant in the Christianity of his day. For this reason, he wished to suggest that the Christianity of his day had it backwards and that they should start listening to the devil's argument. I am suggesting a similarity between Blake's theology and what Lehi is articulating in these verses.

45.   The Book of Mormon traces the history of Lehi's children into the New World and thereby suggests the possibility that at least some of the indigenous peoples of the Americas belong to the lost tribes of Israel. Although the extent of this genealogical link has shifted in Mormon folk understanding over the years, the Book of Mormon played a vital role in promoting Mormon interest in proselyting among Native Americans. Speculation about the location of Lehi's children abounds in Mormon culture, particularly concerning the location of the fabled multiracial city of Zarahemla where the resurrected Christ appeared following his death in the Old World.

46.   In contemplation of the human violence that nature has had to absorb in New World history, Walt Whitman once wrote in "This Compost":

How can you furnish health you blood of herbs, roots, orchards, grain?
Are they not continually putting distemper'd corpses within you?
Is not every continent work'd over and over with sour dead.

Ultimately, he was convinced that nature's capacity to regenerate in the wake of violence was something we could learn from, leading him to conclude that the leaves of grass that grow indifferently were the "flag of my disposition."

47.   Frémont was not the first to discount the legend of the Rio Buenaventura, but his expedition put the rumors to rest once and for all. Prior to his 1843–1844 expedition, Capt. Benjamin L. E. Bonneville had argued against the existence of the river in 1833.

48.   The citations from this voyage are from Smart and Smart's *Over the Rim*.

49.   Also from *Over the Rim*.

50.   *Daily Herald Opinion*, "Petroglyphs vs. Energy," June 6, 2008. http://www.heraldextra.com/content/view/269248/57/.

CHAPTER 11

51.   Walt Whitman was the great voice of democratic love, of the ambitious embrace of all people, but his ideas are often seen today with more skepticism because of what seems like overreach. In his "Song of Myself," he wrote, in longing for the lost and unknown dead on American soils, "it may be if I had known them/ I would have loved them."

52.   From Isaiah 35.

53.   From the previously mentioned Pearl of Great Price, in the Book of Moses 3:9.

Chapter 12

54.   Mormon 7:48.

55.   Moses 1:10. Subsequent citations are from this chapter.

Bibliography

Utah, Mormon History, and the Environment

Abbey, Edward. *Desert Solitaire*. New York: Touchstone, 1990.

Alexander, Thomas G. "Interdependence and Change: Mutual Irrigation Companies in Utah's Wasatch Oasis in an Age of Modernization, 1870–1930." *Utah Historical Quarterly* 71, no. 4 (Fall 2003): 292–314.

———. "Irrigating the Mormon Heartland: The Operation of the Irrigation Companies in Wasatch Oasis Communities, 1847–1880." *Agricultural History* 76, no. 2 (Spring 2002): 172–187.

———. "Stewardship and Enterprise." *Western Historical Quarterly* 25 (Autumn 1994): 340–64.

———. *Utah: The Right Place*. Salt Lake City: Gibbs-Smith, 2003.

Anderson, Ardean C. *Hills of Home*. Woodland, UT: Ardean C. Anderson, 2004.

Arrington, Leonard J., and Thomas G. Alexander. *Water for Urban Reclamation: The Provo River Project*. Logan: Utah Agricultural Experiment Station, 1966.

Briggs, Eliza. "History of Eliza Briggs (Written by Cora Stone Bigler, May 25, 1956)." Manuscript in author's possession. 5 pp.

Brown, Jeanne Kaye, and Craig J. Brown. "Mormon Beliefs about Land and Natural Resources, 1847–1877." *Journal of Historical Geography* 11, no. 3: 253–267.

Carter, D. Robert. *Founding Fort Utah: Provo's Native Inhabitants, Early Explorers, and First Year of Settlement*. Provo: Provo City Corporation, 2003.

———. *Utah Lake: Legacy*. Provo, UT: June Sucker Recovery Implementation Program, 2002.

Cuch, Forrest S., ed. *A History of Utah's American Indians*. Salt Lake City: Utah State Division of Indian Affairs and Utah State Division of History, 2000.

Farmer, Jared. *On Zion's Mount: Mormons, Indians, and the American Landscape*. Cambridge, MA: Harvard University Press, 2008.

Fleming, L. A. "The Settlements of the Muddy, 1865 to 1871: 'A God Forsaken Place.'" *Utah Historical Quarterly* 35 (1967): 147–186.

Geary, Edward A. *The Proper Edge of the Sky: The High Plateau Country of Utah*. Salt Lake City: University of Utah Press, 1992.

Gertner, John. "The Future is Drying Up." *The New York Times Magazine*, October 21, 2007.

Gowans, Matthew, and Philip Cafaro. "A Latter-Day Saint Environmental Ethic." *Environmental Ethics* 25 (2003): 375–94.

Handley, George. "The Environmental Ethics of Mormon Belief." *BYU Studies* 40, no. 2 (Summer 2001): 187–211.

———. "The Desert Blossoms as a Rose: Toward a Western Conservation Aesthetic." In Handley, Ball, and Peck, *Stewardship and the Creation*, 61–72.

Handley, George, Terry Ball, and Steven Peck, ed. *Stewardship and the Creation: LDS Perspectives on the Environment*. Provo: Religious Studies Center, 2006.

Handley, G. Kenneth. "How I Gave Up Farming and Began A New Life in New York City." 1994. Manuscript in author's possession. 27pp.

Hansen, Wallace. *The Geologic Story of the Uinta Mountains*. Guilford, CT: The Globe Pequot Press, 2005.

Jackson, Richard. "Righteousness and Environmental Change: The Mormons and the Environment." In *Essays on the American West 1973–1974*, edited by Thomas G. Alexander, 21–42. Provo, UT: Brigham Young University Press, 1975.

Janetski, Joel. *The Ute of Utah Lake*. Salt Lake City: University of Utah Press, 1991.

Kelson, Aaron. *The Holy Place: Why Caring for the Earth and Being Kind to Animals Matters*. Spotsylvania, VA: White Pine Publishing, 1999.

Lowry, John, Jr. "A Sketch of the Life of John Lowry, Jr.," edited by Olive Anderson. Manuscript in author's possession. 18 pp.

Nibley, Hugh. "Subduing the Earth: Man's Dominion." In *Nibley on the Timely and the Timeless: Classic Essays of Hugh W. Nibley*, 95–110. Provo, UT: Religious Studies Center, 1978.

———. "Brigham Young on the Environment." In *To the Glory of God: Mormon Essays on Great Issues—Environment—Commitment—Love—Peace—Youth—Man*, edited by Truman G. Madsen and Charles D. Tate, 3–29. Salt Lake City: Deseret Book Co., 1972.

Nielsen, Mark J. "The Wonder of Creation." *The Ensign*. March 2004.

Nunes Carvalho, Solomon. *Incidents of Travel and Adventure in the Far West with Colonel Frémont's Last Expedition*. Lincoln: University of Nebraska Press, 2004.

Reisner, Marc. *Cadillac Desert: The American West and Its Disappearing Water*. New York: Penguin, 1993.

Ruess, Everett. *A Vagabond for Beauty*. Salt Lake City: Gibbs-Smith Publisher, 1983.

Shaffer, Stephen B. *Of Men and Gold: The History and Evidence of Spanish Gold Mines in the West*. Spanish Fork, UT: Stephen B. Shaffer, 1994.

Smart, William B., and Donna T. Smart, eds. *Over the Rim: The Parley P. Pratt Exploring Expedition to Southern Utah, 1849–50*. Logan: Utah State University Press, 1999.

Smith, Joseph. *History of the Church*. Edited by B. H. Roberts. Vol. 6. Salt Lake City: Deseret Book Company, 1980.

Smythe, William E. *The Conquest of Arid America*. New York: Macmillan, 1905.

Stegner, Wallace. *Where the Bluebird Sings to the Lemonade Springs: Living and Writing in the West*. New York: Modern Library, 1992.

Stratton, James. "History of James Stratton (Written by Cora Stone Bigler, 1953, from the Diary of James Stratton)." Manuscript in author's possession. 7 pp.

Stratton, Richard D., ed. *Kindness to Animals and Caring for the Earth: Selections from the Sermons and Writings of Latter-day Saint Church Leaders*. Portland: Inkwater Press, 2004.

Stratton, Vern. "Utah Valley Orchards." Interview with April Chabries and Randy Astle, July 30, 2001. Manuscript in author's possession. 55 pp.

Sullivan, Tim. "Bits of History Suggest Utah Is Location of Mythic Aztlan." *The Salt Lake Tribune*, November 17, 2002, Nation/World, A1.

Toelken, Barre. "The Folklore of Water in the Mormon West." *Northwest Folklore* 7, no. 2 (Spring 1989): 3–26.

Trimble, Stephen. *Bargaining for Eden: The Fight for the Last Open Spaces in America*. Berkeley: University of California Press, 2008.

U.S. Department of the Interior: Bureau of Reclamation. "Central Utah Project." http://www.usbr.gov/projects/Project.jsp?proj_Name=Central+Utah+Project. Last accessed 6 June 2010.

Utah's Watershed Restoration Initiative. http://wildlife.utah.gov/watersheds/. Last accessed 6 June 2010.

Utah Reclamation Mitigation and Conservation Commission, http://www.mitigationcommission.gov/index.html. Last accessed 6 June 2010.

Williams, Terry Tempest. *Leap*. New York: Vintage, 2001.

———. *Refuge: An Unnatural History of Family and Place*. New York: Vintage, 1992.

Williams, Terry Tempest, William B. Smart, and Gibbs M. Smith, eds. *New Genesis: A Mormon Reader on Land and Community*. Layton: Gibbs-Smith Publishers, 1998.

Worster, Donald. *Rivers of Empire: Water, Aridity, and the Growth of the American West*. New York: Oxford University Press, 1985.

Young, Brigham. *Journal of Discourses*. 26 vols. Liverpool: F. D. Richards, 1855–1866.

Religion and the Environment (General)

Berry, Thomas. *The Dream of the Earth*. San Francisco: Sierra Club Books, 2006.

Cobb, John. *A Christian Natural Theology*. Louisville: Westminster John Knox Press, 2007.

Foltz, Richard C., ed. *Worldviews, Religion, and the Environment: A Global Anthology*. Belmont, CA: Wadsworth, 2003.

Gottlieb, Roger, ed. *This Sacred Earth: Religion, Nature, Environment*. New York: Routledge, 1995.

Hessel, Dieter, and Rosemary Radford Ruether, eds. *Christianity and Ecology: Seeking the Well-Being of Earth and Humans.* Cambridge: Harvard University Press, 2000.

Northcott, Michael S. *A Moral Climate: The Ethics of Global Warming.* Maryknoll, NY: Orbis, 2007.

———. *The Environment and Christian Ethics.* Cambridge: Cambridge University Press, 1996.

Oelschlaeger, Max. *Caring for Creation: An Ecumenical Approach to the Environmental Crisis.* New Haven: Yale University Press, 1996.

Rockefeller, Steven C., and John C. Elder, ed. *Spirit and Nature: Why the Environment Is a Religious Issue.* Boston: Beacon Press, 1992.

Simkins, Ronald A. "An Introduction: The Legacy of Lynn White." *The Journal of Religion and Society,* 3(2008): 1–26.

White, Lynn. "The Historical Roots of Our Ecological Crisis." In Gottlieb, *This Sacred Earth,* 184–93.

Wilson, E. O. *The Creation: An Appeal to Save Life on Earth.* New York: W. W. Norton, 2006.

ENVIRONMENTAL STUDIES (GENERAL)

Berry, Wendell. *The Unsettling of America.* San Francisco: Sierra Club Books, 2004.

Brower, Michael, and Warren Leon. *A Consumer's Guide to Effective Environmental Choices: Practical Advice from the Union of Concerned Scientists.* New York: Three Rivers Press, 1999.

Clewell, Andre F., and James Aronson. *Ecological Restoration: Principles, Values, and Structure of an Emerging Profession.* Washington, D.C.: Island Press, 2007.

Crosby, Alfred W. *Ecological Imperialism: The Biological Expansion of Europe, 900–1900.* Cambridge: Cambridge University Press, 2004.

Davis, Devra. *When Smoke Ran Like Water: Tales of Environmental Deception and the Battle Against Pollution.* New York: Basic Books, 2006.

Dessler, Andrew E., and Edward A. Parson. *The Science and Politics of Global Climate Change: A Guide to the Debate.* London: Cambridge University Press, 2006.

Elder, John. *Reading the Mountains of Home.* Cambridge, MA: Harvard University Press, 1999.

Falk, Donald A., Margaret Palmer, Joy Ziedler, and Richard J. Hobbs. *Foundations of Ecological Restoration.* Washington, D.C.: Island Press, 2006.

Friedman, Thomas. *Hot, Flat and Crowded: Why We Need a Green Revolution.* New York: Farrar, Straus, and Giroux, 2008.

Goldsworthy, Andy. *Rivers and Tides: Working with Time.* Directed by Thomas Riedelsheimer. New York: New Video Group, 2002.

Graves, John. *Goodbye to a River: A Narrative.* New York: Vintage, 2002.

Grove, Richard. *Green Imperialism: Colonial Expansion, Tropical Island Edens, and the Origins of Environmentalism, 1600–1860.* Cambridge: Cambridge University Press, 1995.

Handley, George. *New World Poetics: Nature and the Adamic Imagination in Whitman, Neruda, and Walcott.* Athens, GA: University of Georgia Press, 2007.

Heidegger, Martin. *Poetry, Language, Thought.* New York: Harper Perennial Classics, 2001.

Hoagland, Edward. "Endgame: Meditations on a Diminishing World." *Harper's Magazine.* June, 2007.

Leopold, Aldo. *A Sand Country Almanac.* New York: Oxford University Press, 2001.

Louv, Richard. *The Last Child in the Woods: Saving Our Children from Nature-Deficit Disorder.* Chapel Hill, N.C.: Algonquin Books, 2008.

McKibben, Bill. *The End of Nature.* New York: Random House, 2006.

Pearce, Fred. *When the Rivers Run Dry: Water—The Defining Crisis of the Twenty-first Century.* Boston: Beacon Press, 2006.

Robinson, Marilynne. *The Death of Adam: Essays on Modern Thought.* New York: Houghton Mifflin, 1998.

Serres, Michel. *The Natural Contract.* Translated by Elizabeth MacArthur and William Paulson. Ann Arbor: University of Michigan Press, 1995.

Schut, Michael. *Simpler Living, Compassionate Life: A Christian Perspective.* Denver, CO: Living with the Good News, 1999.

Slobodkin, Lawrence B. *A Citizen's Guide to Ecology.* New York: Oxford University Press, 2003.

Wilson, E. O. *Biophilia.* Cambridge: Harvard University Press, 1986.

LITERARY WORKS

Arendt, Hannah. *The Human Condition.* Chicago: University of Chicago Press, 1998.

Aridjis, Omeros. *Eyes to See Otherwise: Selected Poems.* Edited by Betty Ferber and George McWhirter. New York: New Directions Books, 2002.

Bishop, Elizabeth. *The Complete Poems, 1927–1979.* New York: Farrar, Straus, and Giroux, 1980.

Blake, William. *Blake's Poetry and Designs.* New York: W. W. Norton and Company, 2007.

Clare, John. *Selected Poems.* New York: Penguin, 2004.

Dillard, Annie. *Pilgrim at Tinker Creek.* New York: Harper Perennial Classics, 2007.

Eliot, T. S. *Four Quartets.* London: Faber and Faber, 2001.

Emerson, Ralph Waldo. *The Essential Writings of Ralph Waldo Emerson.* Edited by Brooks Atkinson. New York: Modern Library, 2000.

Faulkner, William. *Absalom, Absalom!* New York: Modern Library, 1993.

Frost, Robert. *The Poetry of Robert Frost: The Collected Poems, Complete and Unabridged.* Edited by Roberty Connery Lathem. New York: Henry Holt and Co., 1969.

Lewis, C. S. *An Experiment in Criticism.* Cambridge: Cambridge University Press, 1961.

Maclean, Norman. *A River Runs Through It and Other Stories.* Chicago: University of Chicago Press, 2001.

Neruda, Pablo. *The Poetry of Pablo Neruda.* Edited by Ilan Stavans. New York: Farrar, Straus, and Giroux, 2003.

——. *Extravagaria.* Translated by Alastair Reid. New York: Farrar, Straus, and Giroux, 2001.

Rilke, Rainer Maria. *The Essential Rilke.* Translated by Galway Kinnell and Hannah Liebmann. New York: Ecco, 2000.

——. *Letters to a Young Poet.* Translated by Joan M. Burnham. New York: New World Library, 2000.

——. *Rilke's Book of Hours: Love Poems to God.* Translated by Anita Barrows and Joanna Macy. New York: Riverhead Trade, 1997.

Stevens, Wallace. *The Collected Poems.* New York: Vintage, 1990.

Thoreau, Henry David. *Walden and Civil Disobedience.* New York: Signet, 2004.

Wordsworth, William. *Selected Poems.* New York: Penguin Classics, 2005.

Whitman, Walt. *The Portable Whitman.* Edited by Michael Warner. New York: Penguin Classics, 2003.